THE PASSIONATE SHOPPER

THE
PASSIONATE
SHOPPER

Marion von Adlerstein

Illustrations by
Lyndal Harris

LANTERN

an imprint of
PENGUIN BOOKS

LANTERN
Published by the Penguin Group
Penguin Group (Australia)
250 Camberwell Road, Camberwell, Victoria 3124, Australia
(a division of Pearson Australia Group Pty Ltd)
Penguin Group (USA) Inc.
375 Hudson Street, New York, New York 10014, USA
Penguin Group (Canada)
90 Eglinton Avenue East, Suite 700, Toronto ON M4P 2Y3, Canada
(a division of Pearson Penguin Canada Inc.)
Penguin Books Ltd
80 Strand, London WC2R 0RL, England
Penguin Ireland
25 St Stephen's Green, Dublin 2, Ireland
(a division of Penguin Books Ltd)
Penguin Books India Pvt Ltd
11 Community Centre, Panchsheel Park, New Delhi – 110 017, India
Penguin Group (NZ)
67 Apollo Drive, Mairangi Bay, Auckland 1310, New Zealand
(a division of Pearson New Zealand Ltd)
Penguin Books (South Africa) (Pty) Ltd
24 Sturdee Avenue, Rosebank, Johannesburg 2196, South Africa

Penguin Books Ltd, Registered Offices: 80 Strand, London WC2R 0RL, England

First published by Penguin Group (Australia), a division of Pearson Australia Group Pty Ltd, 2006

1 3 5 7 9 10 8 6 4 2

Text copyright © Marion von Adlerstein 2006
Illustrations copyright © eskimo 2006

Design by eskimo and John Canty © Penguin Group (Australia)
Illustrations by Lyndal Harris
Author photograph by Earl Carter
Typeset in Goudy by Post Pre-press Group, Brisbane, Queensland
Printed in China by 1010 Printing International Limited

National Library of Australia
Cataloguing-in-Publication data:

von Adlerstein, Marion.
The passionate shopper

ISBN-13: 978 1 92098 957 6.
ISBN-10: 1 920989 57 9.

1. Shopping – Australia – Guidebooks.
2. Teleshopping – Australia – Guidebooks. I. Title.

640.73

www.penguin.com.au

For Flavia and Lily

CONTENTS

Introduction

SHOP TALK

ONE MORNING, as the *Royal Viking Star* cruised the Yellow Sea towards the port of Tianjin, we were treated to a lecture by a venerable professor with a deep knowledge of China. He gave us a sweeping view of the country's immense history and added useful practical details, such as cautioning us not to be offended if anyone asked how old we were, and not to take photographs of people without first nodding and asking their permission.

This erudite chap wound up his talk by asking us to repeat after him a few rudimentary words to help us communicate once we were in Beijing. *Ní hao*, he said, and we did our best to repeat it. It means hello. *Dui* is useful, we all agreed, because it means yes. *Bù* is a help because it means no. *Xièxie*, which means thank you, would be easy to remember because it's pronounced *si-si*, the way they say yes in Italy and Spain. Most important of all, however, said the learned one, is *shar-ping*. *Shar-ping*, we devotedly repeated. 'Is that something to do with that wrinkly dog?' asked a lady with a Caribbean suntan and a lot of gold jewellery in the front row. No, beamed the prof. This was his little joke. He meant shopping. How well this professor read his audience.

While I'm sure that most of us aboard that slow boat to China had convinced ourselves we were there to tread the Great Wall, tiptoe into the Imperial Palace and queue up at the tomb of Mao, where did we get our biggest thrill? Shar-ping at the Silk Market, where I swathed myself in French navy cashmere for $200. In a department store in Shanghai, little crêpe-de-chine camisoles were the price of Cottontails in a sale at Target, and for a few yuan more, you could take home those long silk neck-to-knees that insulate swishy skiers in Europe (where they cost a fortune). Back at The Palace Hotel, did we speak of the poetry of the Marble Boat moored lakeside in the Park of Nurtured Harmony? No, we bragged about our bargains. Ah, shar-ping, one of the wonders of the world.

Some people travel to see the Falls of the Blue Nile, the chiselled heads at Mount Rushmore, the ruined Mayan city of Palenque, the ancient places of worship at Angkor Wat and the lofty temples of Tibet. For others, magic lies in the castles in Spain and Germany, the Gothic cathedrals of France, the Michelangelos and Leonardos in Italy, the eerie rocks at Stonehenge. And then there are those of us whose purpose is more predatory. We rarely see much more than the insides of Takashimaya in New York, Browns Focus in London, Colette in Paris, Fendi in

Rome, 10 Corso Como in Milan and flea markets in any city, town, village or hamlet anywhere in the world. We know Westbourne Grove, the Marais and West 14th Street as well as we know Flinders Lane and William Street, Paddington. If you don't know who Matthew Williamson, Frida Giannini, H&M, Ozwald Boateng and Zac Posen are, just ask us. But don't look for us in the afternoon; we'll be having a lie down in our suite at The Mercer or The Zetter or The Bulgari.

Down the decades, there have been shoppers who make the likes of you and me seem tightwads, so never feel guilty about being acquisitive. There are more of us than will ever confess to it, so you are not alone.

According to legend, one grand shopper of the past who also inspired the great artists of her day – and John Galliano in recent times – was Marchesa Luisa Casati, one of Europe's richest heiresses, who was born in 1881. She expressed the desire to be a living work of art and, judging by the number of portraits made of her, her wish came true. She knew how to blow the family fortune in style. Before she died penniless in 1957, she owned the Palais Rose, a mansion of red marble outside Paris, and Palazzo Venier dei Leoni on the Grand Canal in Venice. She was dressed by Erté and Fortuny, wore jewellery designed by Lalique and kept monkeys, cheetahs and snakes as pets. Her male servants wore nothing but gold leaf. While many women have worn feather boas, who but the Marchesa could carry off a real boa constrictor around her neck when she walked about Venice with her big spotted cats on a leash?

Another unforgettable prodigal was the Chinese Empress Dowager Ci'xi (pronounced *Tsi-si*), who in 1888 funded an extravagant reconstruction of the Summer Palace and the Garden of Virtuous Harmony in Beijing with money laid aside to establish an entire navy. She had the right priorities. ('Surely a King who loves pleasure is less dangerous than one who loves glory,' wrote the insightful Nancy Mitford, though in quite a different context.) Twenty eunuchs and twenty-eight ladies-in-waiting used to hang around, to indulge Ci'xi's whims. She owned the very first car imported into China, an 1898 second-generation Benz (forerunner of the Merc) – but, admittedly, that was a gift. There's a lesson there, though. She who spends fortune receives fortune, must surely be an ancient Chinese proverb. Patiently, I await at least a tiny reward for trying.

Ci'xi is not to be confused with CZ (pronounced *See Zee*) Guest, who died in November 2003 at the age of eighty-three. This cool blonde American socialite (think Grace Kelly) married a great-grandson of the 7th Duke of Marlborough and was astonished to learn from the fashion designer Oscar de la Renta that not every girl owned a pony. Another big-time fashion designer, Karl Lagerfeld, is no slouch when it comes to throwing his euros around. Some people fit out cellars to store their bottles of wine. He tunnelled under the tennis court at his Biarritz property to make a climate-controlled bunker for his books, numbering 230000 at last count. It's elevating to find an intellectual component to extravagance.

Tsar Alexander III of Russia was imaginative as well as rich. As a wedding anniversary gift to Tsarina Maria Fedorovna in 1885, he comissioned a young jeweller named Peter Carl Fabergé to make her an Easter egg. This was no sweetmeat from Haigh's. In a breathtakingly lavish version of those funny Russian dolls of ever-diminishing sizes inside each other, the enamelled egg held a yolk made of gold. Inside the yolk was a golden hen. Inside the hen was a diamond crown with an egg-shaped ruby. An even more glorious ovum was delivered every Easter from then on, until the revolution in 1917 put an end to the Romanoffs, their chickens and their eggs.

What those Easter excesses cost is anybody's guess, but we assume the Tsar honoured his financial obligations, unlike the wife of King George V of Great Britain. They say that Queen Mary, who died in 1953, was the bane of London's antique dealers because, if she fancied some exquisite little object, she was fond of saying, 'The Queen would be pleased to have this for the royal collection.' What could a shopkeeper do but hand it over? If they didn't, goes the gossip, Her Majesty would just nick it. She was always dressed to the nines, so you can imagine the finery when she went to a wedding. At one such reception, the writer EM Forster is said to have bowed to the wedding cake, thinking it was Queen Mary.

More pedestrian, but a spendthrift in the grandest tradition, is Imelda Marcos, wife of the one-time President of the Philippines, who was so proud of her profligacy she reckoned that, one day, a new word would enter the dictionary, 'imeldific', meaning ostentatiously extravagant. She was also a stickler for accuracy: 'I did not have three thousand pairs of shoes,' she protested. 'I had one thousand and sixty.'

Donald Trump, the American magnate who has often been a bit imeldific himself, advises, 'As long as you're going to be thinking anyway, think big.' But is he a man

of his word? When he wed for the third time, his bride, Melania Knauss, wore a
Christian Dior dress that cost US$100 000. That might sound like a lot to you and
me, but my friend, the writer and fashion authority Marion Hume, reckons it's cheap
by couture standards. She has known couture dresses that set big-spenders back by
as much as US$600 000. Anyway, Ms Knauss had her wedding frock on only briefly.
An overload of hand-stitched crystals and pearls caused the glittering garment's
90 metres of satin to tip the scales at more than 50 kilos – and that's without the
bride being inside. It had to be transported to the century-old chapel at the groom's
Mar-a-Lago private club and spa in Florida, so that Melania, wearing blue lace
panties, could whip into the vestry and pop it on just before the ceremony.

Thinking big does not always entail spending heaps of money, but it usually does.
So if you get into trouble, be comforted by the words of J Paul Getty: 'If you owe the
bank $100 that's your problem. If you owe the bank $100 million, that's the bank's
problem.' But let the last word come from Dorothy Parker, who is said to have said,
'If you want to know what God thinks of money, just look at the people he gave it to.'

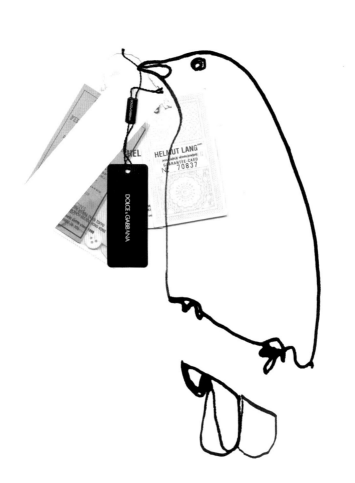

1

MY FASHION
CREDENTIALS

BEFORE I ASK YOU to put your trust in me as someone who knows her way around a shop, let me place before you my fashion credentials.

My progress as a fashion plate started early. At the age of four, decked out in peach-coloured crêpe-de-chine, with brown velvet bows and swirls of coffee lace (every stitch lovingly sewn by my mother), I was named best-dressed girl at the Bankstown Baby Show of 1936. (If you don't believe me, look at the silver cup on the mantel in my ironing room.) I was filmed by Cinesound News giving a cone of ice-cream to the most beautiful baby in the show. Between the two of us, the ice-cream finished up in the babe's lap, she bawled and I felt terribly responsible.

Like both her sisters, my mother was an accomplished dressmaker, so although we didn't have much money, we were rarely without finery. I was always a bit of a show-off ('This one's an actress,' the midwife told my mother when I was born), and I can remember singing 'Daisy' when I was two. Because I was good at recitation, at the age of six I was asked to deliver the farewell speech to our headmistress on her retirement from Bankstown Public School.

At school I rehearsed and re-rehearsed under my teacher's guidance until I was word perfect. Every syllable is engraved on my memory, to this day: 'Dear Miss Barrett, The boys and girls of the school wish you to have this lamp in memory of the many happy years you have spent at Bankstown School. We hope the lamp will radiate as bright a light for you as the light from your face has radiated upon us.' Needless to say, I did not write this flowery prose but I memorised it quite easily, after I had finally remembered to say 'wish' instead of 'want'.

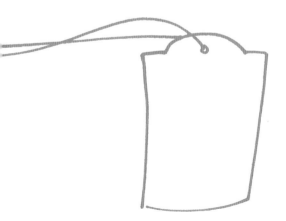

Meanwhile, a fashion industry was in full swing at home, as my mother prepared my wardrobe for the great event. It was winter, so she knitted a frock from mustard-coloured wool and lined it in matching silk. It had a plain bodice, fancy stitching for collar, sleeves and skirt, and eyelets at the waist for the brown velvet ribbon to which my mother maintained unswerving loyalty. A brown Bo-Peep bonnet, beige socks and brown mary janes were bought and put in the wardrobe. The finishing touch was a little green patent-leather pouch bag.

Miss Barrett's farewell was scheduled for the afternoon, so I went to school in the morning wearing my old grey coat and with my hair in curling pins, so that I could go home to change at lunchtime and not risk sullying my new gladrags. That's when tragedy struck. The farewell was brought forward to the morning, so there I stood in my old grey coat with my hair in pins because, even though I'd never heard the thespians' mantra, I knew that the show must go on.

SOON I WAS an adolescent, at a time when there was no such thing as teenage fashion. You went straight from wearing children's clothes to dressing like a grown-up. Denim jeans were still the uniform of American cowboys and coal miners. There were sloppy joes but they were only for walking in the bush or going to the pictures on Saturday afternoon, never to parties or on visits to the rellies. At fourteen my best outfit was a suit of cream Moygashel linen with red polka dots made, of course, by my mother. I wore it to a hop in a church hall at Guildford. After Barry Tolhurst and I had done a bit of jitterbugging, he asked me if he could sit down because the bouncing spots made him dizzy. I had never liked that wretched suit and that killed it for me forever.

But it wasn't as bad as being fifteen and wearing my school break-up dress – mauve voile with tiny white spots, a drawstring neckline and a full skirt – on day one of my first job, at Michell Gee Wilson and Clapin, solicitors, in Pitt Street. What was mortifying to me about my attire was not the dress but my footwear: all I had was a pair of clumping brown-and-black brogues and bobby socks. It wouldn't turn a head today – in fact, it might even get me photographed for Fernando Frisoni's Urban Style page in the *Sun-Herald* – but this was 1948, the era of perfectly matched accessories, seamed stockings and very strict rules for city dressing that did not include frothy frocks with clodhoppers.

In collusion with my mother, I did not take my first pay packet of £2 home on Friday night, breaking tradition for this rite of passage – I spent it on a length of blue-and-white checked gingham and a Butterick pattern at McDowell's in George Street, and took it home on the train so I would have something to wear on Monday. That weekend my mother turned it into a pinafore dress that pleased me so much I thought it looked like a page out of *Seventeen*, my favourite magazine. (If you were lucky, you could find secondhand copies of this and other American magazines, such as the *Ladies' Home Journal* and *Saturday Evening Post*, at Ashwood's bookshop in Bathurst Street.)

At sixteen, I made a two-piece outfit for myself in white linen. It was sensational, a triumph for beginner's luck. The dress was sleeveless, with a square neckline and a full-circle skirt. It teamed with a short jacket that had a kicky flare at the back. It was so successful everyone thought my mother had helped me make it. She hadn't. From the moment I could walk, I suppose, I'd learned by watching her work the old Singer sewing machine, threading it up, inserting the bobbin and, with her feet on the treadle, guiding material under the awesome rat-tat-tat of the needle. Perhaps dressmaking is in my blood. According to family folklore, a distant forebear on my mother's side was transported to the colony with the second fleet for stealing a length of cloth. I bet she'd planned to turn it into something to wear.

By now I'd found myself a job in the advertising department of a department store called Hordern Brothers. That is where I met the catalyst in my fashion life – in my entire life, really – in the form of an incredibly chic Florentine copywriter called Marisa Martelli. She was the daughter of a sculptor who took the family from Italy to Singapore in the early 1940s when he received a commission to work on a civic building. Just before Singapore fell to the Japanese in 1942, the Martellis were deported to Australia and interned somewhere near Bathurst.

Although she cannot have been much older than me, Marisa was light years ahead in experience, sophistication, worldliness, education, culture and style – all the things I desperately wanted for myself without ever having thought about it rationally. She was a gifted designer and poet. Luckily for me, she was also generous and kind. So began my tertiary education under a bewitching tutor. Her avant-garde sketches were turned into couture by her mother, an expert needlewoman, which meant that photographs of Marisa often appeared in the social pages of the newspapers.

In modelling myself on her, my appearance became a little more pared down,
a little sleeker.

It was more than what today is called a 'girl crush', although I was certainly in thrall.
Marisa was my mentor. She taught me the rudiments of Italian language, and took me
to art shows, foreign films and smart parties where there were French diplomats who
talked about being in the Resistance during the war, hiding out in cellars and living
on bread and wine. Oh, the glamour of it! For my first marriage, at twenty, Marisa
designed my wedding dress. I made it on my mother's trusty Singer and my father
measured the length of the train with the slide rule from his workshop. It was quite
nun-like. I've always preferred coverage to a lot of bare flesh.

Fast forward six years to London. Marisa is married and living in Eccleston Square.
Having arrived there in 1957, I have a job as a copywriter at The London Press
Exchange, Europe's largest advertising agency. It must have been in about 1960 that
I kitted myself out in what I truly believe was the first sack dress ever sighted in St
Martin's Lane, where LPE was located. The sack was a tube that ignored the waist
but touched the hips, emphasising the bottom, before it finished at the knee. Its
sexiness came from innuendo rather than revelation because it sort of undulated as
the body moved. The sack had been invented in 1957 by the noble French couturier
of exquisite refinement, Hubert de Givenchy.

Needless to say, mine did not come from Givenchy's atelier in Paris but from my
basement flat in Montagu Place. I made it from cinnamon wool jersey, gave it a
V-neckline faced with black grosgrain ribbon and lined it in silk. It was quite
striking, especially given the times. Although Mary Quant was beginning to
make a name for herself with the mod clothes she sold at Bazaar (her boutique
in the King's Road, Chelsea), most people still clung to established notions of
what was ladylike and what was not.

Not yet acceptable were pantyhose, invented in the US in 1959 to supplant seamed stockings held up by lumpy suspenders attached to corsets or girdles or just dangling from elastic waistbands. One day, at a client meeting in the agency, the managing director of Aristoc Stockings, for which I wrote copy, held forth on the vulgarity of this frightful new seamless underpants-and-stockings hybrid. He told us how it was doomed to failure because no self-respecting woman would step out without seams down the back of her legs. After his harangue, to which we dutifully listened, the creative people were allowed to get back to work. I stood up and walked to the door knowing all eyes were on my unseemly seamless calves.

Will we ever know for sure whether the miniskirt was invented by Courrèges or Mary Quant? Or did it just rise up from the streets of London, an inevitable result of the youthquake? One thing's for sure: it was the making of pantyhose as a mass-market essential. There were plenty of protests, though, usually from men claiming that it wasn't as sexy as a suspender belt and stockings, à la Marlene Dietrich playing the sleazy Lola in *The Blue Angel*. What I believe put the seal of erotic approval on this liberating garment was the soft-porn sequence in Antonioni's 1966 movie *Blow-up* in which David Hemmings cavorts in his studio with two teenage girls (one of whom was Jane Birkin) clad in little more than, as I recall it, pastel-coloured pantyhose. It was about this time that we were titillated by the news that Mary Quant's husband, Alexander Plunkett Green, had cut her pubic hair into the shape of a heart.

Soon I am divorced and living in a maisonette at Swiss Cottage. The outfit I made to face the judge for my divorce is a lesson in appropriateness: a sober grey flannel tunic that covered my hips over a narrow grey skirt that covered my knees. To salute my newfound freedom, Marisa commissioned a jeweller to attach a baroque pearl to my wedding ring.

A COLD CLIMATE brings out the best in dressing, and the fabrics in London were wonderful, especially the tweeds from Scotland and Ireland, and the silks and cottons from France and Switzerland. I chose nubbly red tweed to make into a 'Chanel' suit which, in my naivety, I wore to Paris! There were velvet maxiskirts for at-home wear after I moved into my smart garden flat in Moore Street, Chelsea. Navy hipster pants with bell-bottoms, very much in step with swinging London, were among the first garments I did not make myself. I still didn't give up the sewing machine, though. My Singer and I turned out an impressively tailored charcoal-grey chalk-striped suit, lined in coffee-coloured silk, for my arrival back home in Sydney in 1964 after seven years in London.

I decided to fly home via the United States because, at age thirty-two, I'd seen a lot of Europe but never been to New York. Some moments in life are true standouts, remembered forever; my first sight of the Manhattan skyline was one of those. A Bostonian friend and fellow copywriter in London, Blanche Wheeler, had written me a do-it-yourself day tour and advised me to stay at the Barbizon Hotel for Women, a most respectable establishment uptown at 140 East 63rd Street. (Much later it became The Melrose Hotel before closing in July 2005.) Early in the morning, dutifully following Blanche's advice, I experienced the novelty of buying a cream-cheese-and-pecan sandwich from the Horn & Hardart Automat. But once I stepped onto Fifth Avenue, I forgot the guide because I couldn't take myself away. I stayed all day, ogling department stores I had only read about, from Bergdorf Goodman to Bloomingdale's to Saks to Altmans to Lord & Taylor, where I bought a wide-brimmed black silk hat, like something a Spanish rider might wear, to go with my chalk-striped suit.

Three years later, I was back in New York on a transfer from J Walter Thompson in Sydney to the company's head office in the Graybar Building above Grand Central Station on Lexington Avenue. This time I knew not to take my sewing machine. What was the point, when matchless bargains were to be found in Bloomingdale's basement and at certain little stores on Second Avenue? I returned from New York to marry my second husband, Hans Heinrich Vladimir Sergei Crull von Adlerstein – a German-born baron and the love of my life.

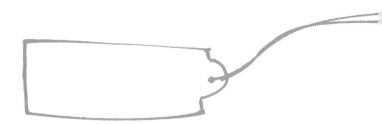

Nothing is quite as empowering as a beautifully tailored suit, the female version of the jacket-and-pants combination that has served men so well for 200 years. Dull? Wrong. I have always thought that a woman wearing a tuxedo or a jacket the French call *Le Smoking* is far more alluring than one who flashes her bits indiscriminately. By instinct more than design, I gravitated to androgynous dressing in the 1970s when Hans and I worked together making television commercials at an advertising agency in Melbourne. Two winter pants-suits from Paris are the outfits I most remember from my years as a serious advertising executive. One was black and svelte. The other was grey, chalk-striped flannel with its own waistcoat. They came from Georges of Collins Street, where else? At that time, no other store, not just in Melbourne but in the entire country, matched it for quality. The carriage trade shopped at Georges for luxuries and at Myer for everything else. By now, my sewing machine had been laid to rest.

By THE TIME recession dressing arrived, Hans and I were back in Sydney and I was writing for *Vogue*. Suddenly, the Japanese designers were making headlines because they gave us completely new kinds of clothing that had little to do with our Western tradition. I adored the rips and patches, the dour colours and flying panels, and the way Rei Kawakubo (for Comme des Garçons) and Issey Miyake swathed us in asymmetrical garments that needed no buttons or zippers but were wrapped and held together with knots. The technique was similar to the exquisite way the Japanese wrap packages.

I was so enraptured by a pair of Issey Miyake black padded cotton pants I bought at Rhonda Parry in Double Bay, they circumnavigated the world many times on my behind before finally wearing through at the knees from my sitting in the lotus position in airline seats. They were drawstring, with fullness around the bottom, and they tapered towards the ankles. When they were quite new, I wore them on a trip to Japan. Seated in the lobby of a hotel in Kyoto, I saw a priest wearing pants that were identical to mine. I didn't dare stand up. If he'd seen what I was wearing, surely it would have seemed a kind of blasphemy.

During my Japanese period (I have never left it, actually) I often travelled abroad in a black kimono-like thing, as light as a parchute, by Junko Shimada. I used to wear it with a clip-on plastic neckband from Fendi, a parody on those winged collars on men's dress shirts. I was decked out in this combination when my flight home to Sydney from Hong Kong was delayed at Melbourne Airport very early one morning. That's when a Texan asked me what order I belonged to. He meant religious. I don't know which of us looked more ludicrous: me in my habit or him in his ten-gallon hat.

I have weathered so many fashion cycles I now know which looks to avoid. I have dropped skirts entirely for pants. Other untouchables are short sleeves, floral prints, floppy bows, fringes and stiletto heels. Although I am still not immune to fashion victimhood, at least I have narrowed my choices of style, cut and colour. And not before time.

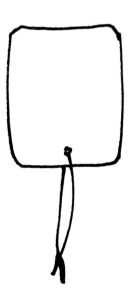

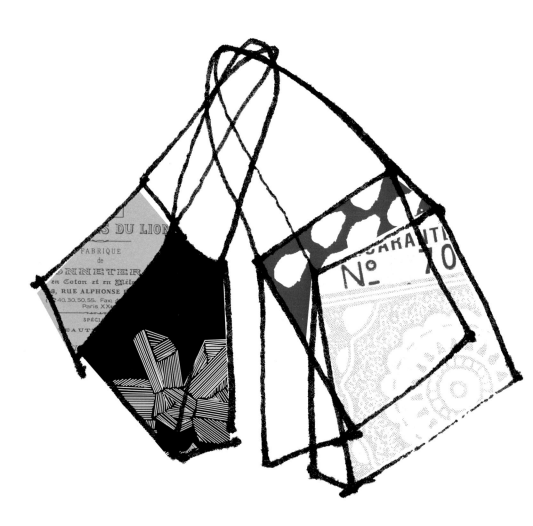

2
FRIENDS

Dearest Marion
sending you all love and
bestest thoughts for
and the New
2006

THIS BOOK OWES most of its shopping secrets not to me but to more than seventeen of my friends and acquaintances; savvy souls who get around the world and gravitate by instinct to wonderful things. They are style detectives in different fields, identifiers of real gold from the stuff of fools, monitors of the next big thing. That takes talent, discipline and experience.

I prevailed on each of them for different things, so when some of them are missing from certain categories, it's because I was reluctant to take up too much of their time with my constant interrogation – I know that, in every case, time is the one commodity they have in short supply. Let me introduce you to the key people, in alphabetical order.

TEMPE BRICKHILL

Tempe was born in London to Australian parents, the war hero and author Paul Brickhill, and his wife Margo, who worked for Norman Hartnell, the Queen's couturier. Although Tempe grew up in Australia, I always think of her as European, not so much because she's lived in London for a long time but because of her character, tastes and temperament. She is thoughtful, non-confronting and creative, with a Bachelor of Music from the NSW State Conservatorium of Music and a Diploma in Stage Management from the Royal Academy of Dramatic Art in London. Acquiring her level of skill in these aspects of music makes for self-discipline and imagination, qualities she has in heaps. Ever since I wrote about her in 1981 when she was a student and fashion model, I've felt an affinity with her. Now I know why. She is managing director for Issey Miyake London; has been since 1998. Now, that's fate.

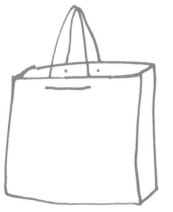

JAMES GORDON

When well-heeled people or the marketers of big-time luxury goods want to put
on a lavish event – say a society wedding, a gala fashion show or a glamorous store
opening – they call James Gordon to theme it. His imagination has no boundaries.
Between putting the finishing touches to one party before flying off to do another,
he paints extraordinarily beautiful pictures, often of everyday objects (kitchen utensils
in one show, ribbons in another) and flowers. His style is quirky and spontaneous. An
iron chandelier painted white (a birthday present from Collette Dinnigan when he
masterminded the opening of her London store in 2000) couldn't be hung from the
ceiling of his flat, so he leaves it lolling on his work table; in December he decorates
it with 'crystals, feathers, bits of this and that' for Christmas. He is amusing and
sentimental. Each time there's a heatwave he remembers his Scottish mum's form of
air-conditioning: a wet tea towel over the open window.

ALISON HANSON

When Alison was a student of design at East Sydney Tech, her instructor said, 'I can't
teach you, I can only open your eyes.' He certainly succeeded in opening hers. Six
years in London working in West End art galleries and on the *Telegraph* magazine
did the rest. After she came back to Sydney, her ability to select served her well as a
trend-spotter and stylist for various *Vogue* Australia publications, and that's when we
first met. Alison's two great passions are literature and her role as a governor for the
World Wildlife Fund for Nature. Although she no longer chooses items for inclusion
in the editorial pages of glossy magazines, she has never given up the habit; it is
second nature.

DAVID HARRISON

If you want to know about modern and contemporary furniture, go no further than this fountain of knowledge. David's passion for furniture led him to forsake his former career as an audio engineer to establish Curve, a business dealing in vintage twentieth-century pieces and contemporary art objects. Given our obsession with buying, selling and renovating our houses, along with the craze for Danish, Finnish and Swedish design, you'd think there would be a booming market for good furniture of this type. Not so, says David. There's a big market for cheap furniture but, he says, according to local architects, 'Ninety-nine per cent of the time, all the money goes on the building, on the renovations, and there's nothing left for the quality of furniture a lot of the buildings probably deserve.' So most people settle for copies or derivatives of period pieces. David writes about interior design for *InsideOut* magazine.

AKIRA ISOGAWA

Never mind that Akira was born in Kyoto, we have claimed him as our own and the feeling is mutual. It is humbling to see how simply this famous fashion designer lives, how restrained his needs and desires. By living in a space the size of some Sydney balconies, with everything on show, Akira makes us question how much clutter one person needs. Few of us will ever attain his level of spirituality, yet he is very much of this earth, with an infectious sense of humour and a liking for hand-cut potato chips from his favourite restaurant, the Balkan. He walks to his studio, and takes a bus to Bondi Beach to put his feet in salt water. By his own admission he is a happy workaholic: 'Work for me is leisure. It's not like work work. It's fun work.'

ILANA KATZ

When she worked at Design Warehouse and I was travel director of *Vogue*, Ilana and I used to compare notes and exchange information on lodgings and destinations. She is one of very few people whose opinion I trust. Her expectation of hotels is high and her judgment of them impeccable. She is either a hotel's dream or its nightmare, depending on how good it is at living up to its claims and Ilana's expectations. Since she opened her lifestyle store, Mondo, in Bay Street, Double Bay, thirteen years ago, Ilana travels twice a year for business, with spin-offs for pleasure. She researches avidly beforehand, loves to go in season when cities and resorts are abuzz with life, books everything a long way ahead and deals directly with her chosen hotels rather than through a travel agent. She is a dynamo.

SUSAN KUROSAWA

Catch her if you can. Susan averages an overseas trip a month, plus what she describes as 'local jaunts', staying in style around the world and reporting on it for *The Australian*, for which she is travel editor. She is so passionate about India, she's been there twenty-nine times, once appearing as an extra in a Bollywood movie. 'India could almost be described as one big emporium,' she says. 'In a world where mass-produced mementoes of doubtful quality crowd the shelves of gift stores, India offers a truly handmade shopping experience.' But it's not just the shopping that draws her back; it's the whole social and cultural experience, hence her nickname, 'Begum of the Bay'. If Susan and her partner, Graeme Blundell, ever find time to get married, she plans to arrive on the back of an Indian elephant. Ever the wit, she muses, 'The older I am getting, the more veils I will need.'

CAROLYN LOCKHART

You've seen her name on many glossy magazines over the years. As a stylist, she has been a force behind influential pictures of many kinds, from tots in T-shirts with zinc cream on their noses, to table settings that break with convention, and dishes that have helped shape our culinary progress for two decades. She has edited a number of *Vogue* publications, including *Vogue Entertaining* and *Vogue Children*. When she edited *Vogue Men*, her name appeared on the masthead as Charlie Lockhart, her childhood nickname, because it sounded blokey. She is the last person to sing her own praises, so some of us must do that for her. During Charlie's eleven-year reign at *Australian Gourmet Traveller*, the magazine's circulation rose from around 33 000 to upwards of 88 000. Under her editorship, *Qantas: The Australian Way* came first in the Avion Awards, winning Best Inflight Magazine for 2004 out of forty-four leading airlines worldwide. Her achievements were honoured by *The (Sydney) Magazine* last year when they inducted her into their Hall of Fame.

EDWINA McCANN

The first time I realised that Edwina McCann was a cut above the regular run of fashion assistants was at Hanoi Airport at the end of a shoot for *Vogue* in 1996. Ed was busy grappling with eight suitcases of clothes, showing the customs officer the inventory that proved we'd arrived with them a week before, and handing out boarding passes to the team. That's when the model from Paris took off all her clothes. Starkers in the middle of the terminal. Did Ed panic? She didn't even blush. Cool as a Bondi Iceberg after a dip in the surf in July, Ed simply marched her into the ladies' room and put what the model called 'my cloze-ezz' back where they belonged before any official had time to notice and call the police to lock all eight of us up in the slammer. All in a day's work when you're in fashion publishing. It's no surprise then that she is now fashion editor of *The Australian*.

MICHAL McKAY

You should see her CV. It starts with a cadetship at British *Vogue*, makes its way through fashion designer for Carla Zampatti, to editor of *Mode*, followed by marketing and development manager for Country Road, then founding editor of *Vogue* Singapore. But wait, there's more. She turns up in New York as corporate creative director for Estée Lauder. As marketing director of Beymen, a sumptuous fashion store in Istanbul, she lived in a yalla, one of those sublime traditional houses overlooking the Bosphorus. And these are only the highlights. Apart from that, just look at her. Have you seen anyone more chic? Michal now lives in Auckland and edits New Zealand's top-selling glossy magazine, *House & Garden*, and its spin-off, *H&G on Holiday*.

CRAIG MARKHAM

We read a lot about the talent drain – Australians who choose to take their flair elsewhere. What I say is, good on them. First, they're fabulous ambassadors for us, breaking down the stereotype of the bronzed yob with nothing on his mind but beer and sport. Second, if you've got what it takes to swim in a bigger pond, why not take the plunge? Craig is a boy from Wollongong who joined a small company called Firmdale Hotels in London as reception manager in 1987. Firmdale now has some of the most beautiful boutique hotels in London, and Craig is its director of marketing and public relations. The company's latest property, The Soho Hotel, was named 'The most glamorous hotel in the world' in the *Tatler Travel Guide 2005*. No wonder we won't be seeing him packing up to come home for good just yet.

ERIC MATTHEWS

Although I do my best not to hoard things – certainly old greeting cards – I have made a few exceptions. Among them is a beautiful hand-painted black-and-gold dove, dashed off by Eric Matthews some years ago as a Christmas card. Out it comes every year, one of a few precious decorations with memories attached that I scatter about the house. When we were colleagues at *Vogue* I found him to be someone of brilliance and sensibility. Since then, others in higher places have recognised those qualities too, along with a leadership ability that I would have thought him too shy to exercise. Any magazine over which he has a measure of control – whether as creative director of *Harper's Bazaar* or editor-in-chief of *Belle* – has consistently formed itself into a superb piece of design. In the case of shelter magazines, each issue he touches is every bit as impressive as the buildings and interiors within its pages. He has a selective eye for form (preferring it to embellishment), something that a couple of years spent working in Japan helped to refine. We love each other dearly but see each other rarely, mainly because he is work-centred. You can see it in the results.

LUCINDA MENDEL

She is the prototype for the contemporary woman of the noughties, the kind many young women aspire to be. Lucinda Mendel is a former beauty editor of *Cosmo*, then of *Elle*, where she was ultimately appointed the magazine's editor. As a respected authority on beauty, Lucinda is in the enviable position of rarely having to buy any skin-care products or make-up, because she is forever required to test them as part of her work as beauty editor of *The (Sydney) Magazine*, a freelance writer for other publications and a sometime presence on the Lifestyle Channel. She is fair in her testing of beauty products: 'I tend to work in blocks of four to six weeks, to really give the product a chance.' She is blessed with good looks, clear skin, trouble-free hair and a confident and optimistic nature. She lived in Italy for a year and is fluent in Italian and French. Her wedding dress was made just for her by Martin Grant. Hers is the epitome of the good life.

MEGAN MORTON

This warm, gifted, excitable enthusiast knows where to source just about anything in the world. She has to, because she's one of the most sought-after freelance stylists in glossy magazine publishing. Everyone loves working with Megan because she is a giver, in every sense. Whereas some professionals are reluctant to tell the world where they get their fabulous props, Megan never hesitates to share her magic box of tricks. Even in her private life, she can turn the everyday into a fantasy. Every Thursday, she and her daughter Millicent, who is seven years old, have Milkshake Night. This means they shower and get dressed up in the late afternoon and, leaving husband Giles at home with five-year-old Sebastian, take the bus to the city. After a chocolate milkshake and some sushi, they go to David Jones to look at the lipsticks and perfumes, then to Belinda in King Street and Hunt Leather in the MLC Building before they catch the bus home again.

JANE ROARTY

Most of us love Paris, but Jane Roarty is an extremist. As far as she is concerned, there is no place in the world to equal it. Not even Milan, which she loves and visits regularly, or London, where she lived and worked as a freelance stylist and fashion editor in the early 1990s. Jane's passion is understandable when you realise that she is an authority on international fashion; the kind who can tell not just what's doing now but what's coming next. Her best friends, all in the fashion business, are either based in the city that gave the world haute couture, or do most of their work there. After six years as style director at *Harper's Bazaar*, Jane has now returned to *Marie Claire*, the magazine for which she was founding fashion director. Sounds quite rarefied, doesn't she? Well, she's not. At twenty-one, Jane joined the anti-bourgeoisie French hippies living in the high country of Provence. She milked goats, took them up the mountain to feed, and made *tomme de chèvre* (tiny goat's-milk cheeses) that were sold in the market of a hamlet in the valley below. Her love of France is deeper and wider than the salons of Avenue Montaigne and the cafes of Boulevard Saint-Germain.

BELINDA SEPER

I would never have picked her for a tycoon when she was that sweet young uni student modelling for *Vogue* in the 1980s, but she's been a smash-hit as a top-end fashion retailer. You only have to say her first name for everyone to know who you're talking about. The great thing about Belinda, and the key to her success, is that she's never played it safe. She takes fashion risks all the time, placing her bets on labels that are unproven newcomers, outsiders in the fashion field. And she wins, if not all the time, then most of it. Belinda looks not only to catwalks but to vintage shops and raggle-taggle markets for inspiration and guidance. She has an understanding of what women will want to wear, and why they'll want to wear it, even if they don't know themselves. Does she create a trend? What a question. I reckon most of us didn't know we wanted it until we saw it on a rack with a big price tag at Belinda. And when we're sick of what we bought, we take it to The Frock Exchange in Clovelly, where her pre-loved pieces find new homes, and swap it for Belinda dollars to buy something new at Belinda. Has she got nous, or what?

KARIN UPTON BAKER

Few of us who knew Karin in her early years at *Vogue* can have been surprised at her ascent to the top of the fashion industry. She has always been clever, capable, efficient, self-motivated and disciplined. Having risen through the ranks to deputy editor, she was wooed by Consolidated Press, where she truly made a name for herself as editor-in-chief of *Harper's Bazaar*. Within the first eighteen months, she and the magazine carried off seven Magazine Publishers Association national magazine awards. Her achievements did not go unnoticed abroad. After the sudden death of Liz Tilberis in 1999, Karin was invited to take her place as editor-in-chief of American *Harper's Bazaar* until a permanent replacement could be found. Since 2001, she has been managing director of Hermès Australia. The glamorous image Karin presents hides a warm, likable and down-to-earth character.

NOTES

3

PACK UP
AND GO

Over lunch at The Book Kitchen when he was in Sydney not long ago, **Craig Markham** gave me a brilliant travel tip about check-in baggage. It is so obvious, I couldn't believe I'd never thought of it myself. 'You Fedex it,' he said. (For me, that would be DHL Worldwide Express, a very efficient crowd.) A bit imeldific? Don't be a skinflint! Think of the benefits. You avoid all the hassles of getting your luggage to the airport, standing in line to check it in, hoping it will turn up on the carousel at the other end and lugging it to the cab rank, before you surrender it to the porter at your hotel and hope it will get to your room speedily. If it's good enough for Donna Karan, it's good enough for me.

Better choose your hotel carefully, though, because your bags must go to trustworthy hands. If you're staying at one of Craig's hotels, the butler will have unpacked your case, cleaned or pressed anything needing attention and put all your things away by the time you arrive. If you'd like to put a soundtrack to that moment, I'd suggest 'The Arrival of the Queen of Sheba', from Handel's oratorio *Solomon*.

Sure it costs an arm and a leg, but if you're paying through the nose to be in the pointy end of a plane to Europe or North America, what's another $600 or so to get the load off your body and mind? I'd rather skip the odd lunch at Le Grand Véfour and forgo the flutes of Taittinger in the bar at Hôtel de Crillon in Paris. But I wouldn't have to, would I, if I resisted the cream blazer at the Chloé boutique on rue du Faubourg Saint-Honoré? There's nothing much below $1000 in this arrondissement.

It's a matter of priorities. Being stingy when you buy goods in one category, in order to splurge on something out of your cash-flow class in another, is defined as 'rocketing' in a cluey marketing book called *Trading Up, The New American Luxury* by Michael J Silverstein and Neil Fiske (Portfolio). There's nothing new about rocketing. I've been doing it for years, saving money on house-brand soap pads at Coles, in order to shop at Mecca Cosmetica in David Jones, where Gino can sell me an eyebrow pencil that costs as much as lunch for two at Sopra, above Fratelli Fresh in trendy Waterloo. But I've strayed from the point. Back to packing.

You have to be well organised to pack up ahead of time, but most savvy frequent flyers know what they're in for. They know how to be efficient. The only big burden that sending your luggage ahead doesn't take off your shoulders is selecting what to take, what to pack it in, and how to pack it. Solutions to these questions are as many and varied as there are travellers, so you have to choose according to your own personality, the places you're going to and your purpose in going there.

Since what you pack to take on holiday is pretty self-evident and of less importance to your survival than what's required on a business trip – when you're an ambassador not only for your country but for your company – we'll stick to guidelines for a working trip abroad.

Here's my formula: packing begins with buying. After all, if you don't have the appropriate clothes, how can you pack the appropriate travel wardrobe? Seasoned travellers make sure they've always got outfits that can take them anywhere, so they don't have to rush out at the last minute, trying to find the right thing. Before they buy a single item, they consider its ability to survive unlimited travel. Linen does not travel well. Micro-fibre does. Wool is a great traveller. So are most knitted fabrics, no matter what the fibre.

Colour coordination is crucial. Choose a scheme and stick to it. When in doubt, make it black. Think teamwork, not loners. If an item doesn't go with others, leave it behind. I know it might sound old-fashioned, but you do not need more than three sets of underwear: three bras, three pairs of panties – one to wear, one to wash, one resting in your lingerie bag in a drawer. You can be a bit more lavish with pantyhose and knee-highs because they're easily snagged and they don't weigh much. Panty liners are better on the plane than a spare pair of knickers, because you can dispose of them, as needed. Who wants to carry unwashed knickers, even if they are in a plastic bag?

Unless you're a shoe fetishist and you don't mind heavy bags, see how many shoes you can do without. I reckon two pairs will see you through. Okay, three max. Toss in those spindly Christian Louboutins with signed red soles if you must, but no more.

Miniaturise your skin-care products. If the brand you use doesn't come in small sizes for travel, transfer enough for the length of your stay from the regular size into tiny plastic pots and bottles with leak-proof lids. Don't travel with glass; besides being breakable, it weighs a ton. All your toiletries should fit into one waterproof clutch.

Pack as much as you can – along with the shopaholic's friend, a collapsible spare bag – into the big bag that you'll check in (or, if you're lucky, send by DHL). Don't weigh yourself down on the plane. Needless to say, any bag that is not with you in the cabin must be locked and the keys kept with you 24/7. Lock every outside pocket, too, in case someone behind-the-scenes is looking for a convenient carrier for something illegal. Simple? Not if you're travelling to the United States. Unless the lock is a type approved by The US Transportation Security Administration, you risk having it busted open by Customs. Log on to **www.howtodothings.com/travel** and read the requirements by clicking on 'Trip preparation & tips', then on 'How to find TSA luggage locks' in the 'Gearing-Up' section. Online retailers include **www. safeskieslocks.com**.

I have been through many suitcases in my travelling life, but I always come back to Longchamp: a plain, soft, medium-sized black bag with the signature brown leather trim, two wheels and a pull-up handle. Nothing big. Nothing fancy. No fiddly fittings or bitsy extra pockets to add weight, just one big outside pocket that unzips for newspapers and folders. A size that's acceptable in the cabin, if you're lucky enough to be going first or business. Otherwise it goes into the hold. I have travelled to Finland with this one bag and survived happily on its contents for three weeks. Admittedly, I was travelling in their summer. I took a warm wrap, though, for those long northern evenings and because I had to get to and from the airport here without turning blue. I love to travel light, at least on the way out. It's not always so on the way home, but it doesn't seem to matter then.

Not only do I identify my bags inside and out, I tattoo them. I scratch my initials into a prominent place on the outside so that they cannot be confused with anyone else's and I can recognise them easily when they're riding on the carousel. You might think this a wanton act – as bad as scrawling graffiti on a pristine wall – but I think of it as a beauty spot, the flaw that emphasises the loveliness of the rest.

How the experts pack

Lucinda Mendel's principle of packing is: bags within bags. Clothes stay with their hangers and bags from the drycleaner. Lucinda has bags for shoes, bags for lingerie, bags for wet cossies, bags for dirty clothes.

She was sent to report on the La Prairie Spa at Hôtel Ritz Paris (all in a day's work), which has the most voluptuous indoor pool in that romantic city. It's modelled on the baths of ancient Rome, frescoes and all, so just entering it makes you feel like an empress. Among abundant amenities in the women's dressing room was a stack of transparent plastic shoe bags with the Ritz crest on them. When Lucinda asked if she could take some, 'The woman handed me this stack. So I have them at home and whenever I travel I take a wad of them.' (The rest of us must content ourselves with ziplock bags from the supermarket.)

Instead of packing a lot of clothes, Lucinda is 'more into accessories. I have a beautiful Prada beaded sort of collar. It changes an outfit, looks great whether it's over a singlet or a dress. That sort of thing. But really I live in [my] black Prada trench, and I've got a basic black Chanel jacket that I can change with a bit of Hollywood Fashion Tape [see box, page 32]. I used to think I'd have to have a different outfit for every day, but really you don't because you're not necessarily seeing the same people all the time.'

These items go into 'a standard-issue black suitcase of durable nylon fabric with reinforced edges, wheels and a fold-away handle'. The brand is irrelevant. 'I'm not a fan of designer luggage. I feel it attracts too much attention. I'd rather spend the money on what's inside. I have a couple of bright pink labels so I can recognise my luggage on the carousel.' One designer bag Lucinda has fallen for, however, is the Longchamp envelope that expands to become a big overnight bag. She has two of them for a trip: one packed away to be used on the return trip, the other to carry on board the flight.

Eight years ago in Singapore, **Eric Matthews** bought the medium-sized black hard-shell Samsonite suitcase with wheels that he's been travelling with ever since. 'It's a fantastic piece of design. Light. You don't need a trolley. You just pick it up from the carousel and run.' He takes on board the plane a strong, lockable Louis Vuitton black Epi leather overnight bag, along with the one by Bally, slung diagonally from his shoulder, that he is never without.

Before any of his clothes go into the bags, they have been dry-cleaned or washed, ironed and hung somewhere well ventilated the night before: 'Although it comes out a bit crumpled at the other end, at least it's vaguely decent when you take everything out and hang it up once you get to a hotel. You can virtually work for a week without having to use hotel irons or laundry services. The better you pack, the better it is at the other end.'

A week before **Edwina McCann** goes on one of her twice-yearly overseas work trips, her packing starts with, 'Basically the entire wardrobe organised on the bedroom floor; five pairs of pants on top of each other, then the tops and whatever.' She tries on all the outfits, before she starts eliminating until she's down to a workable number. Then she adds the shoes that go with them.

She packs them into a big, solid black Tumi suitcase with a pull-out handle and wheels. Although Tumi bags are expensive they're not as obvious as some highly promoted brands that might tempt the light-fingered. Since Ed anticipates a purchase or two during her stay, she takes along a Longchamp bag called Le Pliage, which looks like a wallet but folds out to become an extra bag to carry the spillover.

When **Tempe Brickhill** travels for business – most often to Paris, Milan or Tokyo – her luggage is by Mandarina Duck and Issey Miyake, because 'they are multi-functional and adaptable and don't scream a label. Wheels are a must. As I invariably travel alone, I like luggage that allows me to be independent and self-sufficient. Getting on and off the Eurostar with a laptop, files and luggage is hopeless if you need someone to help you.' Before packing, 'I put everything out that I like wearing, then eliminate to fit the time away. Anything that requires high maintenance, ironing, etc., gets to stay at home; it's too impractical.'

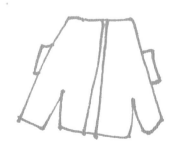

Belinda Seper is a last-minute packer. 'I usually start to think about it a week before and if there's a possibility I might like to take something, I'll take it to the cleaners. I leave everything on their hangers and in the plastic from the drycleaners. If there are four or five together it doesn't matter. Everything just goes in the suitase and gets folded in half. And that's it.'

Most packers put shoes on the bottom, but not Belinda. 'I put all the shoes and lumpy things on top, so all the clothes are flat. And then I put a layer of scarves and accessories on top of all that so when I arrive at the other end it's not this great palaver to unpack. I take out all these hangers and chuck them straight in the closet. Shoes, always in shoe bags, get put straight in cupboards. Underwear's always in a bag of its own with all my tights. Gym clothes in another. If my shirts are a bit squashed I don't care because I'm usually wearing a jacket or cardigan over them anyway. If they're pressed properly they survive.' The trick, she says, is to make sure your suitcase is full. 'If there's room left in a suitcase, they bounce around. Generally, it takes no more than seven-to-ten minutes to unpack, so I can be showered, unpacked, dressed, I'll see you in half an hour. Then we go to our first appointment.'

Tumi is Belinda's favourite brand of suitcase. 'The thing I love about this particular suitcase is it's got a zipper that allows it to expand for all my inevitable purchases.' It also has a large outside pocket where she packs her ankle-length wind coat and a big cashmere wrap. That means she can leave Australia in lightweight clothes and wrap herself up without fuss to wait in the taxi queue in icy Europe.

Ilana Katz is not fond of traditional suitcases, and abhors the ones with wheels. 'You're running in an airport, you look straight ahead and suddenly you trip over them. They drive me crazy.' She tried a detachable set of wheels, some time ago. 'It annoyed me so much I threw it away at the airport.' For the past fifteen years, she has travelled with two unbranded leather bags she bought in Florence. 'They are soft overnight bags which collapse, can be put away, take no room. They are the perfect size because they take a pair of trousers folded in half. They are such a good design; they expand, and a zipper can make them small again. I am constantly looking to find a replacement because I can see that their days are numbered. I'm going to get someone to remake them for me because I can't find anything like them. They are always admired by check-in people and I hope they won't be admired by anybody else.'

A battered and scratched sturdy grey Samsonite, circa 1985, is **Susan Kurosawa**'s loyal fellow traveller. 'I love the fact that it is the sports model, a tiny bit smaller than the norm.' She says the Ralph Lauren tote she picked up in a sale at the boutique in The Peninsula, Hong Kong, in 1980, 'is gloriously worn and looks as if it has been swung from the heights of many a camel'. No doubt it has. She was asked to name her price for it by 'a very elegant French woman at the Palais Jamais hotel in Fez who thought it was "*très authentique*" and would not believe I hadn't stolen it from a passing Berber'. Her third piece is a frivolous handbag of some kind (see chapter 9, 'Pocket power').

The blueprint of the perfect travel wardrobe is well known to **James Gordon**, but sticking to it is the problem. 'I try really hard to do a capsule wardrobe and stay with navy, sky and red, with a bit of black. But I see a hint of orange and off I go. On my most recent trip [to Spain and London] I seem to have had enough separates for three grown men to wear for a month. My solution is to say ta-ta to all large suitcases next Monday.' Two he will not toss out are 'a lovely plaited brown leather overnighter, and a black one I love from Country Road. I don't use a wallet, with the philosophy, "Lose a wallet, lose the lot," so pockets are crammed with cash and credit cards and bits of whatever.' His Prada bag is a clutter of pens and other paraphernalia.

A spare bedroom comes in handy as a sorting-house for **Carolyn Lockhart** when she's planning a trip. 'I put everything on the rack that I think I might need, with the shoes underneath in plastic bags. I do pack very carefully. In my brain I want to take very little but, each time I have, I've been desperately unhappy because I've always got the perfect thing at home. I try to cut back on shoes.'

She has suitcases and bags in lots of sizes, 'but nothing amazing, otherwise people will steal it. I quite like Hedgren. It's not very glamorous but it's terribly practical, lots of handbags with proper slots for your telephone. I've got a couple of those for travel.' Her carry-on bag is from Longchamp.

Paring down presents a problem to many of our most stylish and experienced travellers. Add **Craig Markham** to the list. 'I always try to pack light but it's not in my DNA, so I try not to have suitases that are too large, otherwise I will simply fill them.' He is not fond of 'designer luggage that says to people there are expensive things inside to steal, although some vintage Vuitton has always appealed to me.' An exception to the no-designer rule is the beautiful brown leather Prada overnight bag bought on sale in New York that he carries on board, never checks in.

What goes into his strong, practical black Tumi suitcase for a combined business/ private visit to Australia in summer is well planned and precise. 'There are certain items I always travel with. One is a Rowenta Steamer. It saves on hotel pressing when so often one just wants to freshen up a suit or sweater. I also travel with a black Prada suit, in a lighter weight for Australia. It has a slight stretch in it. It's comfortable, a perfect cut and goes anywhere. Two other light suits – one bitter chocolate, the other beige – by Jil Sander. For work, an extra suit in navy or grey. I bring John Smedley knitwear in black, chocolate and navy sea island cotton; always a couple of white shirts and a stack of cotton Ts, which I pick up at Banana Republic in the US. (Here in Australia I buy up black and white Bonds Ts, which I love.) I pack lightweight Helmut Lang trainers in black, brown and beige, as well as two pairs of sandals (Prada and Jil Sander) in brown and black leather. Also a pair of light chinos and my jeans from paperdenim&cloth, bought on a recent trip to Barneys in Beverly Hills. I try to keep toiletries to a minimum. Day face cream by Rebecca Korner and a new light hair dressing called Second Day by Unite.'

Too big a suitcase is, to **Jane Roarty**, 'a bit vulgar'. She also thinks it's unfair on the handlers. Apart from that, it's just not practical, especially if you're trying to lug it on and off trains. 'I'd rather go with two: one medium and one for me to take on the plane.' Like her clothes, her cases are always black. A soft Samsonite with wheels is the kind she prefers.

Jane is a systematic packer. 'I lay everything out on the bed, coordinate everything and try to be as light as possible. I dislike myself so much for taking things that I do not wear, so I am very strict with clothing and I wear only one colour: black. I cannot stand huge problems with lots of luggage because I know damn well I'm going to come back with so much.' It's not going away that's the problem, it's coming back. The clothes that were neatly folded over each other for the journey out have often been screwed up ruthlessly to make room for the inevitable purchases she brings home. These will not necessarily be wearables, apart from perhaps a pair of shoes and bohemian accent pieces or jewellery to enliven the black. They're more likely to be hefty books, additions to her formidable *batterie de cuisine*, and even light bulbs (see page 114). Although Jane never packs a hairdryer – if the hotel doesn't supply it, she buys one – she always takes adaptors, 'because no-one has Australian adaptors' for her laptop computer.

Predictably, **Akira Isogawa** is the most pared-down of travellers. The soft black unbranded nylon bag with wheels and leather handles that he checks in for Paris does not contain his wardrobe; it's filled with samples or sketches to do with business. The black cowhide shoulder bag – a gift from a friend – that he takes on board has no brand, either. 'I only pack what I really need because otherwise you end up not actually using it. There's no point carrying it. I take really few clothes. Then I can wash them at the hotel, even when there is no washing machine. I can hand-wash everything. I tend to do that in Sydney anyway. Also, I never iron any of my garments. I like the crushed look.' He folds trousers to pack them, 'but business shirts are usually twisted into a small ball'.

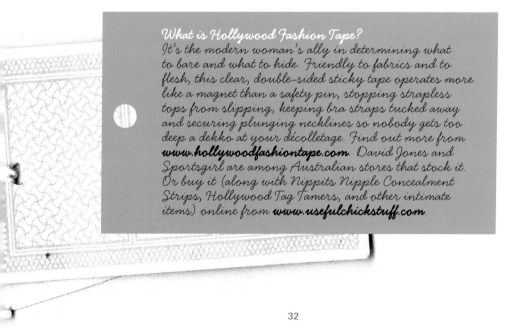

What is Hollywood Fashion Tape?
It's the modern woman's ally in determining what to bare and what to hide. Friendly to fabrics and to flesh, this clear, double-sided sticky tape operates more like a magnet than a safety pin, stopping strapless tops from slipping, keeping bra straps tucked away and securing plunging necklines so nobody gets too deep a dekko at your décolletage. Find out more from **www.hollywoodfashiontape.com** David Jones and Sportsgirl are among Australian stores that stock it. Or buy it (along with Nippits Nipple Concealment Strips, Hollywood Tag Tamers, and other intimate items) online from **www.usefulchickstuff.com**.

NOTES

4

TOUCHDOWN —
THE WORLD

No matter what time of day it is, you revive momentarily. After endless hours on the wing, you and your luggage have been reunited in the arrivals hall of an airport on the other side of the world. The relief is exhilarating! You can tell, just by looking around, that you're on foreign soil. Even a big international airport, sterile though it might be, reflects the character of a country: the hot frankfurts and soft-porn bookshops at Schiphol, Amsterdam; the hucksters offering limousine rides into Manhattan from JFK; the way porters at Leonardo da Vinci Airport, Rome, give every woman the eye, no matter what age she is.

My arrivals in Europe have been, almost invariably, at the crack of dawn. I remember one exception, though. It was mid-morning by the time I arrived at Hôtel de la Trémoille in Paris in mid-winter. The porter, surely no older than fourteen, asked me how long I had been travelling. 'Thirty hours,' I said. 'Thirteen hours!' he exclaimed in amazement.

An overnight journey by rail from Edinburgh to London is no hardship. No seatbelts. A good dinner in the dining car. No jet lag. Refreshed, I got off the train at seven o'clock one morning and took a taxi to the St James's Club, where nobody could find any record of my booking. I dumped my bags there, grumpy that my day had started badly, and walked around the corner to the Ritz. There I explained my predicament to the resident manager, who parked me in a comfortable chair and ordered coffee to be brought while, I imagine, he made a discreet telephone call to the deputy general manager, whom I said I knew. I did not make up this grandiose claim; as travel director of *Vogue* Australia, it was my business to know a lot of people in the industry internationally, and by then Julian Payne had become a friend. Presto! A charming room was mine. When Julian arrived for duty, dashingly turned out in morning dress, he delighted in escorting me to the Club to pick up my bags. I never did stay at the St James's Club and I've had a soft spot for the Ritz ever since.

PASSENGER TICKET

36

Once in my room, I unpack everything immediately. I look for a safe where I can put away my passport, tickets, credit cards, cash and keys. Over the years, my travel wardrobe has narrowed itself down so severely that I can empty my suitcase and have everything hung up or stacked neatly in the wardrobe in the time it takes to run a bath. (Are bathtubs getting bigger or am I getting smaller?) I have a long soak in silken suds, and I love a towelling robe to dry myself in. I don't hurry. I love hotels, especially if they have such luxuries as linen sheets. (In the case of the Ritz Madrid there's so much pure linen even your laundry bag is made of it.) I make telephone calls to confirm appointments. I study a map of the city carefully before I go out. I never open one up in the street. If I get lost, well, too bad; I either find my way back on foot or I look for a taxi. I try to look like a local and, certainly, never like an American – unless I'm in America, of course. I like a topcoat to hide my bag under but, if it's summer, I keep valuables tucked carefully away in the safe or upon my person. Never in one of those horrible bum bags.

Losing your way is easier than finding it in a foreign city, and you can get into a bit of strife when the language is as difficult to understand and pronounce correctly as French. Once in Paris I was invited by Remi Krug to Reims, in the Champagne region to the north-east, to look at his family *cave*, the one that produces what many (including Her Majesty) believe to be the finest champagne in the world, and to join him for lunch afterwards. Talk about living high. I asked the concierge at the Trémoille to book me a return train ticket to what I pronounced as 'Reems'. Just as well I studied the ticket carefully, because he booked me on a train to Rennes, way over to the south-west. When I pointed to Reims on the map, he exclaimed, with a gutteral roll of the r, 'Ah! *RRRRRanz!*' (At least I knew how to pronounce my destination when I boarded the train.)

What a beautiful excursion that was. After the personal tour and before lunch, I sipped Krug in the sitting room of the Krug family maison before we motored to a neighbouring restaurant, lavish with Michelin stars, for exquisite dishes, all accompanied by Krug. When my host put me on the train back to Paris, he popped a bottle of Krug in my bag, and I seemed to float back to the Gare de l'Est on some kind of rosy cloud in the late afternoon.

Then I saw the queue for taxis. Goodness, how mundane was the reality of having to stand in line after I'd been sipping ambrosia with the gods. I was so far above myself, I decided to walk and pick up a taxi on the way. I struck out and suddenly I was in an African ghetto, totally lost and shocked into sobriety. While I felt terribly conspicuous, especially with the top of the bottle of Krug sticking out of my bag, it was important not to panic or to look vulnerable. I adopted my most confident air and marched as purposefully as a sergeant on parade, even though I had no idea where I was going; the light is so diffused on those long summer evenings in Paris you can't tell east from west. How long was it before I saw an empty taxi nosing its way out of a side street? It felt like hours. I've always been partial to a cab, but none has ever been as welcome as that one.

Day one in a new place

Essential for **Craig Markham** when he steps off the plane is 'a person in the arrivals hall holding a sign with my name on it. A pre-arranged car makes all the difference,' especially after a flight from London to Sydney that arrives at 6 a.m., or a trans-Atlantic one that gets to New York at noon on a sweltering day in summer. On his return to London, though, he catches a taxi because he reckons the famous London black cabs are 'the best in the world'. (They are also expensive, about as much from airport to city as the cost of a BA hop from London to Amsterdam.) Essential in a foreign place is 'a hotel room pre-registered from the night before, so that there is none of that boring waiting around in the lobby' for the room to be ready. Whether you're prepared to pay for the privilege depends on your priorities and the size of your expense account. In most hotels, check-in time is not until the afternoon.

When **Eric Matthews** travels to Milan, as he does regularly as part of his job, he usually arrives in the morning. 'Having endured a 24-hour flight, the most blessed thing in the world to me is having a shower, cleansing myself of all that rank plane air, unfurling everything out of the suitase and putting it on fresh coathangers. Washing my hair, washing everything. Shaving.' That done, he goes to a coffee shop for breakfast. 'Then I just walk and walk and walk, buy a copy of the *International Herald Tribune*, have lunch and try to fight sleep until eight or nine o'clock.'

Last year, he arrived in Milan on Easter Saturday morning. 'The whole city was in reverence. Not a soul anywhere, only the sound of all these amazing church bells in the beautiful spring air. Fluttering pigeons on piazzas. I wandered down some of the exquisite lanes, seeing beautiful old buildings and Mamma pegging out the washing.'

There's no rest for **Belinda Seper** when she arrives at her hotel. After her ten minutes of unpacking, showering and changing clothes, she's ready to meet her colleague in the lobby to go to their first appointment. But first of all they'll derive a little spiritual sustenance from a visit to a hallowed place. In Milan, it's the Duomo, which she finds 'a very, very powerful space'. In Paris it's Notre Dame des Victoires, 'the most beautiful old church'. Once inside, 'I say my prayers for a good trip and hope I'll be guided in the right way in the decisions I'm about to make'. Then she gets down to business.

'Most people say they take the day off and wander around, but I want to get straight into it, because I get tired otherwise and then jet lag will set in around three in the afternoon and I might be tempted to lie down.' She never buys anything on the first day; 'I look around and see what else is out there'. Back at the hotel at the end of the day, the fresh flowers she has ordered will be in her room and she'll light the Diptyque candle she travels with, 'So that my rooms always smell like *my* rooms, not like the hotel'.

Carolyn Lockhart always unpacks her bags completely, 'Even if I'm going from place to place and only have one night in each. You always want what's on the bottom.' Hanging things up means you rarely have to press anything and, in Europe, that's a big advantage. Carolyn remembers that, on her first trip to Paris, 'I was so shocked when they said, "No, no, no iron, madame, we'll press it for you", and then I saw the price.' On weekends the service might not even exist, 'So it's three days before you get your clothes back. I don't mind wrinkles as much as I used to. I certainly try not to travel with linen.'

39

Once unpacked, 'I like to go out, find a map and walk to get my bearings, particularly if I do arrive really early. I don't want to lie down, because then jet lag will catch up. I'm a great believer in staying awake until their night time, having a meal and going to bed early. So I often walk, almost all day, then feel really tired and go to bed'.

The time-change is negligible for **Tempe Brickhill** on her business trips from London to Paris or Milan, so jet lag doesn't apply. But the first thing she does is unpack. 'I always need to try to make the room feel like it is mine, and I like to have my things around me.'

Because of her expertise in fashion and beauty, **Lucinda Mendel** often finds herself on assignment in Paris, and it's usually 6 a.m. when her plane touches down. Although she doesn't really expect to be able to get into her hotel room at such an early hour, she always tries. 'If I can't, I leave my bags there. Usually I've organised some sort of [beauty] treatment. Last May it was with the house of Orlane; they have a lovely institute in the 16th arrondissement. Yves Saint Laurent's mother has a treatment there every day. She takes her little dog.'

Lucinda's treatment was just the thing for jet lag. 'They scrubbed me all over and then made me stand and this woman stood behind a barrier and hosed me down with an industrial hose. It was fantastic. I felt as fresh as a daisy afterwards. Then they blow-dried my hair. When I went back to my hotel, the room was ready. I didn't fully unpack because I didn't want to waste the day. I didn't need a shower. Then I was out. I always try to stay up all day and go to bed at the normal time.'

What did she do with the rest of the day? 'I went to my favourite haunts. I went to Martin Grant. I went to the Paul & Joe shop. I always go to Café Marly at the Louvre; it's a bit of a fashion-week hang. I used to go to the Collections and that's where a lot of people go for lunch. I have an omelette and a kir royale on my first day. Then I like going to Colette and having a look. They often have a fantastic sale upstairs – you can tell, because people keep walking up and down the stairs – but they don't advertise it. That's where I bought my beautiful Prada necklace for a reduced price. They have great sales there . . . I always like going on the ferris wheel in the Tuileries Gardens because it has this wonderful iconic Parisian rooftop view.'

For dinner, Lucinda makes her way back to the Marais district where, just around the corner from Martin Grant's shop, is Les Philosophes, 'a gorgeous little bistro that spills out on to the street at 28 rue Vieille-du-Temple. They have a fantastic tomato tart and good duck there, too. I often go there by myself because it's quite buzzy'.

By the time **Jane Roarty** gets to Paris for the Collections, she will have been in Milan for a week, so jet lag is not a factor. She usually arrives at a civilised hour mid-morning. 'I do not, under any circumstances, want to be in a ritzy big hotel; I couldn't stand that. I situate myself around rue Jacob. I want to be in a simple hotel. I am so excited to be there, my adrenalin is working so hard and high, I just walk. The first thing I do is go and see my favourite bookshop in the rue Jacob. It's a food and garden bookshop, which I absolutely adore. I am besotted with books.

'I'll have a cup of coffee at La Palette, which is just around the corner at 43 rue de Seine. It has taken at least five years for them to even acknowledge me with a smile. Basically, I got them to like me because one morning I tripped up and fell out of the restaurant, and I think they were upset and concerned I was going to sue them.' Since Jane is not fond of eating alone in restaurants, 'I find out where the rest of my Australian friends are, or my French friends, and make a lunch appointment.' After that, she just keeps on walking. 'I'm on the go non-stop in Paris. I just love it.'

Travel for **James Gordon** is usually for pleasure, so he stays with friends, but when he checks into a hotel the first thing he does is open the curtains. Then he removes the bedspread, folds it away, checks that the pillows are suitable and helps himself to a vodka. After that, he is restored and ready for anything.

When **Susan Kurosawa** gets to India, she treats herself to 'an oil head massage and pedicure at the hotel beauty salon. It's always professional, pampering and incredibly cheap. Sometimes I get my eyebrows "tidied" (the Indian salons do it with a thread; very fast and no pain). If in Mumbai, I go straight to Nalanda bookstore in the Taj Hotel arcade to pick up the latest novels by Indian writers. It seems to be open twenty-four hours a day'.

For the first hour after **Akira Isogawa** arrives in Kyoto to stay with his father, the two have an 'intense conversation, to cover everything. He's curious about me. How's the business, and stuff like that. Then I tell him things like, "This time I'll be here only three days, so I'd love to chill out, just go to temples." So he takes me out to temples and I take him out to lunch. So we do this bit of an exchange.'

Akira takes his father to the family-run restaurant, Oedo, where he worked as a waiter while he studied at university. Its address is Shijyo Karasuma Higashi Iru. Kyoto is laid out as a grid and the literal translation of this address is Fourth Lane, at the intersection of Karasuma, East, Enter. Simple, if you can read Japanese. One of its specialities is crumbed pork schnitzel. Astonishing though it might seem, this traditional northern European dish was introduced to Japan after World War II and it's been popular ever since.

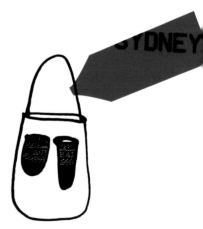

NOTES

5

SLEEPING

AROUND

THE FIRST TRULY grand hotel I ever stayed in alone was Hotel Hassler, at the top of the Spanish Steps in Rome, in the days when its owner, Carmen Wirth, knew each guest by name. She introduced herself to newcomers and invited selected ones to join her little soirées in the comfortable splendour of Salone Eva, beside the bar on the ground floor.

I was so anxious to do the right thing during my stay that I did everything wrong. I over-tipped the concierge, only to find that he was the receptionist. I was so awestruck by the paternal way in which Signor Sabatini looked after me in the splendid Rooftop Restaurant, I couldn't bring myself to tip him at all – it would have been like slipping a few notes to my father.

What the Hassler gave me, apart from a breathtaking view from my room of the dome of St Peter's silhouetted against the dawn, was a taste for the grand old privately owned hotels in Europe that are now rarities and growing even more scarce as big international chains move in and take them over, slick them up and open them up to a wider market.

I am happy to report that Hotel Hassler is still owned by the Wirth family, and is now run by Carmen's son, Roberto. Among other glorious old piles that remain in private hands are the Baur au Lac, which was owned by the Baur family when it materialised beside the lake in Zurich in 1844; and Excelsior Hotel Ernst, built opposite Cologne Cathedral in 1863 and bought by Friedrich Kracht in 1871. Marriage between Friedrich's son Carl and Emma Baur in 1889 ulimately brought both hotels under the same ownership and – hooray, hooray – they are still owned by the Kracht family. Hôtel de Crillon, that gloriously sited eighteenth-century palace lording it over Place de la Concorde in Paris, is owned by the Taittinger family, who produce what happens to be my favourite of all champagnes (though who am I to be picky?). All of these venerable old-timers are members of The Leading Hotels of the World, which you can read about at **www.lhw.com**.

Because of their distinction and a sense of their belonging to a courtlier era, I think of them as providing one-off rather than regular experiences. They are noble anachronisms, to be loved and enjoyed while they last. They can be quite intimidating, though, when you come from a more informal land. If you want to be cosy, you'll be more comfortable staying somewhere less formal, where what you need for dinner comes from a coffee shop rather than a restaurant with two Michelin stars.

In fact, I think the way to appreciate grandeur to the full is to have it as a contrast. I am fond of a family-run pensione or an affordable flat for a few days, followed by utter spoiling somewhere luxurious. It's the best way to intensify the enjoyment of both and to balance the budget, and it's far more rewarding than staying in accommodation that is always at the same level, even if that plane is very rarefied.

Edgy and Intimate

More to today's tastes are the new-concept hotels, some privately owned, set up within the past few years for a hipper crowd. Ian Schrager started this trend a generation ago in New York, first with Morgans, designed by Andrée Putman. It became a clubby bolthole for people who were at what used to be called the cutting edge. But Schrager's first hotel to make the design and hospitality worlds sit up and take notice was The Royalton, in the same midtown block as the old Algonquin. It showcased the brilliance of Philippe Starck, who created a carpeted catwalk the length of the lobby, to make everyone who trod it feel that they were on stage. He made the whole place moody, hard-edged and sleek, like a bullet train or a luxury liner. Everything was custom-made. Dramatic lighting came from hidden sources and from globes shaped like rhino horns. Quite phallic, really. Witness the steel rods thrust through eyelets at the tops of curtains. Hotel lobbies have always been great places for entertainment but this was different. Hush rather than hubbub. So cool, the fashion folk took to it immediately. It became American *Vogue*'s canteen.

Adrian Zecha gave us an Eastern aesthetic we hadn't seen before, in celestial temple-like resort hotels, such as Amanpuri in Thailand and Amankila on the eastern coast of Bali. They are truly sublime. Whereas European service at the highest level can be a bit unnerving, Asians handle it so subtly you never feel uncomfortable.

Small hotels that don't overwhelm but look after their guests in an almost familial way have been around in San Francisco seemingly forever. The boutique idea was also behind Firmdale Hotels in London, although on a much more luxurious and elevated scale than family-run establishments. This trend was slow to catch on in Australia until the McMahon family converted an apartment building in Springfield Avenue, Kings Cross, into the excellent Regents Court Hotel, with self-contained studios. The Schwambergs followed, with the Medusa and the Kirketon (the latter has since been sold) in Darlinghurst Road. The Adelphi sprang up in Melbourne and, later, Hotel Lindrum.

Although it's an international chain, W Hotels interpreted the laid-back concept very well at the Finger Wharf in Sydney's Woolloomooloo before the property was renamed Blue, Woolloomooloo Bay, in 2005 after Taj Hotels took it over. Meanwhile, along came Justin Hemmes, bringing a refined aesthetic to downtown Sydney with The Establishment, a very polished little hotel down a back lane behind his highly successful restaurant/bar/club complex in George Street.

In 2002, when Carla Sozzani added intimate contemporary accommodation to her multi-concept store, 10 Corso Como in Milan (see page 139), she heralded the next big thing in hospitality: think tiny. Her trendy trio of suites is simply called 3 Rooms at 10 Corso Como, **www.3rooms-10corsocomo.com**. Each has its own entrance, balcony overlooking the courtyard garden, living room, bedroom and bathroom. Arne Jacobsen, Marcel Breuer, Joe Colombo, Eero Saarinen, Isamu Noguchi, Gìo Ponti, Charles and Ray Eames and Verner Panton are some of the names behind the design of the furniture and fittings; in other words, a virtual rollcall of twentieth-century interior designers. It's not your everyday fit-out.

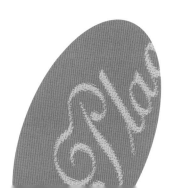

The same may be said of 3 Rooms at 5 Rue de Moussy in Paris. This is fashion designer Azzedine Alaïa's take on a tiny apartment hotel in the building where he lives and works in the Marais district. When he decorated the rooms himself, he threw in a few of his own objects designed by style-setters such as Marc Newson, Serge Mouille and Jean Nouvel. Each spacious suite has its own small kitchen. Email **info@3rooms-5ruedemoussy.com**.

Ilana Katz, our toughest hotel critic

I love hotels, whatever their scale, and I am quite forgiving of them, as long as my room is clean and I have my own bathroom. Not so **Ilana Katz**, who is very clear about what she wants in a hotel. 'I have one philosophy in my head when I travel: I want the place where I'm going to stay, not to be worse than home. Equivalent or better, and usually better. Otherwise, why leave home?' This is particularly true, she says, of resorts. 'It has to have more than a water view, because I have that at home anyhow. If I can't get this, I just don't go, or if I can't afford it, I'm not interested. I sometimes look at people who have the most magnificent homes and then I see where they stay when they travel and I ask myself, why did they even bother to go this distance?'

In her view, **The Four Seasons** at Jimbaran Bay in Bali is worth leaving home for. Its airy pavilions, luxuriant gardens, private plunge pools and impeccable service justify the costly tariffs, **www.fourseasons.com**. And she can't wait to try out a villa at the new **Bulgari** resort designed by Antonio Citterio on the southern tip of Jimbaran Bay, **www.bulgarihotels.com**. Her expectations are based on a close look at the first Bulgari hotel soon after it opened in Milan in 2004. 'It's beautiful, in a wonderful position. You think you are in a holiday resort because they've got beautiful grounds and gardens. It's far from practical. You hear the staff complaining because the floor needs polishing all the time. But the design, the detailing! You have dinner there and everything is perfection. Even the mineral water comes in a designer bottle – they are commercial bottles that you can buy anywhere, but you feel like taking it home and using it as a water carafe. That hotel is absolutely fabulous, so I imagine the one in Bali will be following it.'

The other standard Ilana applies to accommodation is growing more and more difficult for any property to achieve: 'I look for places which are not touristy. Everything is discovered very quickly. A place which is fantastic gets media attention and . . .' there goes the neighbourhood. 'So the big thing is to get your booking in time. I book everything early, so I get in.' She also points out that, even if a hotel has become known to the world but it's a small hotel, say twenty-two rooms, even at full capacity it's never going to be overcrowded.

Ilana now gravitates to 'the new vogue of hotels, the Design Hotels. They are interesting in design – which I am interested in – and they attract a young group of people.' Log on to **www.designhotels.com** to explore.

Hotel Straf 3 via San Raffaele, Milan, is one of them. 'This particular one is very hard-edged – not all of them are – with concrete floors, but the attention to detail and the architecture and design are fantastic. The boy who took us to show us a room was wearing sandshoes, his head was shaved, he wore a T-shirt – that was the uniform. All in black and he looked fabulous.'

Hotel Josef 20 Rybnà, Prague, also belongs to Design Hotels. 'Being in the business of lifestyle and interiors, I appreciated so many fabulous details. Every single thing, even the hangers in the wardrobe, is a design piece. Very cleverly done because the site doesn't have fantastic views but they make it work with design details and internal gardens.'

Neri H&R 5 San Sever, Barcelona. Another in the Design Hotels portfolio, this one is 'magnificent, with old walls and new amenities' and only twenty-two rooms. It sits next to the cathedral and Sant Jaume Square in the old Gothic quarter.

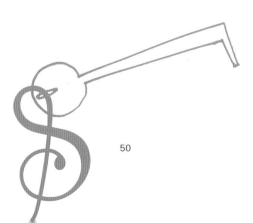

Two others that have earned Ilana's seal of approval are:

Hôtel l'Abbaye Saint-Germain 10 rue Cassette, on the Left Bank in Paris, **www.hotel-abbaye.com**. Ilana has stayed in many top hotels in Paris, such as Hôtel le Bristol and Hôtel Montalembert, but one day, about five years ago, 'I went for a walk and I saw this beautiful courtyard and a sign that said it was a hotel. So I went in. I was taken by the lobby. You could see that somebody cared. The flowers were fresh and white. To see in a three-star [hotel] certain things that you don't usually see gave me a fantastic feeling about it.' She wasn't able to look at a room because the house was full, but she took a risk and booked one for her next visit. 'I've never left it since. The rooms are small, as they are in most hotels in Paris, but they are so well designed around your needs that you can't say that anything you need and want in a room is not there. And the staff are wonderful. So this is my hotel. I don't want to know about anything else.'

Château de Bagnols dates from the thirteenth century and is located in the Beaujolais region, 20 kilometres from Lyon in south-eastern France, **www.bagnols.com**. Ilana says that it is 'most memorable for me and absolutely the best I've ever stayed in' – high praise from a tough judge. 'The antiques and the way the restoration has been done are out of this world. The bed linen is real linen. They've got a flower preparation room, and it's just delightful to see how the girls prepare the flowers in the morning to put in the rooms and the rest of the hotel. The food is wonderful and the kitchen area is enveloped in glass; you can see all the activities and they didn't have to touch any of the architectural features to enclose it.' In her bathroom, Ilana was amused to find that modern technology had put an ancient commode into service as a 21st-century toilet. The whole magnificent conversion was undertaken by Lady Hamlyn. Rocco Forte Hotels now manage the hotel for her.

Susan Kurosawa's top twelve hotels

As you would expect of the travel editor of *The Australian*, **Susan Kurosawa** knows a lot about hotels. She has stayed in more of them than most of us ever will. A serious sybarite, she has a particular fondness for resorts. I am sure you would find no hardship staying in any of the following recommendations. (They are placed in alphabetical order, not according to any ranking, and these are her own words.)

Amangalla Galle Fort, Sri Lanka, **www.amanresorts.com**. The clever Amanresorts group has reinvented the shabby New Oriental Hotel (which has not been new for a while: it opened in 1865) within the walls of the UNESCO-protected Galle Fort. Now it's all polished wood, carefully selected antiques, ceiling fans and planters' chairs, and high-ceilinged white suites that are the last word in faux-colonial luxury. It feels like a more authentic Raffles, without the discouraging doormen and queues for gin slings.

Bovey Castle Devon, England, **www.boveycastle.com**. On the edge of forbidding Dartmoor National Park, Bovey had its heyday in the 1930s during the reign of Viscount Hambledon. It was a spiffing spot for Bertie Wooster-style house parties, with gay young things calling for urgent infusions of Pimms. That period has been taken as the benchmark for a glorious hotel restoration, with lots of clubby corners, a spa and sixty-five guest rooms, including cavernous suites with Art Deco bathrooms in the main wing.

Eichardts Hotel Queenstown, New Zealand, **www.eichardtshotel.co.nz**. This one-time tatty pub in Queenstown's low-rise heart has been a town landmark since the 1870s. Now it's a refurbed gem: its five suites feature beds set on raised platforms and dressed with possum-fur throws. Fireplaces are clad in metal and bathrooms gleam like ice rinks; top Kiwi interior designer Virginia Fisher has a wonderful eye for introducing layer upon layer of rich velvety luxury.

Four Seasons Jimbaran Bay, Bali, **www.fourseasons.com**. Every villa has a plunge pool at this exquisite seafront spread. Also on the room inventory: coralstone-walled garden, outdoor dining and lounging pavilion and the prospect of birds with breakfast. This is real do-not-disturb territory but guests who leave their sanctuary have the choice of two main pools, a casual cafe with pizza oven on the beach, gorgeous spa complex and Bali's best hotel shop.

Kims Retreat Toowoon Bay, New South Wales, **www.kims.com.au**. A family-run Central Coast institution on a picturesque scoop of bay featuring unfussy but stylish timber bungalows hunkered amid stately Norfolk Island pines. The buffets are legendary, with offerings as trendy as sashimi and as homely as pavlova. Splurge on the top-tariff accommodation with direct beach access, broad decks and private pools.

Ngorongoro Crater Lodge northern Tanzania, **www.ccafrica.com**. Call it Masai Versailles or Bushveld Baroque: the rooms are full of red roses, everything is silk and velvet, ruby crystal chandeliers and trays of buck's fizz. Perched on the rim of a prehistoric and wild game-filled crater, as improbably as a jewel box, this is Africa's most extraordinary safari camp – and make that high camp. Guest cottages have palm-thatched conical roofs and tipsy mudbrick chimneys that give them the look of a flimsy movie set.

Oberoi Resort Mauritius, **www.oberoi-mauritius.com**. On this scented island's north-west coast, this divinely detailed resort is set on a sunset-facing headland over a brilliant aquamarine bay. Of its seventy-six rooms, twenty-six are villas surrounded by weathered ochre stone walls, some with large private pools, and all the accommodation is strung through bird-busy gardens dotted with statues and bright with bougainvillea and coral trees. The spa offers coconut-husk body exfoliations and treatments with tamarind, ylang ylang and coconut oils that nod to the Creole culture of Mauritius.

Peninsula Hotel Hong Kong, **www.hongkong.peninsula.com**. Quite simply, the world's finest five-star city hotel. The sense of history and heritage, the immaculate service, the carefully thought-out rooms, the vast pool and spa, the arcades of premium boutiques – and then there's Earl Grey and ribbon sandwiches every afternoon in the gilded lobby, or slip into retro-Shanghai mode at Spring Moon restaurant with its Chinese tea bar and Hong Kong's best Peking duck.

Rajvilas Jaipur, India, **www.oberoirajvilas.com**. The flagship of Oberoi's Vilas (meaning 'homes' in an Indian dialect) range, this ultra-luxe caravanserai offers Rajput fortress architecture, Mughal pleasure ponds and teak-floored campaign tents. Outside the fabled 'pink city' of Jaipur, Rajvilas appears as a shimmering mirage in a red desert. The faux-garrison buildings are unified by emerald lawns, orchards and ornamental pools. A pigeon dispatcher with a white flag on a long stick has the sole duty of swiping at the birds so they don't deposit droppings on rotundas and rooftops.

Soneva Gili The Maldives, **www.sixsenses.com**. Tsunami damage has been rectified and this exceptional resort is back in business. Its pixie-hatted villas all sit over the water on stilts and virtually come with an ensuite aquarium – slip off the lower deck and dip in the fish-filled lagoon. Seven villas are dubbed Crusoe Residences, 'moored' offshore like the hermitages of mad monarchs of the sea, and a rowboat is required to reach them. One must go with someone very special.

Taprobane Island Weligama, Sri Lanka, **www.taprobaneisland.com**. My all-time favourite hideaway, loved for its eccentricity and the almost preposterous means of arrival – guests wade from shore at low tide or, if they prefer, are carried aboard an elephant. A white villa occupies the entire rocky little island in Weligama Bay, like a tropical Mont Saint-Michel. Paul Bowles, favouring leopard-print slippers, used Taprobane as a writing retreat, but it was the mysterious Count de Mauny, on the run from Europe, who built it in 1929, keeping houseboys, a mongoose and two cats, and making his shore transfers carried in an armchair.

Yasawa Island Resort Fiji, **www.yasawa.com**. The friendliest staff in the Fijian islands look after guests as if they were family, and housemaids decorate with hibiscus as if competing in flower-strewing Olympics. Super-spacious bures – luxurious interpretations of traditional vernacular architecture – are a towel's toss from a long, lovely beach. The resort is Australian-owned and food and wine are taken seriously, with the occasional stellar guest chef swapping his or her pressed whites for a sarong.

Armchair inspections

I couldn't estimate the number of times I have been ushered through hotels on inspection tours of deluxe suites, superior rooms, cocktail bars, fine-dining restaurants, gyms, spas, business centres, conference rooms and ballrooms. Some were fascinating, others were tedious, and all of them took a lot of time. Not so when you visit hotels on the web. These are some sites I find worth viewing.

Firmdale Hotels London: **www.firmdale.com**
Guides de Charme: **www.guidesdecharme.com**
Small Luxury Hotels of the World: **www.slh.com**
Tablet Hotels: **www.tablethotels.com**
The Charming Hotels of the World: **www.thecharminghotels.com**
The Crown Collection: **www.crownluxurytravel.com**

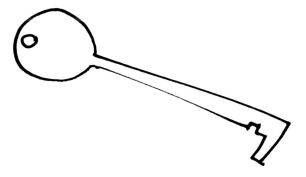

ISSEY MIYAK

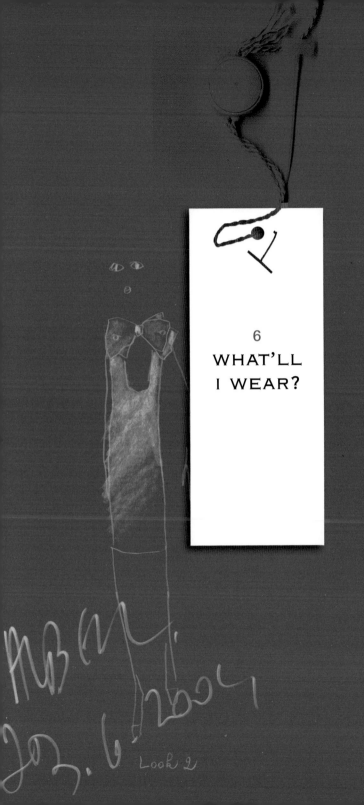

6

WHAT'LL
I WEAR?

WHAT WOULD YOU wear to a business meeting with the fashion legend who made the immortal declaration, 'Pink is the navy blue of India'? Before flying from Italy to New York in 1978 to interview Diana Vreeland at her post as arbiter of excellence at the Costume Institute of The Metropolitan Museum of Art, I had lingered six weeks in the noble shopper's paradise of Florence. What better city to spoil me for choice?

It was the beginning of the battledress look, of gigantic shoulders, jackboots and military stickpins. The coming winter season's colours were olive and bordeaux, and I heard the names Giorgio Armani and Claude Montana for the first time. I fell for it all completely, had to buy two new suitcases for my loot, which included (from the boutique Raspini) an Armani suede jacket that I still cannot bear to part with, poor old crumpled thing.

But, while all the paraphernalia of the new swaggering *alta moda* combat gear found its way into my suitcases, something told me not to strive to be a fashion plate in front of Mrs Vreeland. I reckoned she could spot the fad from the fashion without even looking. Although I knew I would be out of my depth, it was important not to come over as a neophyte or a fashion victim. I also wanted to feel comfortable in what I had on, and I hadn't practised getting through the door in shoulders worthy of Mr Universe.

Research had told me that she liked nothing better than cleanliness (she made a habit of wearing cotton gloves to read the newspaper), neatness (she had her money ironed, though not laundered, let me hasten to say) and simplicity. She espoused the view that 'elegance is refusal'. This belief was borne out by her choice of 'uniform' for the office: a little something in beige from Balenciaga or Yves Saint Laurent, names that were totally out of my class.

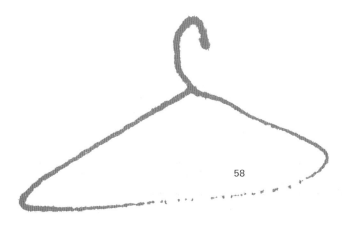

So, I refused flamboyance in favour of reserve. In an elegant little emporium called Principe, in via Strozzi, a tiny street running off Piazza della Repubblica in Florence, I found the most endearing Italian version of the English schoolgirl look in what, to India, is the pink of the West: navy blue pleated skirt, a pristine self-striped white cotton shirt and a navy-and-white fair-isle cardigan with mother-of-pearl buttons. I bought navy opaque pantyhose as well, though I stopped short of navy knickers. It was so restrained. So full of refusal. Yet Italian, therefore not what you'd see among the hockey sticks on the playing fields of England.

A few doubts still lingered. Had I refused too much? Might this outfit come over as unimaginative to the woman who had been the twentieth century's most influential fashion force at American *Harper's Bazaar* and *Vogue*, and who had, along with her late husband T Reed Vreeland, been made a lifetime member of America's best-dressed list? My gesture to individuality was a pair of bordeaux suede brogues from Beltrami and a narrow suede belt that tied in a bow; pretty pathetic now that I come to think about it.

The outfit did its job, though. DV gave me great material for the piece I wrote for June McCallum at *Vogue* Australia, and my questions, in the main, were not too stupid, except for one. Do we ever forget our blunders? Among the exhibitions she had put on for the museum was one called American Women of Style. 'Was anybody offended at not being included?' gurgles gullible one. 'I can't imagine so,' DV replies, pausing to take a draw on her Lucky Strike cigarette. 'They're all dead.'

Fashion fast forward

Refusal is not very fashionable today. I don't dare think what La Vreeland would make of what finds its way onto the backs and off the buttocks of the fashion plates of the noughties. Any old bit of tat, as long as it's been sewn by overworked and underpaid hired hands, is making squillions for those who fossick for it. They stitch it up with offcuts into garments your grandmother would have been too ashamed to give to the poor, and flog it off under a ditsy brand name with a huge price tag at a chic boutique. I'm pretty sure nuns and mothers did not have that kind of thing in mind when they taught us girls tacking, hemming, patching and mending.

Reworking and mismatching yesterday's wearables that have fallen on hard times and found themselves in flea markets and charity stores is big business now. The more imperfect the better. Witness the moth-eaten look, the kind of thing that happens to your best cashmere if you don't seal it in a ziplock bag. The look makes the fetching raffishness of Sally Bowles in pre-war Berlin and Edith Piaf in post-war Paris look positively bourgeois.

In a recent email, **Tempe Brickhill** made the passing remark, 'I hate secondhand shops. They depress me. Everyone seems to call it "vintage" now but, for me, vintage is best when it is something that I bought when I was twenty and still love today. Or, even better, something wonderful that my mother or grandmother bought at twenty. I don't want anyone else's "vintage".' Until she told me that, I had never admitted to anyone that I feel precisely the same way. I like to know where things have come from before I want them next to my skin. Besides, no amount of dry-cleaning or washing can take the lived-in air from tired old clothes. I ask myself: Where Have They Been?

Cathy Horyn's reports for *The New York Times* from Paris on the autumn collections in March 2005 gave me hope that an era of refinement and polish is on the way. At least Stefano Pilati for Yves Saint Laurent and Alber Elbaz for Lanvin are having a good try. I am particularly heartened to learn that the name of Jeanne Lanvin, who was born in 1867 and apprenticed to a dressmaker at the age of thirteen, is again associated with elegance, dignity and discretion. During World War II, while Coco Chanel fraternised with the enemy, the loyal house of Lanvin made uniforms for the women of France's mobile ambulance units. How noble. 'Mr Elbaz's primary concern is that women wear his clothes and feel comfortable in them,' wrote Ms Horyn, adding, 'Now there's a novel concept.' I'll say. But will anybody take notice, or will the street take to the barricades to defend its entrenched right to reveal bra straps, belly buttons and buttock cleavages? I know which side I'm on.

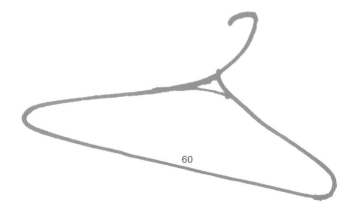

60

Obsession

Other people count sheep when they can't sleep. I count my Issey Miyakes. As I lie there in the dark, it calms me to itemise the precious pieces, one by one. You probably know that many of the garments this Japanese genius makes are so light and flexible and practical, they constitute the perfect travel wardrobe. It is one of life's ironies that, now that I've achieved this state of peripatetic grace, I don't feel tempted to travel anymore, except on the 301, 2 or 3 bus to town. But that's another story.

When I count my Issey Miyakes, I think of where I bought them. One, two, three, four early ones came from the master's shop at Aoyama in Tokyo. From there you can walk to Omotesando, the buzzy boulevard leading to the Meiji Jingu Shrine on sunny Sundays to see how completely Nipponese girls and boys adopt a style and put it together with wit and ingenuity.

Five, six, seven, eight, nine, ten svelte little pleated numbers were a scoop from Issey's signature store in Manhattan at the corner of Madison and 77th, and from Bergdorf Goodman – for me the best fashion department store in New York. (The hairdresser upstairs at Bergdorf's sells a Miami-produced nail strengthening line called Nailtiques, the only products that have ever done anything to stop my fingernails from splitting and breaking. English beauticians on the QE2 first told me about it; they stockpile the stuff every time they land in America. It does exist in Australia but it has so few stockists, it's best to get it direct from the importer in Melbourne, Panache Salon Supplies, telephone (03) 9417 4822.)

How easy it is to digress. Back to counting Isseys. Eleven, twelve, thirteen, fourteen, fifteen, umpteen stunning pieces came from sales at Belinda, Double Bay; I topped them up with four more at Cose Ipanema in South Yarra, when both stores stocked the label.

Then there are the two art pieces, both from Five Way Fusion in Paddington before it closed. I've named the first one The Marsh King's Daughter, after the creepy Hans Christian Andersen story, because it's like the carapace of an exotic sea serpent, a fantasy on a marine theme. I have worn it only twice because there aren't too many places in Sydney where you can go looking like a creature from the bottom of the lagoon. This trophy was gained when I was early for lunch at Bistro Moncur one

Melbourne Cup Day, so I hopped off the 389 on the way. It was love at first grasp. It was on sale. It was on my back before I could say Emma Chizzit.

The second piece of art is not so flamboyant, but it is both divine and wearable. I waited a year for its exorbitant price to be reduced to semi-affordable proportions, by which time it was slightly larger, because I think half the eastern suburbs of Sydney had tried it on and found it either too small or too expensive. It is a diaphanous jacket of two differently coloured bubbled layers that float as I walk. When a friend first saw it, she said, 'It looks as though it was spun by fairies.' I have no doubt that it was.

My Issey Miyake hoard at this moment amounts to thirty-seven items, including bags and scarves, and depending on whether I count the Plantation (an old spin-off label) overcoat as one or two: the outside is made of gabardine and its tweed lining can unbutton to become another coat of a very different kind, similar to the long cardigans they used to wear in the 1930s. This clever twosome is vintage, as fashionistas would say, which means it's so ancient it should have been sent to St Vinnies seasons ago.

And therein lies a problem: clothes are like people – after too many outings, they start getting tired. Even Miyakes, which are all but indestructible. Who stocks Issey Miyake in Australia anymore? As far as I know, only the signature store, **Issey Miyake**, at Shop 2, 177 Toorak Road, South Yarra, telephone (03) 9826 4900. So, unless I feel like getting on a plane – and I'd rather not – I'll just have to rely on the www.

Amanda Love – magnificent minimalist

Halfway through the writing of this book, I happened to be gabbling on about it to an urbane New Yorker named Gene Silbert, who owns an apartment in Sydney and spends each summer here. 'If it's not too late, you must speak to Amanda Love,' he said. I knew Amanda as a curator, valuer and art advisor who loves and understands Australian and international contemporary art and puts together private art collections through her company, Amanda Love Art. When Gene described her disciplined attitude to buying clothes, I knew she was essential to this book. If anybody embodies refusal it is Amanda.

Like Gene, she is a minimalist, in her house, her travels and her shopping. What happens is this: 'I shop twice a year. I don't browse. I buy a couple of things and wear them to death. It's my uniform for the season.' This principle worked particularly well when she could sell the pieces off before she bought the next season's two things. Someone who made a living out of it 'came to the house with garbage bags, gave you back the coathangers, left you with a cheque and sold the clothes on the Internet.' Sadly, she seems to have disappeared, maybe scared off by the case of a girl in New York who was caught for doing that kind of thing without declaring it to the tax office.

The clothes Amanda chooses are from avant-garde designers whose work goes into museums, as well as selected high-end retailers. Her favourites vary. She has a current craze for Belgian designer Martin Margiela; she buys from his shop in Bruton Place, London. Her shoes come from Yohji Yamamoto in Conduit Street. In New York, she shops at Comme des Garçons and at the worldwide headquarters of Issey Miyake in a historic cast-iron building (with a titanium sculpture by Frank Gehry) in Tribeca. If she buys in Sydney, it will be at **Robby Ingham**, 424 Oxford Street, Paddington. (The store is also a personal favourite of SBS's Fashionista, Lee Lin Chin, who shops there for Junya Watanabe.) Black has always been the mainstay of Amanda's wardrobe, although she has 'branched out' into navy, beige and brown. As for anything brighter: 'I tried to wear red for a day and it gave me a headache.'

These pieces come together in a wardrobe that can take her anywhere, and she travels with hand luggage only. Last time she unpacked in London, a friend asked, 'Amanda, where are your clothes?'

Australian fashion

What can I tell you about our own big names in fashion design? You know them as well as I do. Akira Isogawa, **www.akira.com.au**, and Collette Dinnigan, **www.collettedinnigan.com.au**, who regularly show in Paris, are not only highly regarded on the international fashion circuit, they are household names at home. And they are not alone.

Look at the worldwide success of Tsubi (Ksubi internationally), **www.tsubi.com**, dreamed up by four irreverent Sydney beach boys thumbing their noses at convention. Australians are nothing if not enterprising: witness Heidi Middleton and Sarah-Jane Clarke, first noted for jeans with a Sass & Bide label and a 5-centimetre zip, **www.sassandbide.com**. You've heard the legend about them but, like all good fairy stories, it bears repeating. In October 2001, these two sassy Aussies came upon a crew shooting an episode of *Sex and the City* in New York. In a flash, Sarah-Jane had whipped off her Funky Thompson jacket and sweet-talked the security guard into giving it to Sarah Jessica Parker. The rest is a happy beginning, rather than a happy ending; anything seen on the back of the most emulated television superstar of the early twenty-first century was a guarantee of most-wanted status. Being bought out by a big company is another sure measure of success, especially if you stay on as creative director; ask Peter Morrissey, who sold the label that bears his surname to Oroton in December 2000, **www.oroton.com.au**.

Then there are the perennials, such as George Gross, **www.georgegross.com.au**, and Carla Zampatti, **www.carlazampatti.com.au**, whose focus on quality and consistency has earned them a devoted following. Their staying power is all the more creditable when you consider the skittish nature of the industry.

CONSCIENCE CLOTHING

Sometimes Australian designers turn up in surprising places. North-west Pakistan, for instance. That's where Cath Braid and Kirsten Ainsworth live and work, to create clothes under the Caravana label, www.caravana.com.au. The garments are designed by Cath and made by local women from hand-loomed, hand-dyed cottons and silks in brilliant colours. Many are embroidered in patterns depicting everyday life in the remote region where the women live. Through this worthy enterprise, which is partnered by the Aga Khan Foundation, scores of Sunni Muslim women who would otherwise have no chance of paid work are able to earn regular money. As well as taking on the fashion capitals, Aussies are at the frontier where fashion meets fairness.

Fashion runs in Lee Mathews's family. Her grandmother was a dressmaker, so Lee reckons she's been designing clothes 'sort of forever', at least since she learned to sew on her gran's treadle machine. She started designing professionally in 1989 and, 'Funnily enough, little has changed, except perhaps a hem length or a sleeve detail. I have always loved the same simple shapes and natural fibres.' Plenty of other women feel the same way, and that prompted Lee to open a workroom with a shopfront at Newport, on Sydney's northern beaches, in 2002. Three years later, her second signature store opened, this time at 1059 High Street, Armadale, a stylish shopping area in Melbourne. Although her work is cut on simple lines, she does it with flair, using earthy yet noble fabrics, such as pure linen and silk, in neutral tones. Everything is beautifully finished. Her pieces have a look of quality, that indefinable something the Americans call 'class'. See **www.leemathews.com.au**.

As for Martin Grant, his considerable achievement goes far beyond having long ago moved on from Melbourne to set himself up successfully in Paris. His superlative and understated clothes have earned him: acclaim from American *Vogue*; the friendship of Naomi Campbell and the elegant Lee Radziwill (Jacqueline Kennedy Onassis's sister); and clients as illustrious as Cate Blanchett, Oprah Winfrey and our own **Lucinda Mendel**.

The incidence of Australian labels turning up in smart boutiques and department stores in the world's fashion capitals happens so often now that it hardly counts as news. Melbourne designer Kit Willow has sold her dresses under the Willow label through outlets such as Selfridges in London and Barneys in New York. If you're looking for the work of Tina Kalivas, **www.tinakalivas.com**, or Alice McCall, **www.alicemccall.com**, in London, try Browns and Browns Focus. Dresses, bags and spa indulgences sporting the Ginger & Smart label, **www.gingerandsmart.com**, have turned up at Austique and Browns Focus; they are the work of Sydney sisters Alexandra and Genevieve Smart. Antipodium, **www.antipodium.com**, Austique, **www.austique.co.uk**, and Coco Ribbon, **www.cocoribbon.com**, are London boutiques that do great business in Australian fashion labels.

BAROQUE FROCKING

The window of an old shop on the corner of
Francis and Yurong Streets, East Sydney, is not
where I expected to find an elaborate dress
that looked as though it was about to be worn
by an heiress to her birthday party. Close
inspection revealed it to be what its young
designer (and the shop's owner), Ben Smith,
described as 'sportswear meets couture'. On
a base of beautifully cut and finished cotton
organdie, with little French seams, Ben had built
a collage of neutral-coloured bits that ranged
from silk organza to cotton interlock. The frock
was beautiful and imaginative in a thoroughly
contemporary way, so that 'I've had girls try it
on with jeans,' he told me. He did concede that
'You've got to have attitude to wear it, so it
doesn't wear you.'

In playing the elements off each other, Ben hasn't
just redefined baroque, he's turned it into cubism.
Braque meets baroque. More restrained garments,
each impeccably finished, grace the rails inside
his little salon. Since he never makes more than
three pieces of the same design, Ben describes his
work as 'demi-couture'. He also designs to order.
Enquiries, telephone (02) 9331 4888.

The way Michelle Jank makes cohesiveness of disparate pieces from many eras and geographical sources to create exquisite one-offs has put her into the top ten since she graduated in fashion design from the Sydney Institute of Technology in 1999. The elegance of Scanlan & Theodore, **www.scanlantheodore.com.au**, the meticulous finish of Easton Pearson, the superb tailoring of Toni Maticevski, the refinement of Kirrily Johnston, **www.kirrilyjohnston.com**, and the cheeky swagger of Lover, **www.loverthelabel.com**, are hallmarks of Australian designers of singular talent.

What have they got on?

For **Edwina McCann**, 'certain things' are of particular value: the cut of a Stella McCartney suit, the perfection of Chanel ballet slippers, the clever way Melbourne designer Toni Maticevski does 'that soft and hard thing' and the wearability of his clothes. 'I am truly as excited about him as I would be about Narcisco Rodriguez.' She is also a fan of Alessandro Dell'Acqua and Sandra Thom. But, like others whose job means keeping an eye on every nuance of fashion trends, Ed gravitates to homewares in her time off. 'I don't get as excited about the clothing side of it.' Too much like work.

Eric Matthews cuts an elegant figure, especially when you see him fold his tall, lean frame as neatly as a piece of origami into his Smart Car, the tiny environment-friendly two-seater from the makers of Mercedes-Benz. What a match they make: two examples of design excellence tootling around Sydney.

In relation to his clothes, Eric says, 'I don't like pattern in any way, shape or form.' He prefers a sober colour palette of black, navy, brown, charcoal and pehaps olive, offset by 'a crisp white shirt'.

Last time we met he wore the superbly tailored Hermès trousers he bought at a sale in Sydney, with a jacket by Chiodo of Melbourne that never failed to attract attention when he wore it at the Milan Furniture Fair. 'Virtually on a daily basis, one person would stop me and say, "Where did you get that jacket, Comme des Garçons?" I was proud to say, "No, no, no, it's an Australian design." I really like what these local lads do. They're very unassuming. They do classic stuff with a little Yohji [Yamamoto] influence – he's my master – so there'll be a detail, a slight eccentricity but not too tricky, or trying too hard. Their store in Little Collins Street also has edited stuff from other ranges, such as the best knits from Comme des Garçons.'

The T-shirt he had on under the jacket that evening was one of two by Giorgio Armani that he wears 'all the time. You can't go wrong.' Although it's difficult on the bank balance upfront, long-term, the value is there. 'You dry-clean them and they never lose their shape.' An Armani T is 'a perfectly designed garment, plain as daylight. You can wear it morning, noon and night and not have to go home and change.'

A beautiful black roll-neck Yohji Yamamoto sweater **Michal McKay** bought in Paris has been in her wardrobe 'for years'. Along with pieces by Issey Miyake, Yamamoto's designs are 'truly investment dressing because they have a unique style not marked by date. I'm still wearing them because they are timeless.' Harvey Nichols is on her itinerary in London, Max Mara in Milan, and 'in New York, I love going downtown and fossicking in interesting shops,' although it's hard to drag her away from the stores on upper Madison Avenue. Her favourite shops in Singapore are Issey Miyake, Jil Sander and Donna Karan in the Hilton Arcade. 'I quite like having things made, as well. If I have a pair of pants that have been fabulous, I will get my tailor to make up another pair.' She sometimes designs her own pieces and has them made to order.

WHAT'S SO WONDERFUL ABOUT PETIT BATEAU?

In 1893, Monsieur Pierre Valton set up a small knitting company in Troyes, France. After manufacturing long johns for soldiers during World War I, Valton created the first short-legged knickers for children, naming them Petit Bateau after a nursery song that roughly translates as, 'Mama, the little boats on the water, do they have legs?' The brand remained an unglamorous bread-and-butter line for children during subsequent decades until 1996 when Karl Lagerfeld sent his models down the runway wearing Petit Bateau T-shirts under their Chanel suits. The effect was electrifying, the demand immediate. All the company had to do was produce the basic T in larger sizes. In three years, the sales of Petit Bateau Ts for adults increased 1000 per cent. The garments are made of 100 per cent cotton and are fine, soft, comfortable and durable. See **www.petit-bateau.com**.

Colleagues and acquaintances who admire the way **Carolyn Lockhart** always has the right thing to wear might be surprised to learn that, 'I don't really have any grand brands or luxury items. I do love shopping but I hate having to shop because I need something.' She prefers to rely on a few people who bring samples to show in private houses or hotel rooms (see page 81).

One of them is Gay Naffine, who works from what Carolyn describes as 'a beautiful old house in Adelaide'. Twice a year Gay does a circuit of our capital cities, to show her new season's designs and colour palette. Carolyn says, 'Because I buy from her every season, everything works with what I bought the season before. It's not outrageously priced because you're missing the middle man.' Apart from the quality of the fabrics and their tailoring, another advantage is that pieces come in three sizes, so you can choose to have the top in one size and the bottom bit in another. **Gay Naffine**, telephone (08) 8379 2566.

Another of Carolyn's sources is Maria Barkley, who used to buy all the fashion for the second floor of what we now term 'the old' Georges of Melbourne. She is the clever person of Italian heritage behind Europe Express, a movable feast of fashion she has chosen from 'what's being worn on the streets of Paris' and air-freighted to Australia. Her business, promoted only through word-of-mouth, has been thriving for ten years. Twice a year Maria shows her latest collection at home in Melbourne and on her 'travelling trunk shows' in private houses or boutique hotels in Brisbane, Perth and Sydney. Her target audience is women from thirty-five onward. 'That's me,' says Carolyn. 'Her things are a little bit quirky and she does some nice knits. She buys labels you've never heard of, and she's got a really good eye.' The best thing about it is, 'You see it, you buy it and you take it away.' Maria keeps a permanent stock of Petit Bateau T-shirts (black or white, long or short sleeves), the brand no self-respecting Frenchwoman can do without. By appointment only, telephone **Maria Barkley**, 0419 317 411. In May 2006, Maria opened a boutique named **Madame B**, her 'little touch of Paris in a boho chic area' at 6 Inkerman Street, St Kilda, telephone (03) 9534 3348. Its temptations include French accessories, candles, toiletries, notebooks and cute gifts for babies.

A 'really lovely shopping experience' for Carolyn is a visit to **The Diva's Closet**, in a charming house in Paddington, where its director, an American called Regina Evans, shows her collection of vintage clothes and accessories imported from America.

'When you go in,' says Carolyn, 'you have tea and homemade cookies on a tray. Everything is immaculately displayed in a special attic. You know how vintage can be a bit grotty? This is anything but that, and it's not too precious. If she knows you and your taste she'll select things for you when she's shopping. She's a treasure.' Personal appointments only, telephone (02) 9361 6659.

Although Carolyn is 'fairly careful of vintage because it looks a bit like it might be your old things, I do have one coat. It's brown brocade, with embroidered gold rosebuds and a big wide belt, like a proper trench. I've pretended I bought it in London in a vintage shop but, actually, it was my going-away coat for my wedding.'

James Gordon is not alone in his belief that 'A bit of Prada never goes astray. However, I only have my bag, a great pair of pants and three pairs of shoes.' Nothing wrong with that. If his cash flow permitted, 'I would wear Marc Jacobs for Louis Vuitton.'

Ten minutes by bicycle from where **Akira Isogawa**'s father lives in Kyoto is Toji Temple; here on the twenty-first of each month is a flea market where Akira often finds kimonos to rework. A second flea market springs to life at Kitano Tenman-gu on the twenty-fifth of each month. Both markets start early and finish by four o'clock in the afternoon. The department store Bal, 'the equivalent of Barneys but not Barneys', is also on Akira's beat in Kyoto for what's new from Yohji Yamamoto and other Japanese designers.

When **Ilana Katz** is on a buying trip, 'I look at myself at the end of the day and think I must be a nut. How can anybody spend so many hours without stopping and not be hungry? I don't eat breakfast, just a cup of coffee, and I never stop for a drink. How could somebody be so affected by shops?' Not that she is a reckless buyer. Far from it. 'I know that I'm only going to buy, at the end of the day, about three things because I don't need more. So I look. Without planning, I find I end up with a whole lot of Japanese designers. [Yohji] Yamamoto, Comme des Garçons and so on are still my favourites.'

Tubbable trench

For ingenuity and practicality, Australian designer Josh Goot
is a standout. Before the silvered collection he presented in
May 2005, who would have thought of doing a tailoring job on
cotton T-shirt material to create garments such as a washable
trench with a metallic finish? Supremely wearable, as well as
stylish. Many designers seem to be more interested in making
a fashion statement with a capital F than in clothing the
wearer, but Josh Goot's clothes can be worn by women who
get on a bus, push shopping trolleys, pick up children from
school and still have their pictures taken for the social pages.
See **www.joshgoot.com**.

Noir

One of the most irritating clichés of current fashion reporting is the nomination of
some colour as the 'new black'. There is no new black. There is no old black. There
is just black. There are other colours but they are not and never will be black. I hope
that is the end of it, just as I hope that some computer nerd will design a software
program that will blow up the next headline writer attempting to tap out 'Size does
matter'.

Black is the epitome of urban style because it looks as though you haven't tried too
hard, even though you might have preened for half an hour in front of the mirror
and spent a fortune on the Yohji Yamamoto skivvy you are wearing under your Paul
Smith cashmere jacket. Black is the uniform of those in the fashion business who,
just about every season, try to sell you on another colour, although they'd kill rather
than wear it themselves, even just to get a bottle of Shape and the paper at the corner
shop on Sunday morning. Black has dignity and drama. It is both sexy (satin lingerie)
and sober (traditional widows' weeds). It is formal and informal. It makes fat people
skinny and skinny people svelte. It teams with everything, even navy. Australian

fashion designer Robert Burton, who now has a small fashion emporium at 42–44 Queen Street, Woollahra, once famously declared that the only colours to hold their own after dark are black, red and white, although 'on occasion, navy blue and emerald green' may be acceptable. It's true. You watch, next time you're somewhere smart at night.

Black has been the backbone of a style-aware wardrobe since 1926 when American *Vogue* presented to the modern woman a black crêpe-de-chine dress designed by Coco Chanel as the solution to looking chic without fuss. For simplicity and impact, the little black dress has never been superseded. It is the uniform of the incredibly chic women who set the style in New York. I still have a black dress somewhere in a cupboard, although I gave up skirts for pants years ago. You never know when you're going to need one. If you do, I'm sure Didier Ludot has just the thing at La Petite Robe Noire (see page 114). Closer to home, try The Diva's Closet (see page 69).

It's been a very long time since my twenty-fifth birthday, but the year was 1957 and I was living in London. I had the tickets of my dreams, to Wagner's *The Ring of the Nibelungen*, *The Mastersingers*, *Tristan and Isolde* and *Parsifal* at the Bayreuth Festival, way over near the Czech border in Germany. Third-class private accommodation had been booked for me there. I had just one problem: cash flow. My funds were so scanty, the frugal way of getting there was to hitchhike, a practice that was not as foolhardy then as it is now. Besides, I was part of a duo.

I have never been the type to burden myself with a rucksack – or to hitchhike, for that matter – so I bought an all-purpose black wool jersey tube dress at Jaeger in Regent Street. It had a kind of loose polo neck that extended to become a hood; most useful in northern Europe. It proved to be as infinitely adaptable as I had hoped. After I'd worn it to thumb rides with my nifty little overnight bag and check into youth hostels and modest inns for a week, I stepped into high heels and slung beads around my neck for my great and memorable nights in the Festspielhaus (festival house). By the time I went back to Bayreuth the following year, this time alone, I was affluent enough to take the train and stay in second-class private accommodation – and to have a satin dress with a balloon skirt and shoestring straps to wear to the opera. Was it black? What a question. Black has been the basis of my travel wardrobe ever since.

DIY creases

At the opening of a thrilling exhibition called 'The Cutting Edge: Fashion from Japan' at the Powerhouse Museum in Sydney in September 2005, we paid our respects by wearing whatever Yohjis and Isseys and Commes and Junyas we could find in our wardrobes. Kathleen Phillips, who produced the video that accompanied the show, looked very attractive in a soft blue crinkled skirt that I assumed was Nipponese. But, no. It started out as a straight Simona skirt that she had dampened slightly, then wrung lengthwise, like a bit of washing, and left tightly screwed-up for a week or two. When she shook the skirt out, it had taken on the irregularly pleated look we associate with the land of the rising sun. Simple and ingenious. The trick is not to moisten the fabric too much before you crumple it up, or it might go musty. Pressing with a steam-iron should be enough.

So it was that when I went to live in Venice in January 1991, I took with me a black wool crepe shift with an enormous stand-up collar of black lace stitched in parallel rows on to white satin, with cuffs to match. It was the apotheosis of the little black dress. This magnificent creation was the handiwork of the late Hall Ludlow, the New Zealand-born couturier who made his name at the Paris end of Collins Street, Melbourne, in the 1950s.

There are not too many occasions, even in Venice, when a dress of such drama is the appropriate garb, so it didn't occur to me to wear it to a party in the late afternoon of New Year's Day in 1992. It was dark at five o'clock as I made my way from Campo Morosini through the back gateway to Palazzo Barbaro. A small candle had been placed on each worn step leading up to the entrance. As I climbed that staircase it slowly dawned on me that I had missed my moment. The whole palace was lit by nothing but candles, which made everybody look like works of art, especially in their finery. I had the perfect thing to wear, hanging in my wardrobe at home.

The perfect white shirt

Only one garment equals the timelessness, impact and simplicity of the little black dress: the perfect white shirt, at its best with black pants. Sure, it's the traditional garb of penguins, currawongs and headwaiters. That only goes to show what a winning combo it is. In the late 1980s and early 1990s, it was the only thing I wanted to wear, and I gradually assembled enough beautiful white shirts and blouses to fulfil my wish every day. It wasn't particularly fashionable. I've never been too slavish in following fashion but, as you may have noticed, I do love clothes.

My white shirts came from various sources. Some were costly, some not. Until I donated them to a worthwhile charity last year, I held on to two beauties bearing the meticulous parallel stitching that was the trademark of Hall Ludlow's exquisite couture. I remember a pin-tucked one I bought at Chloé in Paris and one with a dropped shoulder and balloon sleeves from Banana Republic in San Francisco. Although it is now threadbare, I can't bear to part with a pleated cotton one by Issey Miyake. A white cotton or linen shirt was the first thing I used to look for when I found myself in the shopping streets of any city in the world.

There are a few conditions attached to wearing a white shirt. It must be pure white; that rules out synthetics, which are usually not-quite-white, or else they go off the dazzle with wear. It must be immaculate, which means you should wear it only once before it goes into the wash. And, with the exception of deliberately crumpled finishes at which the Japanese excel, it must be beautifully ironed. These three imperatives tend to put a lot of people off. Hands up who among us wants to iron a shirt anymore? I do, I do!

People who know me well know that I am never happier than when I'm at the ironing-board. I wield the simplest possible, lightweight iron that cost something like thirty dollars at Bing Lee in Bondi Junction. I've had it for years, far longer than any of its expensive predecessors. Its only sophistication is temperature control. No steam facility or other complication, so there is virtually nothing to go wrong with it. With a plastic spray bottle of Fabulon, another of L'Occitane Verbena Linen Water and my trusty radio tuned to 2MBS-FM, I am in heaven, spraying and smoothing the wrinkles out of a spotless shirt, an embroidered pillowslip, a linen handkerchief with a hand-rolled edge. Yes, I do iron the sheets.

It was during my white-shirt period that I went to live in Venice for a year. I was so worried that I would never be able to buy a spray-on ironing aid in that foreign place, I squirrelled several plastic bottles of Fabulon in my luggage before I left home. Once I had settled into my flat on the Giudecca I discovered that Vanni, my local grocer, stocked an Italian version called Stira e Ammira. It translates 'iron and admire', although Leo Schofield's interpretation, 'iron and shine', is more lyrical.

With Stira e Ammira at my elbow, the white shirt became my signature look in the wily old Italian city that ignores fashion but respects individual style. I realised one day that my shirts did not go unnoticed. It happened like this. The great American-born diva Regina Resnik lived nearby. We had mutual friends and we often exchanged pleasantries when we met on the quayside. After we parted one morning, she must have turned around to watch me, because a rich mezzosoprano voice boomed out along the *fondamenta*, 'You must have used a whole can of Stira e Ammira on that shirt.' She was almost right.

I do have a couple of white shirts now, but their line is narrow, in keeping with the current trend. Skimpy, you know? Just a bit *ordinaire*. For greatest impact, a white shirt needs volume. It has to dominate the look, not be subservient. Its time will come again.

75

7
FABULOUS
FIBRES

Cashmere

LET ME GIVE you some advice about terminology when you're a bit hard up. Don't say you're short of money, low on funds, poor, can't afford it, it's beyond your means, or that sort of derogatory remark. Borrow a term from the business pages: call it a cash flow problem. That's what big spenders say. When I told a friend, not long ago, that I had a cash flow problem at the moment, he replied: 'When a friend of mine has a cash flow problem, he sells a vineyard.' Well, I wouldn't sell my vineyard. Even if I had one.

So it was that one nippy autumn day when I was most worried about money, I found myself walking along Castlereagh from King to catch a bus home after I'd been to the Art Gallery. Just before I got to David Jones my feet took a sharp left, as though with a will of their own, and marched me straight into the House of Cashmere. I defy anyone to go into that soft, hushed cocoon and come out again without a box of treasure. Mine was a hyacinth-blue roll-neck sweater.

It was not my first purchase in this rarefied environment, nor will it be my last. While my pieces are few, they are treasured. Last winter I treated myself to black pants and a big roll-neck black sweater, perfect at-home wear with velvet slippers for a soirée with mulled wine beside the log fire.

Cashmere comes from the underbelly and saddle of a breed of goat that roams the icy wastes of desolate places in Mongolia, China, Tibet and other countries where the bitter cold causes the goat to grow a thick, windproof overcoat that guards the incredibly soft hair inside. The higher the altitude and the drier the climate, the plusher the cashmere inside the protective outer coat. In spring, when the goats begin to moult, their down is collected by combing or shearing. The next step is 'dehairing', a procedure that filters out the coarse fibres, leaving only the finest ones. They say it takes the down of three goats to make one cashmere sweater.

But that is not the end of it. Not all cashmere garments are the same, even if they are of similar weight, ply and density. There is a process of refinement and quality control, through all the steps of production, at which Scotland excels. Spinners such as Todd & Duncan, **www.todd-duncan.com**, located on the banks of Loch Leven in Kinross-shire, have been doing it for more than a century, and they're very fussy. They use only virgin fibre, meaning fresh from under the goat's guard, rather than anything that has been processed. The fact that they dye the fibre before it has been spun is said to intensify the colour and to result in a softer feel. Read all about it at **www.cashmeremadeinscotland.com**.

The best Italian cashmere products, including Malo, are made from fibre processed by the Scots. Twenty years ago when I bought a cashmere muffler at Lanvin in Paris to give to my host in London, he was thrilled when he read the label: 'Fabriqué en Ecosse' (Manufactured in Scotland) seemed to him a triumph of Britain over France. Speaking of the best of British, three boutiques specialising in superb cashmere are in the Burlington Arcade in London (see page 149): **Berk Cashmere** at number 6 and 46–49, **House of Cashmere** at 8–11, and **N Peal** at 37–40, 71 and 72.

A splurge on cashmere is not an extravagance, it's an investment in happiness. Few tangibles in the world can comfort, cosset and care for you the way cashmere can. Diamonds, I hear you say? They're okay on your ears or in a bank vault for a rainy day, but they're no good to snuggle up to when you need a bit of tactility. Imagine the bliss of sleeping under a king-sized cashmere blanket when a chilly southerly moans in the eucalypts. All that stands between you and such a state of grace is about the cost of a return business-class ticket to Bangkok. One-time fling or a lifetime of wintering in luxury?

My cat Missy wouldn't have had a moment's hesitation in her choice. I once caught her reaching up to claw down the cashmere cardigan I had left to dry on a clothes horse just inside the back door. When it comes to comfort, nobody is more discriminating than a feline. Even when a cashmere sweater is old, sagging, pilled and worn to holes, it is still wondrous to touch. I plan to turn mine into cushions – one for my chair at the computer, one for Tiger to purr upon – when they are just too threadbare to wear.

If you'd rather someone saved you the bother of making your own cashmere cushions, pop into one of Christopher Fischer's shops next time you are in America for ones with words such as 'Live', 'Love', 'Laugh' (or all three) knitted in. While you're there, finger the rest of the cushy merchandise for women, men, houses – even babies, with a collection called 'Little Christopher Fischer'. You will find **Christopher Fischer** at 80 Wooster Street (between Spring and Broome), SoHo; 67 Main Street, East Hampton; 52 Job's Lane, Southhampton; 103 Greenwich Avenue, Greenwich; or log on to **www.christopherfischer.com**.

Naturally, the **House of Cashmere** in Sydney and Melbourne acknowledges the needs of the newborn with bunny rugs and hand-knitted bootees. When I went there to buy a little something to send to twin girls born to a friend I think of as my daughter in icy Munich in January 2005, it was not a time for restraint. I left with two grown-up pashmina wraps in glowing colours. Each came with a signed certificate of authentication that included the child's name. Browse online at **www.house-of-cashmere.com**.

Softer than cashmere?

Escorial is an incredibly lightweight wool that comes from a breed of small, curly sheep whose lineage dates back to sixteenth-century flocks that grazed at Philip II's Escorial monastery palace, 55 kilometres north-west of Madrid. Australia and New Zealand grow the fibre but in such small quantities that the annual yield is only 0.1 per cent of that of cashmere. Escorial has been used by fastidious fashion houses such as Chanel, Louis Vuitton, Comme des Garçons and Chloé in garments that are less than two-thirds the weight of cashmere. The sole accredited producers of Escorial woollen and worsted cloths are members of the British Escorial Guild of weavers. Their products are promoted through Holland & Sherry of Savile Row, London, **www.hollandandsherry.com**.

On the subject of babywear, Sara McCartney and Sue Franklin, two clever young working mothers in London, produce a wonderfully practical and pretty collection of clothes for babies and young children made from top-quality fabrics, such as Scottish cashmere, Liberty lawn, Irish linen and Australian organic cotton. It's called **Pelirocco** and is available on the web at **www.pelirocco.co.uk**, and they ship to Australia.

Cashmere's fan club

'There's something about cashmere next to the skin,' **Carolyn Lockhart** told me last time we talked about that fabulous fibre. 'I'd have every colour if I could afford it.' She's getting there. When **Virginia Monahan** first came to Sydney from Melbourne to present her pure cashmere knits to a handful of private clients in 2004, Carolyn bought two sweaters. 'As I put my sweater away in the drawer after wearing it the other night, I thought, "I could throw everything else away and just have a few cashmere pieces".' Although she particularly likes the stunning colours Virginia Monahan produces, 'I must say, the ultimate would be white cashmere, which I've always wanted.' See **www.virginiamonahan.com.au**.

Eric Matthews is still wearing the cashmere jumpers he bought in Beijing six years ago. They cost next to nothing; needless to say, they were not *'Fabriqué en Ecosse'*, but on cashmere's own turf in China. This is everyday cashmere, as opposed to the masterly pieces Eric has seen at the **Malo** store at 7 via della Spiga in Milan. Eric comments, 'If you think Hermès is expensive, this is deadly.' We already know how inspired the Italians are at creating and making fashion of all kinds, so imagine what they do when they get their hands on cashmere. Since it was launched in 1972 Malo has lifted cashmere out of its conservative, ladylike rut and put it at the forefront of thrilling, of-the-moment fashion. White cashmere trench, anybody? Or maybe you prefer ice blue. A Malo boutique is also at 4b–c via Borgognona in Rome, and elsewhere in Europe and United States; check **www.malo.it** for details.

In March 2004, Alfredo Canessa (who established Malo) and Massimo Alba (its creative director) bought **Ballantyne Cashmere**, the label attached to some of the best-quality Scottish cashmere knits for a hundred years. The two were already behind

Ballantyne's new and unmistakably Italian style that began to appear in 2003 and drew **Megan Morton** to its stores in Japan and London. 'It's now on the Net and, oh my god, wait till you see the colours!' she emailed me the other day. Don't wait. Log on to **www.ballantyne-cashmere.co.uk**.

James Gordon possesses 'an incredibly luxurious Hermès triple-ply cashmere blanket in charcoal, but I use it for nothing because it's too hot.' It's certainly not stuck in a drawer somewhere, though. 'It lies languidly over a chair, so I simply look at it and shake it at random.'

Craig Markham travels with the grey cashmere eyemask he bought at Banana Republic to soothe his sleepy peepers in-flight. Isn't that the last word in discreet luxury and status? Not quite. The ultimate indulgence of this sort is to ask Colette (see chapter 11, 'The pick of Paris') to commission Marko Matysik to make one for you. Marko makes out-of-this-world scarves, belts and other drop-dead desirables, such as a zippered mink headrest for each seat in Donatella Versace's private jet. Inside the mink is a hot-pink satin eyemask.

The trouble is that this totally sublime fibre spoils you for life. Lambswool, mohair, angora and alpaca are all beautiful, natural, warming fibres, but they are not cashmere. The only wool in its class is the rarefied Escorial. Whenever someone asks **Megan Morton** what she'd like for her birthday, she thinks, 'I want ten crappy presents to turn into one cashmere something.' And so say all of us.

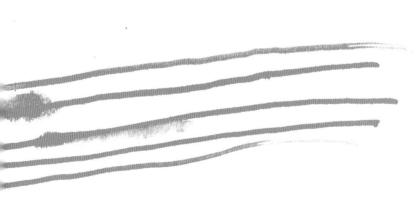

Linen

The summer equivalent of cashmere is linen. This light and airy fabric, long associated with purity, has swathed the pharaohs of ancient Egypt and clothed the altars of churches, as well as adorning the bodies, beds and dining tables of the privileged ever since.

Linen is made from the stems of the flax plant, an annual that produces a blue flower before it goes to seed. In Ireland, they call it the 'wee blue blossom'. It resists dirt, dries quickly and crushes easily, which is how you can tell pure linen from blends and synthetics. Creases are linen's badge of authenticity, so wear them with pride.

I count myself among linen's greatest admirers and I don't mind the hard work its upkeep takes. No household chore gives me as much satisfaction as ironing hand-embroidered linen (on the wrong side, to throw the pattern into relief on the right side) and placing it over a clothes horse to air in balmy breezes on the balcony. The beautifully embroidered linen sheet I bought in Madrid years ago adorns a window instead of a bed so that the light filtering through it emphasises the finesse of the needlework. I don't dare go near **Lucienne Linen** at Mosman – 539 Military Road, telephone (02) 9969 4946, **www.luciennelinen.com** – because I know how susceptible I am to a pure linen bed sheet. At **Iris & Hazel** – 87 Paddington Street, Paddington, telephone (02) 9328 3396 – last spring I couldn't resist a Lee Mathews crumpled 'Tibetan' jacket made from three different shades and weights of pure linen, with seams on the outside. When I got it home, I had to repeat to myself the mantra, 'Don't iron it, don't iron it, don't iron it . . .' I compromised by ironing the lapels.

For me, there is no kitchen cloth to equal a pure Irish linen tea towel. I treasure the ones I bought some years ago at the Irish Linen Centre at Lisburn Museum in Northern Ireland. They are mercifully without pattern, except for a woven blue stripe with the words 'Irish Linen Centre' running down the middle. I have rarely sighted an Irish linen tea towel, before or since, that is without something garish or kitschy printed all over it, defacing this beautiful and noble cloth. I don't iron my tea towels, though, because I love their rough, thirsty quality after they've been dried in fresh air. According to the website of the superb Belgian brand Libeco, **www.libeco.com**, linen is capable of absorbing 20 per cent of its weight in moisture before it feels damp.

James Gordon shares my love of the yield of the wee blue blossom. He loves drying it in the fresh air, too, pegged to his trusty Hills Hoist. Years ago, when BBC Hardware had a shop in George Street, between King and Market Streets, James told me that it carried bolts of white pure linen sheeting, which he turned into bed sheets. I was there with the speed of a madcap courier on a bicycle. It was 2.5 metres wide and cost something like $20 a metre. Lavish lengths of it have floated over the French doors upstairs ever since.

Spain has joined the handful of James's favourite places in the world since he visited Barcelona for the first time in 2004 and discovered the exquisite linen at L'Arca de l'Aviva, at Banys Nous 20. Spain is still a stronghold of the ancient female skill of hand-embroidery, but who knows for how long? In Madrid, it's rewarding to walk the length of the boulevard called Serrano to check out the bed-linen stores. Double-bed sheets are called *ropa de cama matrimonial*, as though you have to be wed to bed in a double. Isn't that quaint?

Once when I asked the Queen's former dressmaker, the now late Sir Hardy Amies, his idea of luxury, he replied, 'Darned sheets. You only get them in grand Irish houses now.' He meant linen, of course, justifiably the pride of Ireland. There was not a darn in sight at The Savoy in London, though, when its beds were made with pure linen sheets. They were changed for fresh ones after every sleep, even if it was only a ten-minute kip in the afternoon. I tested this claim and found it to be true in the years when the service in this great, historic hotel was unsurpassed for discretion.

When *Les Miserables* was fairly new to London's West End I happened to spend a few days at The Savoy. Grand hotels always make me a bit over-excited so, rising to the occasion, I asked the concierge to book two seats for me and invited a dashing young male friend to be my guest at the theatre. To make a properly festive evening of it, I had a confabulation with the butler about something to eat beforehand. We decided on smoked salmon and chilled chablis served at a small table beside the window in my suite overlooking the Thames. The evening got off to a splendid start and we made it to the theatre just as the lights were dimming. Afterwards, my friend walked me back to the hotel, we had a nightcap in the bar, he went home and I returned to my suite. It was pristine. Everything had been cleared away. And the linen topsheet had been turned down on both sides of the bed.

NOTES

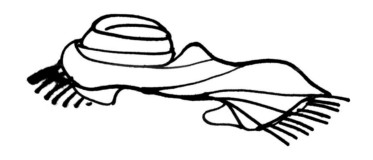

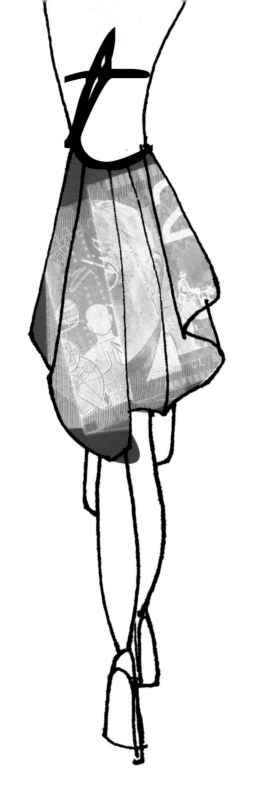

8

TEETERING

If God had meant us to walk on stilts, She'd have welded Jimmy Choos to our soles at birth. But most of us don't learn that lesson until very late in life. I spent the best years of my life wobbling around on high heels, risking sprained ankles, fractured fibulae, mangled malleoli and loss of face. My toes have been squeezed into shoes so pointy, they'd be confiscated as weaponry if you tried to wear them on a plane today.

At the age of sixteen, soon after I got a job in the advertising department of Sydney's Hordern Brothers, I bought myself a New Look suit in brown wool for winter. Although Christian Dior invented the New Look as fashion's reward to women for having put up with skimpy frocks during the austere years of World War II, my suit did not carry his august name. It was what the ads in American trade magazines such as *Women's Wear Daily* and *Retail Advertising Week* described tactfully as a 'line for line copy' – in other words, a rag-trade knock-off.

Nevertheless, I loved it because it was the first outfit I ever wore that had not been made by loving hands at home. The jacket had a peplum with two pleated inserts of red-and-brown tartan and two tartan bows. The skirt was an enormus full circle that swirled around me from nipped waist to ankles. The footwear that gave the seal of approval to this look was a pair of high-heeled brown suede ankle-strap platform soles that I wore with sheer brown stockings with seams up the back. It was as grown-up and of-the-moment as it was unsuited to the job I had to do.

Hordern Brothers sat between Curzon's and Way's, roughly where HMV is now, before this part of Pitt Street became a mall. Twice a day, I was required to go to the offices of the daily newspapers, all within a few blocks of the store, to buy the latest editions, bring them back, cut out Hordern Brothers ads and paste them in a big guard book.

You are probably familiar with that handsome bull-nose building at the junction of Pitt, O'Connell and Hunter Streets? Long before it became the Radisson hotel, it was the headquarters of the *Sydney Morning Herald* when the paper was owned by the Fairfax family. These days, you enter and leave the building through side doors but, back then, you trod the impressive stone steps from Hunter Street, a truly grand way to go in and – you're ahead of me, aren't you? – the cause of my memorable downfall on the way out one morning. There I landed, spreadeagled on the footpath with scattered broadsheets and laddered stockings, mortified.

It wasn't enough to put me off ankle-wreckers, though. In London ten years later, when I should have known better, I wore my best new winklepickers with metal-tipped stiletto heels on my first day in a temporary job as assistant to Miss Midwinter, who was assistant to Mme Garrigues, the *soignée* French fashion buyer at Simpson Piccadilly, a fashion store of quality.

At the end of the day, I walked out of the shop, thrilled to join the peak-hour crowds and feel part of the workforce in the pulsating City of Westminster. Two steps and I knew I was in trouble. My feet were slithering under me on the greasy pavement. I wobbled along with my shoulder propped against the shopfronts. You can imagine the sight from behind. I don't know how I tottered to Piccadilly tube station and down those lethal steps without collapsing in a crumpled heap. Some moments in life are really painful to look back on. Ultimately, stiletto heels were banned in lots of public places, not because of broken legs but because, wherever they went, pock-marked floors were sure to follow.

Miss Midwinter was as bleak as her name, although she was quite pretty in a tightly controlled, ladylike way. She would never have worn anything as extreme as winklepickers. Sensible courts with medium heel – the kind that are still around – were her preference. She didn't really approve of Mme Garrigues, not just because she was French and statuesque, had been a model for Christian Dior and wore perilously high heels, but because her chum in going to the couture collections in Paris was the man who bought fashion for Marks & Spencer. Miss Midwinter nearly had a heart attack the day Mme turned up in a frock from Marks & Spencer to prove how chic that mass-market store was. It was seen as a frightful insult to Simpson Piccadilly, where the tone was hushed and the air rarefied. When my six-week term came to an end, Miss Midwinter became quite choked-up. She told me she would miss me because, she said, 'You're so . . . you're so . . . *English*.' It was the greatest compliment she could think of.

By the time cork-soled wedgies hit the pavements in the 1970s, I was living in Melbourne. Chapel Street had the best little boutiques selling zippered jumpsuits with bell-bottoms designed to fit over the most grotesque of cumbersome footwear. You'd think only someone with a fetish would fall for the Minnie Mouse look but, no, every girl with any pride in her appearance was seen clumping along Collins Street trying to keep her balance. Footwise, this stage passed quite uneventfully for me, although these doorstops lingered on, mainly among bank tellers, long after the clothes they were meant to accompany had become passé.

Then it was 1981 and I discovered Andrea Pfister pumps with Louis heels in Paris. They were sludge-green, lined in gold kid. A pattern had been cut out of the green to show little teardrops of gold. These sumptuous slip-ons were so gorgeous I bought the matching bag, as well. From then on, what my shoes lacked in height they gained in quality. Well I remember those Mario Valentino brogues in navy snakeskin, especially the day I'd got off a plane at Los Angeles airport. I wore them with a dark mulberry knitted tube dress by Jean Muir, a belt by Kai-Yin Lo and a grey-and-white bird's-eye jacket from Ralph Lauren. As I waited for a taxi, a big African-American man came over and said, 'You dress real sharp.' He was in the fashion business. I felt I'd hit the big time.

My last pair of really pricey shoes were by Stephane Kélian, bought in the 1990s when androgyny arrived and never went away – at least for me. They are a kind of parody on a man's loafer with huge black treads and polished uppers. They have been resting in shoe bags for some time now because they are literally too heavy for me to drag my feet around in. I still love them enough not to be able to give them away. Not just yet anyhow.

Now all my shoes come from **Giallo, www.giallo.com.au**. I buy a basic black flat pair by Filippo Raphael that bounce along gently on soft, sensible soles that are flat to the ground, because I have learned my lesson, and I did it the hard way. One day, I was seduced by a hip version of this basic slip-on, one with a chisel toe, an elevated sole and a very streamlined shape. It cost me dearly, though not in its upfront price. Sprinting back from the supermarket one morning, I swerved around one of those

wheelie bins, missed my footing on the curb outside a drug rehabilitation centre and found myself on the pavement with my right hand sticking out the wrong way. Broken wrist. Kind people rushed out to help me inside and call an ambulance. Picture the paramedics carrying me out of drug rehab sucking on a tube of morphine. I count myself lucky that Ros Reines and the paparazzi were somewhere else that day.

Stepping out in style

One shop **Jane Roarty** hotfoots it to in Paris is **Christian Louboutin**, 38–40 rue de Grenelle, not necessarily to buy, but for observation and entertainment. He was a protégé of the late Roger Vivier, who gave the world the first stiletto heels in 1954, made crocodile boots that clung to Rudolf Nureyev's amazing thighs, and shod Catherine Deneuve in Pilgrim pumps for her role in Luis Buñuel's scandalous 1967 movie *Belle de Jour*. (The Roger Vivier label is now owned by Tod's, which opened a boutique bearing the Roger Vivier name at 29 rue du Faubourg Saint-Honoré in March 2004. The fit-out was done by Inès de la Fessange. Bruno Frisoni is the shoe designer. Within the 500-square-metre space is an archive of Roger Vivier originals.) Louboutin makes fantasies on skyscraper heels with shiny, scarlet soles that are not for any woman with vertigo. 'Next door to it,' Jane confides, 'is a shop where you can get shoes which are one season out. Of course that doesn't matter to us Australians. So I walk up and down the rue de Grenelle for all the shoes. French shoes I really love.'

Then Jane crosses the Seine and steps into the vintage couture shop of **Didier Ludot**, 20–24 galerie de Montpensier, Jardin du Palais Royal, where she is sure to find something irresistible, usually in the way of shoes, although it might be a dress by Balenciaga or Patou, or a pre-loved Hermès Birkin or Kelly bag.

Each April, when **Eric Matthews** goes to Milan, he visits the **Bally** store at via Montenapoleone 8: 'It's got exquisite things and it's beautifully laid out. I bought shoes there last year and a bag. They called my hotel to ask if I was happy with my purchases, said they have the means to pressurise the leather from the inside of the shoes, if I needed it. This girl was extraordinary. Perfect English. She said, "Travel safely back to Australia." They recognise you, which I think is wonderful.'

Edwina McCann was thrilled when 1920s T-bar shoes with chunky heels came back into fashion in 2004. 'They were exactly the shoes that were in when I started at *Vogue*. And I've been able to pull out Michel Perrys that I've kept because I never throw anything away. I wore them at Fashion Week and people said, "Fabulous shoes, where did you get them?" "Well, actually, ten years ago".' Recycling works, if you've got the space and the patience to hang on to things long enough.

Although she's 'not a fan of department-store shopping', Edwina went to Barneys when she was in New York to buy Manolo Blahniks for her sister to wear with the wedding dress Georgina Weir had made for her in Melbourne. 'Australia is the land of no shoes and we couldn't find the perfect thing. I knew they had to be Manolo Blahniks because he – and Jimmy Choo – make the best.'

At the moment, Edwina's favourite label for her own shoes is Chloé, but now that Phoebe Philo no longer heads the design team, Edwina will have to wait and see if the aesthetic remains the same.

Most of **Craig Markham**'s lace-ups and loafers, in black or brown for business, come from Prada. When he flies home to Australia for Christmas, he brings three pairs – black, brown and beige – of Helmut Lang trainers, a pair of black Prada sandals and a pair of brown sandals from Jil Sander.

Last time he was in Kyoto, **Akira Isogawa** treated himself to a pair of orange canvas shoes by Junya Watanabe at the Comme des Garçons boutique. (Perhaps he'll team them with Comme's fuchsia-pink pants he bought in Tokyo the year before.) The Kyoto boutique is in an unlikely location for a fashion label, a residential area surrounded by traditional Japanese houses. As Akira approached, 'Suddenly I saw this black stone. Smooth, not rough. No windows or anything in the curved walls. It's two-storey but all you see is this black wall.' The entrance is tucked away at the back of the curved wall. Akira is a fan of Junya Watanabe because 'He does a great men's collection.'

When **Michal McKay** prepared her move from Sydney to Auckland, even the packer remarked on the astonishing size of her collection of footwear – and that wasn't even half of it. 'He had no idea of the ones in storage,' and Michal didn't tell him. She says that her shoe fetish 'probably stems from having slightly tetchy feet, which require nurturing and comfort, along with style.' Not for her the clumpy look. 'No matter what the fashion, I could never get myself near the heavy-heel look. The platypus toe came and hovered but never landed in my wardrobe.'

What has found its way there is a hoard of some of the great names in high-stepping style, including Dolce & Gabbana, Sigerson Morrison, Tod's, L'Autre Chose, Joan & David, Kate Spade, Prada, Marc Jacobs, Coach, Bally and Bottega Veneta. In her view, 'Harrods and Saks are the best department stores for shoes.' In London, Joseph and Russell & Bromley are trusted standbys. In New York, she has 'a blitz on Barneys' whenever she can.

Overall, Michal says, 'I look for whimsy and sexiness, so a heel helps. I love the unexpected in colour and fabrics and delicacy.' She is a modern shoemaker's dream.

Tall stories

When she was under contract to MGM in the 1930s, the elegantly elongated Katharine Hepburn wore purpose-built shoes when she went to talk to her bosses in the Front Office. These clumpy platforms made her about 10 centimetres taller and umpteen times more confident, so she always got her way. Talk about tower power.

According to an in-depth study of Manolo Blahnik on *Hello* magazine's website, the celebrated shoemaker 'revealed a flair for shoe design' as a child at home in the Canary Islands when he shod his pet dogs and monkeys in muslin, tied with pink cotton ribbons. 'One dog would lie on his back and stick his paws up in the air for me while I tied the bows,' Blahnik said of this metaphorical preview of the adoration he now enjoys from his two-legged customers. Rather than who wears his fabulous footwear, the question should be, 'Who doesn't?'

If it hadn't been for Tamara Yeardye Mellon, sometime accessories editor for British *Vogue*, Malaysian-born Jimmy Choo might still be turning out custom-made shoes in modest circumstances in North London. Since the pair joined forces and opened their first boutique in Knightsbridge in 1996, the Jimmy Choo label hasn't put a foot wrong, although its namesake has long since sold his stake. His greatest unpaid publicist was Diana, Princess of Wales, who bought so many pairs, even Jimmy Choo lost count.

If you think flatties are too goody-two-shoes to be sexy, the Paris-based Spanish designer Maloles has variations to lure even the most serious stiletto stalwarts down from their killer heels. Jennifer Aniston, Catherine Zeta-Jones and Julia Roberts have allegedly fallen for them. In any case, like her flamboyant snub-nosed sandals, Maloles's website is whimsical and wonderful and worth a passing glance, as you will discover at **www.maloles.com**.

I don't know whether you're brave enough to buy and wear the colour-crazy shoes Ashley Dearborn designs, but dangle your toe into **www.ashleydearborn.com** just for fun. As for cool elegance, Loeffler Randall is the new name to watch. The label is attached to boots and shoes that are both sexy and refined, a delicate balance achieved by fashion designer Jessie Randall and art director Brian Murphy in New York. Browse the current season at **www.loefflerrandall.com**, but buy online at **www.shopbop.com**.

If you have feet that refuse to fit into a standard size – or you have two left feet, like Eugene Levy in the adorable doggy movie *Best in Show* – have your shoes handmade in Italy. Start your trip in Rome or Florence and ask the people who run your hotel to recommend custom shoemakers. Find your way there, let them fuss over your feet as you deliberate on style, leather and colour, then spend a couple of weeks doing business or having fun in Europe before you step blissfully into your bespoke footwear and board a plane for home.

Do not dream of altering your feet to fit the shoes, even if they are Blahniks, Choos or Louboutins. Toe-shortening by laser and collagen shots in the heels are some of the surgical procedures now favoured by the foolish and the flighty in New York. No good will come of it. Haven't they read *The Little Mermaid*?

SHANGHAI'S SILK SLIPPERS

When certain fashion insiders cross the world to Shanghai, their first stop is Suzhou Cobblers Boutique, just off the Bund, for hand-sewn silk slippers that make the wearer feel like the empress of China. They are the work of local graphic designer Huang Mengqi (aka Denise) and her nimble-fingered team. If you're not planning a trip in that direction soon, log on to www.suzhou-cobblers.com to see how adorable they are, and to shop online.

9

POCKET
POWER

EVER SINCE FASHION caused silly handbags to oust sensible shoulderbags at the end of the last century, I have been astonished at the way grown-up women like you and me are happy to carry prissy little purses more suited to five-year-olds than to corporate queens and domestic divas. The timing could not be more inappropriate. Just when it's foolish to walk around the streets of any big city with your cash, credit cards and house keys slung wantonly over your arm, fashion gives us bags that say, 'Look at me, aren't I flighty? Go on, snatch me.' I guess the people who make accessories had to find a way of surviving what could become an industry crisis if somebody had the commonsense to put pockets into clothes again.

One couturier who knew the importance of putting proper pockets into women's clothes was Yves Saint Laurent. The day I read that he had finally quit designing for the label his brilliance had made so famous, I happened to find myself on the seventh floor of David Jones in Elizabeth Street, Sydney. They do have sales up there where the astronomically priced imports live, but unless you prowl about, you wouldn't know. When you get out of the lift, veer right, glide across the cushy cream carpet, and start looking in corners. Hanging on the odd rack you'll often find things that are 'marked down' – they're never 'on sale', because that kind of terminology is for lesser garments on lesser floors.

Anyway, on this day, there on a rack was probably the last sighting of the master's own handiwork Sydney will ever have – and it was marked down. The garment was a pair of heavy pure linen trousers in a wonderful shade of deep teal blue. Did they have pockets? Did they ever. YSL saw no reason why women's wear shouldn't have the same dignity and detail as men's. These pants have deep side pockets, plus two back pockets with loops that button them down. But, get this: the buttons are on the inside of the back pockets, making them virtually pickpocket-proof. (I will not permit myself to get cranky about the trouble I have fiddling with them, because I think it's such a clever idea.)

The pants were too big for me but I bought them anyhow. I could not resist the quality, the style, the craftsmanship. When I got them home, I took out the old cigar box in which I keep scissors, needles and thread, and I painstakingly took the back apart to rework them to fit my waist while I listened to some soothing sounds from 2MBS-FM. Never mind that they are oversized and someone unkind might think my appearance resembles that of a street urchin, up to no good in baggy breeches (though I am without a balaclava disguised as a beanie). I love these pants, and the fact that I had a hand in sewing them makes them truly my own.

Another thing about David Jones on seven: it has the best public rest room in Sydney, bar none. When you get out of the lift, turn left immediately and walk along a calm, softly lit passage. For obvious reasons I don't know about the men's, but the ladies' room has a carpeted anteroom, with two easy chairs, side lamps and a certain air of benign neglect. How wonderful to find a spot that's been saved from modernisation and allowed to keep its spacious and shabby gentility. A few steps lead down to the loos. In each cubicle, apart from the lavatory, there is a wash basin and a mirror, so you can repair your face and hair in privacy. No noisy blow-drying of the hands, either, because paper towels are provided. So hushed. So civilised. There's a similarly old-world retreat off the lobby of The Windsor in Melbourne, but I think it's a bit plusher.

We were discussing pockets, though, not powder rooms. Prowling around Max Mara on Chifley Square one day, I came upon a beautiful white jacket. I wanted this jacket but it had no pockets; no place for a bus ticket, much less a wad of notes or a stack of cards. 'No problem,' said the saleswoman, applying those two over-used words appropriately instead of mindlessly, as others do. She summoned a dressmaker called Joanna Lichi, who was with us in ten minutes. Each side of the front of the jacket had a horizontal seam at the waist. In twenty-four hours this expert needlewoman had unpicked the middle bits, slotted in two pockets and finished it all perfectly for $30. (Where to find Joanna? At Sew Special, level 3, 61–63 Market Street, opposite Centrepoint, telephone (02) 9261 3550.)

Who's with me to bring back pockets? Cargo pants, hideous though they are, are a crude version of the idea. I'm thinking of something elegant, cultivated and secretive, like the pockets hidden inside men's suit jackets, and fob pockets off the waistband of trousers, to slip coins and cards into. Pockets are practical in any garment, although they do tend to go against the current fashion for skin-tight everything, with every bulge and bump clearly delineated. Some clothes are so skin-tight, if you squeezed a pocket in, any bystander would be able to read the number on your Medicare card. Who's for a bit of leeway again, a swathing of the body, a bit of mystery instead of all this revelation of bits that do not bare well, unless they belong to Elle or Sarah?

Ditsy dollies and other old bags

Even I, who profess to scorn itty-bitty bags, do own a dollybag. It is by Issey Miyake and its pleats are in two shades of blue: iridescent turquoise on the outside, jacaranda on the inside. Its turquoise strings are tipped in silvery metal, just like shoelaces. This tactile little pouch is my sole evening bag, unless you count the tiny black silk one, edged in gold, that I bought for the equivalent of tuppence-halfpenny in Mumbai.

But those are the only gestures to levity among my handbags. The others are sensible, as dour as pursed lips. One is a Donna Karan black fabric number I bought at Bergdorf Goodman in New York seven years ago. It's slick and plain with big stainless-steel loops to anchor the handle. I still own an old (oops, vintage) Fendi made of woven navy leather I bought on a trip to Rome at least twenty years ago, when the brand was little known outside Europe. You had to scamper down the Spanish Steps (you were staying at the august Hotel Hassler, of course) to the shop on via Borgognona. But the bag I carry most of the time is a seriously practical travel satchel by Issey Miyake. It is a mini filing cabinet with pockets for everything – it even holds a fold-up umbrella and, at times, a bottle of wine.

So, if you're after a lift to the spirits, don't ask me. Ask **Susan Kurosawa**, whose handbags are 'always frivolous. I love brightly coloured cloth bags with a bit of tizz that can expand to carry my camera or double as evening bags. I'm mad about Lisa Tilse's handmade **Egg Star** bags and totes. She's an Australian graphic designer who mixes and matches fabrics and trims for a gorgeous vintage look, including toile de Jouy, kimono fabrics and shabby chic paisleys.' For information on her clever fully lined, zip-pocketed limited-edition handbags and totes, email lisa@eggstar.com.au.

When in India, follow Susan's trail to Delhi's central Janpath thoroughfare for 'fun totes with images of goddesses Lakshmi and Kali'. Turn into Janpath Lane and scan the stalls for bags 'sparkling with beads and inset mirrors'. And remember, bargaining is expected.

If you're brave (or foolish) enough to venture into the truly baroque, log on to **www.toastaccessories.com** and know the true meaning of overdone. These bags are complicated and as kitsch as mulga-wood ashtrays. Ask yourself: Do I really want to walk around with one of those? You might even say yes.

Log on to **www.thestylegroup.com** for a very useful monitor of what's considered the best in big-ticket items in most luxury categories, from spas to bags. The group names its Top 10 handbags twice a year. Early in 2003, the Hermès Birkin was in the number one slot. By February 2006, a classic tweed bag from Chanel had taken its place, with Céline's Boogie Bag running at number four and Salvatore Ferragamo's Gina handbag coming in tenth. By mid 2006 Céline's croc-trimmed Farouche was number one and the Rene Caovilla Borsa bag sat at number five. If a tizzy tote made of python, encrusted with topaz-tinted crystals, can find its way on to the list, who knows what we're in for next? This site could drive you mad if you took it seriously. Think how you'd feel if you'd forked out squillions on, say, an Hermès Kelly, only to find it dropped from the magic ten.

Still, great labels, especially one with the history and reputation of Hermès, rise above fads to enter a kind of handbag hall of fame. Ponder this, if you please . . . On 22 January 2004, *The Washington Post* devoted a sizeable article to the fact that Martha Stewart had taken her eleven-year-old Hermès Birkin with her to court on the first day of her trial. It advised its readers that the price of a Birkin started at US$6000 but could reach as high as US$85 000 for one in crocodile with diamonds studding its solid-gold locks. There was no shortage of potential buyers, either. Quite the opposite. The waiting list, said the *Post*, had grown so long, the company had closed it, except for a chosen few (celebrities, that is), so money alone could not buy one. 'For Stewart,' declared the *Post*, 'carrying a bag that is surrounded by such a thick cloud of wealth and privilege was ill-advised.' (It doesn't seem to have impeded her progress, though. Hasn't she come up trumps?) When a handbag catapults itself out of the fashion pages and into court reporting, in a newspaper as ethical as *The Washington Post*, it must be the ultimate in successful branding.

Bliss for the discerning bag lady is to clutch an art piece by the French couple Benoit Jamin and Isabelle Puech, for their label, **Jamin Puech**. But their website, **www.jamin-puech.com**, is so slow and ethereal, you might as well hotfoot it to their shop at 61 rue d'Hauteville in Paris, or to the one at 247 Elizabeth Street, New York. Or maybe just hop down the road and see what **Belinda** has in her shop at 39 William Street, Paddington, (02) 9380 8728, or to **Christine** in Melbourne (see box opposite).

A new Australian label that strikes a brilliant balance between seriousness and surprise is **Eclettica**, **www.eclettica.com.au**. It embodies 'European styling with the Sydney lifestyle,' according to Paolo Gnecchi Ruscone, who, along with his wife Alexia, creates the products they first introduced to the market in October 2004. Using the best-quality Italian leathers and fabrics sourced from France, Japan and elsewhere, they make the bags of a style and finish I thought only came from Italy: practical business bags with space for the laptop, stepping-out bags in singing colours of lipstick pink and sky blue, and totes for summer in straw or deck-chair canvas. Instead of a flashy logo, they prefer their signature to be hidden until you open the bag; each is lined in the colour of the inside of a ripe papaya, with pockets for wallet, mobile, keys and whatever. Avoiding what Paolo calls 'the black hole' is a stroke of genius. True to its name, which means 'eclectic' in Italian, Eclettica also produces a limited line of other contemporary classics, such as beautifully finished shirts with mother-of-pearl buttons, leather sandals, panama hats and the perfect long-sleeved white cotton T-shirt. For stockists, email info@eclettica.com.au.

UNDERGROUND AND OVER-THE-TOP

Is it a *boîte*? Is it a speak-easy? No, it's **Christine**
behind that red metal door in a gloomy alley behind
The Westin Melbourne. It has no identification except
a street number and a skinny little shop window
displaying a few fripperies. It is so self-effacing,
I couldn't even find it the first time I tried. Persevere.
It's worth it.

When I saw what was in there, I didn't have the
heart attack **Megan Morton** predicted, but I did
experience the kind of flutter I haven't felt in years.
The gritty streetscape makes what's inside all the
more opulent. Once that red door is open, you proceed
down the stairs of an entrance lined in red plaid and
lit by a sumptuous chandelier to find a rich hoard of
wondrous wearables for the entire self, from Philip
Treacy *chapeaux*, to Eclettica bags, to Robert Clergerie
blunt-toed mary janes. Last time I was there I found
fantastic sequinned and beaded clutches from Anya
Hindmarch and an absurdly fanciful bag shaped like
a corselet from Jamin Puech – one-offs, all carefully
hand-picked. Nothing was predictable, not even from
long-established labels such as Sonia Rykiel and
Missoni. Gloves, scarves, wraps, mufflers, cuffs, capes,
jewels, outré Etro jackets and wildly coloured lapin-fur
cuffs were some of the temptations. When Megan goes
there, 'My treat is to buy a pair of Chantal Thomass
stockings, a winter thing, in chocolate tweed and
houndstooth.' Not everything is imported. Melbourne
fashion designers Sandy Star and Lorena Laing are
among the locals whose originality is showcased here.
Bring your plastic. Only the iron-willed leave here
without loot. You'll find Christine at 181 Flinders Lane,
Melbourne, telephone (03) 9654 2011.

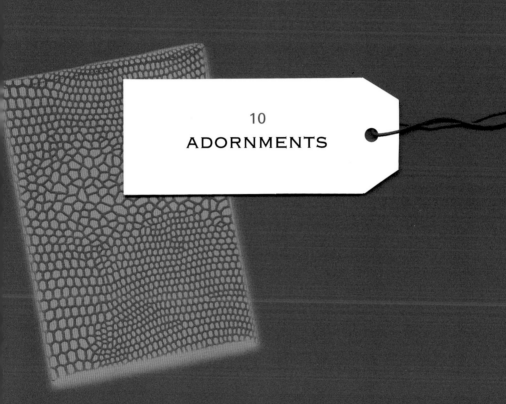

10

ADORNMENTS

When I was the rouseabout in Hordern Brothers' advertising department, one of my chores was to go to the Viennese cake shop at the top end of the old Imperial Arcade and buy snail buns to take back to the office for morning tea. The Arcade was precisely where its namesake is today, although it could not have been more different. With shopfronts similar to those that still exist in the Strand Arcade, the old Imperial Arcade bore the finely detailed craftsmanship and architectural grace of the late nineteenth century. Even the way it sloped down gently from Castlereagh to Pitt Street gave it a kind of civility. No awkward steps and certainly no escalators.

One morning, as I left the shop with my hands full of warm brown-paper bags, the rope of jet beads slung lavishly around my neck broke and all the beads went running down to Pitt Street. I froze, mortified. Kind shopkeepers and passers-by chased the fugitives and gave me back whatever they could salvage.

It was a lesson learned the hard way. I had been told often enough that when stringing beads you must tie a little knot between each one, but I was too impatient in my teenage years to do anything so thoroughly. All I was after was the effect, but this was not the one I had planned.

Does it seem strange to think that we strung our own beads? Oh, we did more than that. World War II had finished only a few years before, so it was still a do-it-yourself era. Every established suburb in Sydney had a local haberdasher, a shop selling everything from press studs, buttons and knitting wool to scissors, tape measures and cloth by the yard. The haberdasher was to women what the hardware shop was to men: the place to rummage for raw materials. The ground floor of each department store stocked haberdashery (known as 'haby'), dress materials, coloured thread, skeins of wool and trimmings for the home dressmaker, knitter and embroiderer.

June Millinery in Pitt Street specialised in everything to do with the making of hats: blocked and unblocked shapes in straw or felt, hatbands, frothy feathers, ribbons, all sorts of veiling, fancy braids, satin bows, glistening sequins and silk roses. You could buy all the elements and take them home to concoct your own headwear, or you could sit on a stool at the counter and have one made for you, a kind of chapeau-to-go. Thanks to June Millinery, I had a red pillbox long before it came to fame on the head of Jacqueline Kennedy. Cocktail hats with little veils that just covered the eyes were very popular, as were bunches of imitation violets and single organza camellias. Every time I made a new dress, I made a hat to go with it.

My adornments were always of the inexpensive kind and I guess they still are, possibly because I jinxed myself when I swapped my sapphire-and-diamond engagement ring for ten quid at a hock shop in Oxford Street, London, and never went back for it. On a trip to Ethiopia with my second husband in the early 1970s he bought me a truly beautiful and very intricate Coptic cross on a gold chain. Because it was crafted from solid gold, the jeweller in Asmara weighed it on old-fashioned scales to determine its value. Fifteen years later somebody nicked it. That was a sad day. What finally convinced me not to strive for expensive trinkets, though, was the loss of my Van Cleef & Arpels watch on a trip to Morocco. A perfectly adequate, uncovetable, plain, androgynous and easily replaceable Swatch suits me perfectly.

On the other hand, if, like me, you have never been on the receiving end of the kind of presents that emperors lavish on their wives, and plutocrats bestow upon their fancy ladies, you probably share my fascination with expensive adornments. I'm thinking not only of diamonds as big as ice cubes and rubies the size of walnuts, but of rolling real estate and art by Rubens and Picasso. For the ogle of your life, log on to www.christies.com and search for upcoming jewellery sales, preferably in Geneva, where a pair of diamonds of exceptional luminosity and clarity, weighing 27.72 and 33.83 carats respectively, went for more than $5 million not long ago. That kind of thing goes to auction there several times a year. Then visit www.sothebysrealty.com and click on 'Find a Property'. Fancy a penthouse overlooking Place des Vosges on top of a seventeenth-century mansion in Paris, or would you prefer a sixteenth-century Medici estate in Tuscany? Prices upon request, so first check your bank balance.

Our lust for loot must surely be appeased by the thought of the insurance, the upkeep, the anxiety attached to such priceless treasures, and leave us pondering the purpose of possessions and grateful for the simple things in life. Make mine a single row of whopping big baroque pearls around my throat and a ring on my finger that is of greater sentimental than monetary value.

Think global, shop local

If I were thinking of owning something precious again, there is no shortage of places in the world to accommodate my needs, from Cartier in Paris, to Harry Winston in New York, to the gold market in Dubai. But, first of all, I would drop into Anne Schofield Antiques, 36 Queen Street, Woollahra, **www.anneschofieldantiques.com**, or catch a plane to Melbourne to see what's doing at Kozminsky, 421 Bourke Street, **www.kozminsky.com.au**, which has been dealing in untold treasures since 1851 when it was set up as an antiquarian jeweller by Simon Kozminsky, the son of a Prussian immigrant.

I'd call on **Jan Logan** at her boutique at 36 Cross Street, Double Bay, or 90 Collins Street, Melbourne, **www.janlogan.com.au** (a fabulously informative site), where her pieces are varied, original and not overpriced. According to a friend of mine, who does possess a fine hoard of real jewels, no job is too humble for Jan Logan. She'll repair or remodel with all the care she puts into her inspiring new designs. I'd also be tempted by ropes of pearls from New Zealand fashion designer **Karen Walker**, although I think I prefer a lion to a skull-and-crossbones on the diamond clasp – see which you prefer at **www.karenwalkerjewellery.com**. I guess our pearly king would have to be **Paspaley Pearls**, the family business located in the far north of Australia that farms, wholesales and retails South Sea pearls and has some exquisite jewellery designed around them. Browse online at **www.paspaleypearls.com**.

A different kind of precious

For size and spectacle, costume jewellery gives us a lot more for our money than real gemstones, and there's no anxiety attached to wearing or storing it. By turning resin into glowing and richly coloured bangles and necklaces, Louise Olsen, Stephen Ormandy and Liane Rossler have decked out the internationally famous with their one-offs for Dinosaur Designs. Their pieces are strong and contemporary with staying power that puts them above passing fads, so they become collectors' items. Explore **www.dinosaurdesigns.com**.

There was a time in the 1980s when hoop earrings grew to elephantine sizes. The threesome behind Dinosaur Designs were just starting out, with a little stand at Paddington Markets, but they were at the forefront of the trend, loading our lobes with globular resin that looked good enough to eat. In Hong Kong, I bought a pair of white enamel discs the size of coasters to dangle from my ears. These I alternated with a pair in white ceramic, 8 centimetres long and shaped like teardrops. Both pairs went well with a voluminous black-and-white striped wrap by Norma Kamali, whose clothes were as relaxed as they were trend-setting. This garment, which I bought in a shop at the bottom of the Spanish Steps in Rome, was shaped like a giant space-age version of an old-fashioned hug-me-tight, with big rip-out shoulderpads stuck on with velcro. It was a wonderful garment for travel, a great big Linus blanket.

Charlie's dangles

I'm about to quote **Carolyn Lockhart** here, but I'm going to call her by her nickname, Charlie, to avoid a confusion of Carolyns, as you will see.

One of Charlie's favourite treasures in her jewelbox is a 'wonderful thing for the neck, all black beads and lots of coloured things hanging from it' from Carolyn Rowe, who imports costume jewellery from Paris. These bagatelles are not cheap but they are spectacular: 'Whole swags of crystals, or masses of stone-washed buttons, all beige and white.' **Carolyn Rowe Design**, Harris Arcade, 12 Cross Street, Double Bay, telephone (02) 9363 2947.

Charlie also loves the semi-precious neckpieces made by **Carolyn Roberts**, a former high-powered marketing executive who, says Charlie, 'has never been happier [than she is] making lovely things by threading semi-precious stones and odd-shaped pearls.' Her jewellery is not sold through a shop but through what Charlie calls 'upmarket Tupperware parties. Glen-Marie Frost invites a few nice people to the house, you have a glass of champagne, you're not obliged to buy anything but you can't help yourself. Lovely drop earrings, nothing outrageous.' When Charlie was editor of the *Qantas* magazine, she featured one of these pieces. There was an immediate telephone call from a man who said, 'Oh, look, just send it. This is my credit card number.'

ugie se consu-
façon régulière
fond du ver...
enez soin
ue la mèche
t centrée a...
le l'éteindre. Il
rtant de bien
r la mèche
e rallumer la
e la placez pas
ourant d'air ni
urface de verre
rbre. N'oubliez
teindre lorsque
absentez.
ez jamais une
allumée sans
ce.

ue - paris

bougie parfumée
scented candle

d i p t y q u e   -   p a r i s

Choisya

e 190 g - 6.5 oz

11

THE PICK
OF PARIS

SOMEHOW, NO MATTER who we are, or what we want from travel, just about all of us have a soft spot for Paris. I have lost count of the times I've been there, but it's never been for longer than a week at a stretch, and that has always seemed too brief. The first bidet I ever saw in my life was behind a curtain in my poetic room in a tiny hotel in rue Thérèse, off Avenue de l'Opéra, in 1957. The view from my window of a narrow street with eighteenth-century houses made me imagine I was playing a part in *Les Enfants du Paradis* (still my favourite movie of all time, although it was made as long ago as the 1940s).

A few years later, when the advertising agency where I worked in London sent me to the couture collections in Paris, they put me up at the more salubrious Hôtel Louvois, north of the Palais Royal. I felt so posh, even the Ritz itself couldn't have given me greater pleasure. Which reminds me. Each of the collections that season was shown in the couturier's salon, and, from my possie on a gilt chair at Chanel in rue Cambon, I saw Coco herself, sitting high on the curved staircase, watching us all. As we know, her permanent home was a suite at the Ritz, just around the corner in Place Vendôme.

Nearby, that same day, I discovered Le Soufflé, the little restaurant in rue du Mont Thabor that I have visited every time I've returned to Paris. Where else in the world can you order a true spinach soufflé – incredibly light, crisp on top, soft inside – in civilised surroundings with linen-decked tables for one? Only in France.

Much later still, I stayed on the Left Bank at Hôtel de Saint Germain, 88 rue du Bac, **www.hotel-saint-germain.com**. In those days it was quite shabby, but very clean. Titus, the pure-bred boxer of the house, spent his days reclining on a hand-crocheted patchwork rug on a chaise-longue in the foyer. The hotel has since been renovated but, while I can't imagine that Titus is there anymore, it doesn't seem to have lost its enchantment.

I wonder if Restaurant des Ministères is still at 30 rue du Bac? It was marvellously old-fashioned, with wood-panelling, banquettes and dim lighting. Its menu was strictly traditional, with Escargots de Bourgogne, Oeuf dur mayonnaise, Sole belle meuniere, Pieds de porc grillé Sainte Menehould. When I ordered the Tête de veau ravigote, the waiter asked me if I knew what it was. 'Mais, oui,' says I with aplomb, expecting some kind of galantine. What arrived was half a calf's face, boned, and mercifully smothered in sauce. Did I eat it? Of course. I was not about to lose my face, as well.

One of the most thrilling weeks I have had in Paris was when I stayed in a studio flat at Résidence Orion Les Halles overlooking Place des Innocents, fulfilling my dream of keeping house in Paris, if only momentarily. Just like a local, there was I buying baguettes, brioches, bottles of *vin ordinaire*, slabs of whiffy cheese and rich pâtés from small shops on rue Saint-Honoré and rue des Lavandières-Ste-Opportune. I discovered the nurseries selling potted blooms along Quai de la Mégisserie. For me the best sightseeing is not nature's scenic marvels or man's monuments to power and glory, but life in the streets of big, knowing cities.

Paris has some of the world's very grand hotels, and I've been fortunate to have stayed in some of them and to have eaten in some awe-inspiring restaurants. But in this elegant city, I truly prefer something small, family-owned and family-run. Of course, there is the odd exception. One of them is the exquisite restaurant Le Grand Véfour, 17 rue de Beaujolais, at the north end of the gardens of the Palais Royal. It is to restaurants what Fauchon is to grocery stores (see page 118). It's not for every day, but if you want to go to town, this is the place to do it.

Why they love Paris

JANE ROARTY

In ranging far and wide across Paris, over a long period of time, Jane has refined her shopping list to the following very personal selection.

Galignani 224 rue de Rivoli, opposite the Tuileries Gardens, for American publications and the latest books on fashion.

Bazaar de l'Hotel de Ville (aka BHV), 51 rue de Rivoli, between rue du Temple and rue des Archives. Since the fashion writer Maggie Alderson introduced her to it, Jane heads for the hardware department in the basement for 'wonderful things for my house that I can't purchase in Sydney' including silk lamp cords, door numbers and even light bulbs, because 'they are big and they give off beautiful tones of light'.

Ladurée 16 rue Royale, a tearoom dating from 1862, and the newer version at 21 rue Bonaparte, Saint-Germain-des-Prés, **www.laduree.com**.

Dehillerin 18–20 rue Coquillière, at Les Halles, where Jane adds to her *batterie de cuisine*: 'I've slowly collected dishes and cookware and humble kitchen things from this special place.'

Papier 9 rue du Pont Louis Philippe, for wonderful stationery.

Parfums Caron 34 Avenue Montaigne, one of the world's oldest perfumeries, where Jane buys Narcisse Noire for her mother. It's a scent that brings back memories of childhood because her father gave a flaçon to her mother every year.

Didier Ludot two shops at 20 and 24 galerie de Montpensier, for vintage couture. She usually finds a pair of shoes too beguiling to resist, before walking across the Palais Royal Gardens (thinking of the writer Colette, who spent her last years in an apartment there) to Ludot's third boutique, aptly named La Petite Robe Noire, 125 galerie de Valois, devoted to little black dresses. Some are vintage, some are new but styled and finished like vintage pieces. See **www.didierludot.com**.

Caviar Kaspia 17 Place de la Madeleine, full of old-world Russians tucking into the best caviar and champagne. Joan Burstein, the force behind Browns and Browns Focus in London, introduced Jane to that heady experience.

Across the Seine, on the Left Bank, Jane stays at the **Millesime Hôtel**, 15 rue Jacob, **www.millesimehotel.com**, in the vicinity of some of her favourite haunts. Her friends know to look for her in the bookshop directly opposite the hotel. And in the following places.

Brasserie Lipp 151 Boulevard Saint-Germain, **www.brasserie-lipp.fr**, time-honoured meeting place for a glass of wine. 'When I dine there, it's for sole, or when it's really cold, the choucroute.'

La Palette 43 rue de Seine, for morning coffee. (Avoid the toilet, unless it's a dire emergency.)

J Leblanc 6 rue Jacob, where Jane collects stoneware jars of walnut, pistachio and hazelnut oils. Simon Johnson imports them to Australia but Jane finds it more glamorous to buy them in Paris.

Flamant 8 rue de l'Abbaye, is 'like walking through a house. It's a wonderful store for furnishing, paints, plants, everything.' She also seeks out the designs of Pierre Frey and Manuel Canovas in fabric shops lining the cobbled streets of the Left Bank.

TAX-FREE SHOPPING

Provided you are a visitor living outside the European Union, you're eligible to receive a tax refund if you spend more than 175 euros in a shop that participates in the scheme – that means most department stores and some boutiques. You must be prepared to show the goods, and the paperwork involved, at customs immediately before you leave the European Union. A caution: this may be inconvenient if you've shopped big because, depending on the rules in the country of your departure, it could mean you have to keep the goods in your hand luggage on the long haul home.

TEMPE BRICKHILL

Ladurée 16 rue Royale, is also a favourite of Tempe, who goes there for tea, pastries and 'the best macaroons'.

Mariage Frères 30–32 rue du Bourg-Tibourg, is a refined tea salon that also sells related products, such as ceramic teapots, biscuits and jams. It serves 'the best tarte Tatin in Paris'. Tempe advises us to 'order it hot'.

Detaille 10 rue Saint-Lazare, **www.detaille.com**. If the Countess de Presle hadn't owned one of the first motor cars of the twentieth century, Detaille would not exist. The wind caused her skin to dry, so she consulted a chemist, and a moisturiser called Baume Automobile was born and sold to Europe's nobility. The 1905 boutique has enjoyed a clientele of quality ever since. According to Tempe, it is 'a lovely old-fashioned shop selling its own fragrances and powders'.

CRAIG MARKHAM

Colette 213 rue Saint-Honoré, corner of rue du 29 Juillet, **www.colette.fr**. Here you will find 'the most fabulous selection of the latest objects, accessories, fashion, and so on. There's a Harvey Nichols food store and cafe downstairs, but I like to buy music. They have the best selection of CDs from the hottest DJs' – selected by Adelaide-born Linlee Allen. Colette's website is very entertaining, with witty sfx.

Modénature 3 rue Jacob, **www.modenature.com**. Craig's favourite furniture designer is Christian Liaigre (see page 151), and this store has 'clean modern furniture in the same design direction, but it's not as expensive. I have a tall bookcase at home, but the best buy would be the chocolate goatskin rug, which I think I might just have to have in my new apartment.'

Diptyque 34 Boulevard Saint-Germain, **www.diptyque.tm.fr**, a taxi-ride away from Brasserie Lipp and the street's other famous haunts. Craig calls it 'the Rolls Royce of the scented candle. I love this classic little shop that has the most personal of service. The product is available all over the world but there is something special about stocking up on my favourite Baies [a combination of blackcurrant leaves and Bulgarian roses] candles from the original Paris store.'

Christian Tortu Carrefour de l'Odéon, and 17 rue des Quatre Vents, on the Left Bank, **www.christian-tortu.com**. Craig loves freshly cut flowers – he often sends them to friends – and some of the best blooms in the world are arranged here in monochromatic bouquets.

Hôtel de Crillon **www.crillon.com**, is an eighteenth-century former palace grandly sited at Place de la Concorde. It is Craig's favourite hotel in Paris.

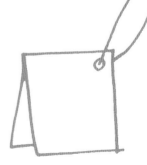

LUCINDA MENDEL

Martin Grant 44 rue Vieille-du-Temple, in the Marais, **www.martingrantparis.com**. This ex-pat Australian is such a favourite of Lucinda (and of Lee Radziwill, sister of Jacqueline Kennedy Onassis), she commissioned him to make her wedding dress. 'He does a beautiful classic cut with just a bit of a twist. I love his things because they fit me really well. Whenever I go to Paris I always go to his little atelier and find something.'

Galeries Lafayette 40 Boulevard Haussmann, **www.galerieslafayette.com**. 'There's a great little sandwich shop there, Lina's, and they do nice coffee. My feet are always killing me at this point, so I like to have a half-time break in there. You can have a basic sandwich or salad and it's not too expensive.' Another attraction is the tax-free scheme, especially if you're buying big-ticket items like Prada, Chanel or Chloé. 'They've got a fantastic kids' section. I always buy presents for people with children. And I end up buying my Petit Bateau T-shirts that I live in. I used to be a bit of a snob about department stores but I've found myself going back to them.'

Fauchon 26 Place de la Madeleine, **www.fauchon.com**, established in 1886. In this city of gastronomic delights, Fauchon is a standout. 'I always bring little treats back for my husband.' In the same culinary class is **Hédiard**, at 21 Place de la Madeleine, **www.hediard.fr**; it predates Fauchon by thirty-two years.

Hôtel Pont Royal 7 rue de Montalembert in Saint-Germain-des-Prés, **www.hotel-pont-royal.com**, is a traditional haunt of the literati. Lucinda loves it, 'particularly if it's on somebody else's budget'.

Hôtel Costes 239 rue Saint-Honoré, **www.hotelcostes.com**. A stylish rendezvous near Place Vendôme where it is not unusual for the fashion-conscious to survive on a plate of steamed *haricots verts* for dinner.

Café Ruc 159 rue Saint-Honoré. 'It's owned by the Costes brothers, it's very central, a bit more low-key than [the restaurant at] Hôtel Costes and not as expensive.' Its proximity to Carousel du Louvre, where the shows happen, makes it another fashion hang-out and a great place for steak and pommes frites.

Café de Flore 172 Boulevard Saint-Germain (famed for its former clients Simone de Beauvoir, Jean-Paul Sartre and their fellow existentialists), and Les Deux Magots next door, are shrines to the Left Bank's past intelligentsia. Lucinda knows that the coffee is 'over-priced' but thinks the experience is worth it. Another fashion insider tells me that, despite it being touristy, locals still go to what is commonly referred to as 'The Flore' for champagne or hot chocolate and little snacks, but they sit inside or upstairs, ignoring the tourists on the pavement. One of the reasons it is still held in affection is because the Nazis never went there during the German occupation of Paris during World War II. Caution: there is always an attendant in the loo, so don't attempt to venture in there without a euro to hand over.

WHAT DO THE FASHION EDITORS WEAR TO REPORT ON THE COLLECTIONS?

Is there a uniform? According to **Edwina McCann**, 'The shooting fashion editors, like Grace Coddington [creative director of American *Vogue*] wear black pants and sandshoes – it's actually quite anti-fashion, in a way – whereas Anna Wintour [editor-in-chief of American *Vogue*] will have the outfit on, with the jewels, the whole look. You can pick the Americans: they've got high heels on because they've got cars to get them from A to B.' Australians are not often on that kind of budget. 'I wear flat shoes because you've got to run. I take a tweed skirt, a pair of black pants and one long leather coat that will go over everything. But I wouldn't dress as casually as Grace Coddington. I guess, as an Australian, you still try to impress a bit.'

MICHAL McKAY

Colette (see also Craig Markham's recommendation on page 117). In Paris, it's definitely boutique shopping for Michal. At this concept store 'they spot trends. Products change according to what's new and what isn't. Upstairs, you get the pick of Prada. They have such clout, they can pick any brand name and select whatever they want, irrespective of the fact that, round the corner, Prada might have its own store.'

L'Eclaireur 3 ter rue des Rosiers, in the Marais. Another highly selective concept store, with labels such as Comme des Garçons, Ann Demeulemeester, Dries Van Noten and Easton Pearson. Michal finds it every bit as good as Colette.

EDWINA McCANN

Stella Cadente 93 quai de Valmy, beside the Canal Saint-Martin in the 10th arrondissement (north of Place de la République), and at 4 Quai des Célestins, beside the Seine in the 4th, **www.stella-cadente.com**. Jewellery and accessories designer who has amazing ways with crystal, fur and feathers, handmade in her workshop. (In January 2006 a Stella Cadente store opened at Islington in London.)

Jamin Puech 61 rue d'Hauteville (see page 102) is another of Edwina's favourites.

BELINDA SEPER

Marché de la Porte de Vanves This famous Sunday-morning flea market is in the south, way beyond Montparnasse. Don't look for Belinda in the swish boutiques, because, 'I'm just passionate about trawling endless flea markets, antique markets, junk shops.' What does she search for? 'Just stuff. I've found brilliant old handbags. I've bought umbrellas, hats, scarves, stickpins, earrings, bracelets, beautiful old bakelite pieces, glassware, baskets. I've brought back mirrors and fire screens.'

Hôtel Le Tourville 16 Avenue de Tourville, on the Left Bank, **www.tourville.com**. Belinda prefers small hotels but, after staying happily at this one four times a year for the past seven years, she is about to change. She needs a gym and a swimming pool, which means sacrificing charm for the facilities of a bigger establishment.

NOTES

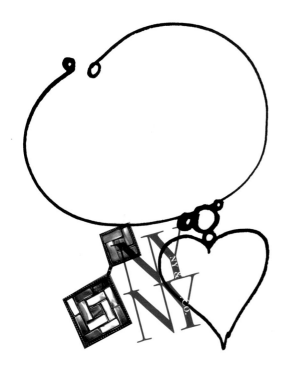

12

UPTOWN,
DOWNTOWN
NEW YORK

However convincingly Manhattan tries to pass itself off as a hard-edged megalopolis, it doesn't fool me. I know that it's just a collection of villages – neighbourhoods, the locals say – in which New Yorkers cocoon together in defiance of the forests of skyscrapers designed to intimidate them.

All that *attitood* in the streets is just a garb they put on, along with their designer puffer jackets, the minute they triple-lock their apartments to walk their Dobermans. Underneath, they are village people, whether they live uptown, downtown, east side, west side, lower Manhattan, upper Madison Avenue (I always think of it as Catwalk Kilometre, so prevalent are the big-name fashion boutiques located there) or the swanky stretch of Fifth Avenue known as Museum Mile.

All cities change, but none seems to do it as quickly, efficiently and definitively as New York. Adventurous, creative people lead the drift into forgotten or neglected districts and smarten them up for the establishment to follow. Look what happened to SoHo (the name stands for South of Houston Street, pronounced 'Howston', not 'Hooston', as it is in Texas). It nudges Greenwich Village, Little Italy, Chinatown and TriBeCa (which is short for 'triangle below Canal'). Canal is not a canal but a street. (I do not wish to be pedantic but, as a would-be Manhattanite, you have to know these things.)

Artists moved into this neglected little pocket because its warehouses, with their spidery fire-escapes, were cheap to rent, and their palatial Italianate and Frenchified facades of pre-fab cast iron (the modish construction material of America between 1850 and 1890) were full of character. Art galleries, fashion stores, bookshops, restaurants, cafes and boutique hotels followed; by the time Rupert Murdoch became a resident (he has since sold his loft for US$25 million and moved uptown), SoHo had become so expensive the artists had to move out. A night at **The Mercer**, a terribly trendy designer inn at 147 Mercer Street (Craig Markham loves it), **www.mercerhotel.com**, costs almost as much as one at **The Carlyle**, uptown at Madison and 76th Street, **www.thecarlyle.com**, the hotel many experienced travellers regard as the finest in the city.

Where did the artists go? Over to Hell's Kitchen or to Gansevoort Market, commonly known as the Meatpacking District. They are today's hot spots, although Meatpacking is further advanced in its gentrification.

Hell's Kitchen

Bordered by 59th Street, Eighth Avenue, 30th Street and the Hudson River, Hell's Kitchen covers a lot of ground on the west side. A former industrial area and home to successive immigrant populations from many parts of the globe, it is thought to have been named after one of the violent gangs spawned there in the nineteenth century. It is still disreputable but it's hovering on the brink of betterment, since the re-invention of Times Square. I know at least one eminent person who lives there: John Loring, the distinguished design director at Tiffany & Co., and author of many of its books. A good excuse to check it out is **Hell's Kitchen Flea Market**, operating on Saturdays and Sundays from 10 a.m. to 6 p.m. on West 39th Street, between Ninth and Tenth Avenues, **www.hellskitchenfleamarket.com**.

Another reason is a tiny cafe and bakery called **Amy's Bread** at 672 Ninth Avenue, between 46th and 47th Streets, **www.amysbread.com**, where Amy Scherber set up business in 1992; she now has three stores in Manhattan and more than 200 wholesale customers for her wonderful breads, cakes and pastries. And a third reason is **Bistro du Vent**, Mario Batali's new restaurant nudging the Theatre District at 411 West 42nd Street, between Ninth and Tenth Avenues, **www.mariobatali.com**. Casual but still classy enough to attract theatregoers is **Eatery**, 798 Ninth Avenue at 53rd Street, **www.eaterynyc.com**, serving modern American cuisine.

The Meatpacking District

Under the heading 'You Paid How Much for That Haircut?', the 21 November 2004 edition of *The New York Times* carried a very amusing piece by Alex Kuczynski on the cost of a haircut at **Orlo**, a third-floor salon on Gansevoort Street, in the Meatpacking District. Its owner, Orlando Pita, charges US$800 to sculpt a head of hair into a work of art. Among other hairdressers whose opinions the writer sought was Kenneth Battelle, the man behind the famous **Kenneth** salon in the Waldorf-Astoria hotel, who charges US$150, does not accept tips and has shorn the locks of such luminaries as Jacqueline Kennedy Onassis, Marilyn Monroe and Lauren Bacall. Kenneth decreed:

'Anyone who pays that much money to go to the Meatpacking District to have their hair done is a meathead.' Doesn't it go to show, though, how the old slaughterhouses have come up in the world? Talk about a silk purse from a sow's ear.

What's there, apart from wholesalers hefting dead animals in the daytime? Well, the fashion world's most covetable accessories are at **Jeffrey**, 449 West 14th Street. Alexander McQueen's own boutique is at 417 West 14th Street. Even vegetarian and animal-rights champion **Stella McCartney** braved the smell of carcasses to set up shop at 429 West 14th Street, so that tells you how stellar the district is. A few doors away is sexy Italian lingerie at **La Perla**. Those pretty frocks across the street at 408 are the work of Israeli designer Yigael Azrouel, and the flamboyant ones are from his Brazilian counterpart Carlos Miele. Their address is also shared by **Design Within Reach**, a space stuffed with mid-twentieth-century furniture. **Bodum** is on 14th Street, too, at number 415. **Diane von Furstenberg** is at 385 West 12th Street. The online store **Girlshop** has materialised in a former art gallery at 819 Washington Street, between Little West 12th and Gansevoort Streets; this is where you can see some of the rising young names in fashion. If it weren't for all the attractive clothes displayed at **Charles Nolan**, 30 Gansevoort Street, you might think you had stumbled into somebody's living room. **Rebecca & Drew** at 342 West 13th Street (near Hudson) has revolutionised the sizing of quality shirts for the female form by making them in widths according to bra size – they go from 32A to 38DD. Isn't that brilliant? For all the details, go to **www.rebeccaanddrew.com**.

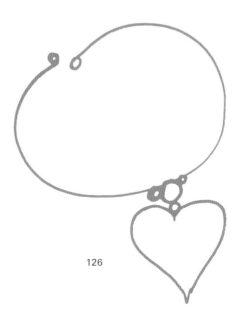

Vitra has a vast furniture showroom at 29 Ninth Avenue for iconic pieces, including those by Charles and Ray Eames, Frank Gehry, Isamu Noguchi and Philippe Starck. **Lars Bolander's** converted warehouse at 72 Gansevoort Street is filled with Swedish and other European antiques. At 15 Gansevoort Street is a totally seductive childrenswear and toy shop. This list is far from exhaustive and it grows by the month. Despite its name, **Boucher** at 9 Ninth Avenue is not a butcher (although countless chooks lost their heads here in the old days), but a much swankier store where an ex-employee of Tiffany & Co. sells her handmade jewellery.

As for eating, there's nothing like an affordable plate of good steak frites, caesar salad or crab cakes at **Restaurant Florent**, 69 Gansevoort Street, between Greenwich and Washington Streets, **www.restaurantflorent.com**, the local French bistro that never closes. Truly. It opens twenty-four hours a day, seven days a week, thanks to its French owner Florent Morellet. **Lucinda Mendel** remembers having an omelet there at 3 a.m. with her husband after an uptown wedding at The Knickerbocker Club. The onion soup gratinée is very restorative when you're on the way home at 4 a.m.

Bright red awnings over **Pastis**, on the corner of 9 Ninth Avenue and Little West 12th Street, **www.pastisny.com**, enliven the flinty grey streetscape and flag a more expensive French bistro than Florent but one that is equally popular. Lucinda says, 'The food is great but the restaurant is very hard to get into. I often used to go at the end of a night for a slice of lemon tart and a coffee.' In May 2006 Sascha Lyon, a former sous-chef of Pastis, opened **Sascha**, an ambitious and handsome three-storey restaurant, bistro and deli nearby at 55 Gansevoort Street.

Not long before that, two state-of-the-culinary-art chefs and restaurateurs, Jean-Georges Vongerichten and Gray Kunz, opened **Spice Market**, their mammoth Asian eaterie at 403 West 13th Street. Book or you'll never get in, telephone (212) 675 2322. Del Posto, at 85 Tenth Avenue between 15th and 16th Streets, attracts the glitterati, but if your funds are running out, US$20 goes a long way at **The Diner**, 44 Ninth Avenue at 14th Street.

The old **Gansevoort Market** is certainly the place to see and be seen. And if you do have a bad-hair day do not despair, blow your top, or beggar yourself at Orlo. Drop into **Blow**, 342 West 14th Street between Eighth and Ninth Avenues, where you don't need an appointment. I'm told they'll get out the hair dryer and tame your unmanageable mane for less than US$50. Another possibility is to make an appointment to have an apprentice give you a model cut for a similar price at the Antonio Prieto Salon, 127 West 20th Street, between Sixth and Seventh Avenues, telephone (212) 255 3741. Sure, it's in Chelsea, but the neighbourhood is only a hop, step and a jump north of Meatpacking. If it's after office hours and you're not short of a dollar, you could always go to the Red Market Salon & Lounge, 3rd floor above 32 Gansevoort Street (between Hudson and Ninth Avenues), which is open until after midnight Thursdays to Saturdays, until 10 p.m. on Sundays, and till 11 p.m. Monday through Wednesday. Have no qualms about their coiffures – co-owners David Cotteblanche and Reynald Ricard trained with celebrated uptown stylist Frédéric Fekkai, 15 East 57th Street, so they should know how and when to wield the scissors.

Hit the town

CRAIG MARKHAM

Craig's circuit in the Meatpacking District is all worked out: 'After breakfast at Florent, or lunch at Pastis, or before drinks at Soho House [a private club at 29–35 Ninth Avenue, corner of West 13th Street, telephone (212) 627 9800], or before dinner at 5Ninth [5 Ninth Avenue between Gansevoort and Little West 12th Street, telephone (212) 929 9460], head to Jeffrey (details page 126). It has the most cutting-edge fashion collection. It sells the things you see on the runway but so rarely see on rails. It's directional, innovative and low key in design. It feels a bit like shopping on sale. I buy my Helmut Lang trainers there.'

Takashimaya 693 Fifth Avenue, between 54th and 55th Streets, is 'the most beautiful store in New York'. Because of its Japanese origins, 'the fashion, home accessories and furniture have a strong Asian flavour. Buy travel guides and oversized cashmere scarves on the first floor but, best of all, send flowers to your best friend from the ground-floor florist. In my mind, it is the best in the world. Originally operated by Parisian Christian Tortu [see page 117], it is now run along the same lines by the in-house team. The presentation is perfection.' So is the ladies' room upstairs, and there's no attendant there expecting a hand-out. James Gordon, who also loves

Takashimaya, describes it as 'the most fantastic small department store: chic, witty and wonderful.'

Waterworks 469 Broome Street, SoHo, **www.waterworks.com**. 'I love bath products, and this store (there are others in the US) sells everything, from the chicest bathroom accessories to full bathroom furniture. Divine! I buy the classic body cream, which comes in a ribbed frosted-glass bottle.'

Moss 146 Greene Street, SoHo, **www.mossonline.com**. 'The very best selection of classic modern design, from a Jean Nouvel chair or a Cappellini sofa, to the latest Swedish glassware designer. Everything is displayed behind glass, therefore it takes on an almost museum-like feel.'

Comme des Garçons 520 West 22nd Street, near Tenth Avenue, Chelsea. Divided into rooms that look like moonscapes, the space is 'all white inside and the stock reveals itself behind panels as you wander through. Truly unique. I buy the sneakers in black and white, and the shirts.'

Lucinda Mendel

Because she happened to be there on September 11, 2001, Lucinda feels a special affinity with New York. 'It was an amazing thing to see, good and bad. I saw such a different side to New York. I'd been there six or seven times for work but this time I'd been on holiday with my husband. He'd just flown back the day before and I stayed in town because an expat friend of mine was having her first child. And then I got stuck there. It was a New York that obviously I had never seen before. Nobody had, given the circumstances. It became the most friendly, warm place. You don't always associate that with New York. In cafes, I met something like six groups of people who offered me a place to stay when they heard my accent. I went to give blood. I almost felt a bit privileged to be there during that time.'

Our award-winning chef's favourite New York restaurants

Hamish Ingham, now head chef at Billy Kwong in Sydney, won the Josephine Pignolet Award for 2004. That's how he came to spend six and a half weeks in the United States, three of them in New York, helping out in the kitchens of some famous restaurants and dining in others. Here are his recommendations.

Amy's Bread 75 Ninth Avenue, between 15th and 16th Streets, **www.amysbread. com**. Hamish had a day as a baker in the Chelsea Market shop and cafe, where the loaves are handmade from the best of ingredients, including organic flour, grains and seeds.

Artisanal Fromagerie and Bistro 2 Park Avenue at 32nd Street, **www.artisanalcheese. com**. A cheese-lover's heaven, so inspiring that Hamish dreams of having a special cheese room when he has his own restaurant, some day.

Babbo 110 Waverley Place, between MacDougal Street and Sixth Avenue, **www.babbonyc.com**. Mario Batali's modern Italian cuisine in Greenwich Village.

Lupa Osteria Romana 170 Thompson Street, between Bleecker and Houston Streets, **www.luparestaurant.com**. Mario Batali's lively trattoria with Roman family staples on the menu.

Otto Enoteca Pizzeria 1 Fifth Avenue at 8th Street, **www.ottopizzeria.com**. Mario Batali serves up a superior pizza and a choice of 600 wines in the vicinity of Washington Square.

Balthazar 80 Spring Street, between Broadway and Crosby Street, SoHo, **www.balthazarny.com**. 'For atmosphere, I couldn't fault it. It looked as though it had been shipped in from Paris.'

Gramercy Tavern 42 East 20th Street, between Park Avenue and Broadway, **www.gramercytavern.com**. Neil Perry arranged for Hamish to spend a week in the kitchens of Tom Colicchio's restaurant, famous for the freshness of its ingredients and the respect they're given in the cooking.

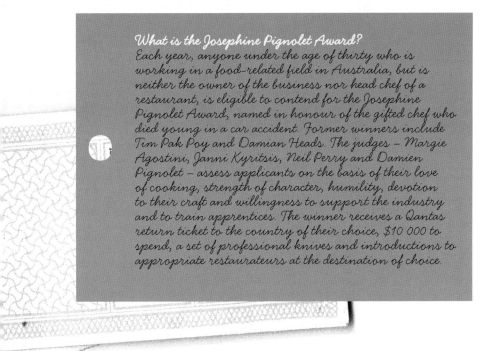

What is the Josephine Pignolet Award?
Each year, anyone under the age of thirty who is working in a food-related field in Australia, but is neither the owner of the business nor head chef of a restaurant, is eligible to contend for the Josephine Pignolet Award, named in honour of the gifted chef who died young in a car accident. Former winners include Tim Pak Poy and Damian Heads. The judges – Margie Agostini, Janni Kyritsis, Neil Perry and Damien Pignolet – assess applicants on the basis of their love of cooking, strength of character, humility, devotion to their craft and willingness to support the industry and to train apprentices. The winner receives a Qantas return ticket to the country of their choice, $10 000 to spend, a set of professional knives and introductions to appropriate restaurateurs at the destination of choice.

Craft 43 East 19th Street, between Broadway and Park Avenue, **www.craftrestaurant. com**. Hamish spent his second working week in the kitchens here at Colicchio's newer restaurant. 'It has a sort of do-it-yourself menu. I don't mean that you cook your own food, but you design your own course. When you order, say, fish, that's the only thing that will arrive on the plate. You choose whatever else you want to accompany it.'

If you want to mingle with the chefs, go to the **Union Square Greenmarket**, Broadway at East 17th Street.

Musts of Manhattan

1) I know you are far too sophisticated to join a package tour or to feel compelled to view the city from the observation deck of the Empire State Building (like Cary Grant and Deborah Kerr in that horribly mawkish old movie), but there is one touristic activity you owe yourself, at least once: circumnavigate Manhattan Island in three hours on a Circle Line Ferry from Pier 83 in the Hudson River at the end of West 42nd Street, **www.circleline42.com**. Apart from making geographical sense of where you are and giving you a close-up of the Statue of Liberty, the cruise has a commentator on board whose patter is as witty and gossipy as it is informative. Take sunscreen if you plan to sit outside. Food and drinks are at hand and the whole ride is very civilised. If you time it to finish at dusk, seeing the entire city light up will give you goose bumps.

2) You cannot qualify as a Manhattanite unless you have eaten pastrami on rye. This delicious and generous Jewish sandwich of smoked corned beef with a pickled cucumber on the side may be found at: **Carnegie Deli & Restaurant**, 854 Seventh Avenue at 55th Street, **www.carnegiedeli.com**; **Katz's**, 205 East Houston Street, **www.katzdeli.com** (instead of 'skip the intro', which appears on lots of websites, you have to love Katz's for substituting 'cut the drama – let me in already'); and Artie's, 2290 Broadway at 83rd Street, **www.arties.com**. All of them claim to be the best, so you be the judge. If you happen to be in the vicinity of Barneys, Bergdorf's and Bloomingdale's – and why shouldn't you be? – you can always tuck into pastrami on rye at **Kaplan's at the Delmonico**, 59 East 59th Street. Don't you love the name? It's so 1940s.

3) As **Tempe Brickhill** has wisely observed, 'The French don't understand department stores, whereas the New Yorkers have perfected them.' For verification, visit two all-time greats: **Barneys New York** at 660 Madison Avenue (it's even better than the original downtown store), **www.barneys.com**, and Bergdorf Goodman, 754 Fifth Avenue at 57th Street, **www.bergdorfgoodman.com**. When **Lucinda Mendel** shops at Barneys, she looks at the racks around the edge of the floor because that's where they put their marked-down pieces, although they don't draw attention to them. I have been so stultified by overchoice at Bergdorf's that I had to leave the store empty-handed, cool down and go back later. If you have a taste for department-store shopping, try: **Macy's Herald Square**, 151 West 34th Street, **www.macys.com**;

Saks Fifth Avenue, 611 Fifth Avenue, **www.saksfifthavenue.com**; and Bloomingdale's, 59th Street and Lexington Avenue, **www.bloomingdales.com**.

4) **Radio City Music Hall** on Sixth Avenue, between 50th and 51st Streets, began life in December 1932 – the Rockettes who made it famous are still the standard by which synchronised high-kicking choruslines are measured. Their top performances are at Christmas and Easter. Like the Vienna Boys' Choir, they have become a symbol of their home city. Read all about it at **www.radiocity.com**.

5) Although Radio City has been called 'a palace of the people', **The Rainbow Room**, **www.rainbowroom.com**, was never meant for the masses when it opened on the 65th floor of the most imposing building in the newly constructed Rockefeller Center in 1932. With a panorama of New York in three directions, a revolving dance floor surrounded by dining tables, and a live band playing toe-tappers, it's glamour all the way. Pricey for dinner, though. Go for a drink between 11 p.m. and 1 a.m. instead.

6) **The Oyster Bar** at Grand Central Terminal, **www.oysterbarny.com**, is much more than a bar, it's an institution. Since it opened in 1913, it's been serving scrumptious oysters and other seafood dishes in sumptuous surroundings.

A seventh essential experience would have been Afternoon Tea in the Palm Court at The Plaza, but Oh My Gaahd, the hotel was sold in August 2004 for US$675 million to Elad Properties, which is turning it into a hotel-apartment-shopping complex. Who knows what will happen to the Palm Court when the place re-opens at the end of 2006? Will there still be exquisite linen, flutes of Moët, the tinkle of teacups, delicate morsels brought to your table on a three-decker cake stand, attentive service and sweet sounds from the orchestra in the afternoon? Or will this totally upscale experience, which made tea at the Ritz in London seem touristy and pedestrian, be lost forever?

nne West

invites

to

RED
LABEL

Winter 1 MADE IN ITALY

Cher M

prie .... M

13

MARVELS
OF MILAN

WHEN I LIVED in Venice, I could board a train with a small overnight bag and arrive in Milan a few hours later, to stay a couple of days in Italy's pulsating centre of design and commerce, so different in character from the gloriously serene and decadent backwater I then called home.

On one of those visits, I spent a day with the expat Australian fashion expert Vivien Egge, walking around what is known as the Golden Quadrangle. A heady concentration of all that is covetable and costly lies within the borders of via Montenapoleone, via Alessandro Manzoni, via della Spiga and Corso Venezia. I defy any woman, except perhaps a Parisian, not to be intimidated by the style of what is on show in shop windows and being worn with incomparable flair and individuality by Milanese women. Italians not only know how to make clothes, they know how to wear them at no matter what stage of life they happen to be. And they know how to accessorise – every big city in Italy has wonderful bags and shoes, but none surpasses Milan.

Vivien also introduced me to a marvellous designer outlet called Il Salvagente at 16 via Fratelli Bronzetti, where big-name items were discounted to ridiculously low prices. A generous price-cut is even more attractive – if not imperative – now that Italy has the euro, which is not as kind to our dollar as the lira used to be. More recently, Vivien tells me, another designer outlet, called Dmagazineoutlet, has opened in a much more convenient location, 26 via Montenapoleone. Check it out next time you're in the vicinity or log on to **www.dmagazine.it**.

I remember enjoying a panorama of the Duomo from my table in the cafe on top of La Rinascente (the sort of Myer of Milan), **www.larinascente.it**, where Giorgio Armani did time as a window-dresser in the late 1950s. Today's fashionistas buy their homewares there.

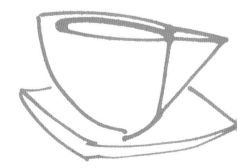

But apart from *la moda Italiana*, what remained in my head after that visit, because it seemed to symbolise the exquisite refinement of this extraordinary city, was something I spied in the window of a family business of cutlers, G Lorenzi, at 9 via Montenapoleone. It was a set of *midollo* scoops, little silver implements for extracting the marrow (*midollo* in Italian) from osso buco. Is that not precious? It belongs in the same category as the tiny asparagus-shaped silver tongs that Pepe Garcia brought to the table if you ordered asparagus at Maxim's in Melbourne in the 1970s. Totally unnecessary, an exquisite frippery, like the rose petals floating on the honeyed milk in which Miss Frou Frou bathes **Edwina McCann**'s tootsies (see page 264).

Browse about

To adjust to *la dolce vita* Milan-style, start with the following, then follow the trail of our stylesetters.

Cova at 8 via Montenapoleone has been making the rich Viennese cake, Sacher Torte, since 1817, but **Tempe Brickhill** likes to go there for 'a gin and tonic and a nosey look at people', who no doubt include the fashion crowd tempted by tiny, bite-sized Italian cakes dubbed 'sugar-rush canapés', and the hot chocolate. Beware of the prices, though; they are 'exorbitant', says one fashion insider.

Pasticceria Marchesi is in a lovely nineteenth-century building at 11a via Santa Maria alla Porta. No seats. You rub shoulders at the bar with the locals taking an espresso and a sandwich or buying cakes.

Da Giacomo is a modish trattoria at 6 via Pasquale Sottocorno. Go there for the fish, the stylish surroundings and maybe a sighting of some big names in fashion.

Mimma Gini 21 via Santa Croce at Piazza Sant'Eustorgio is where you will find the former furniture designer's marvellous hoard of furnishing fabrics from all over the world. Many finish up on the backs of fashionistas.

Nilufar at 32 via della Spiga is home to antiques and all kinds of inspirational interior design pieces.

Buccellati 8 via Montenapoleone. Family jewellers since the middle of the eighteenth century, Buccellati are now known internationally, from Hong Kong to Beverly Hills.

Pettinaroli 2 Piazza San Fedele (the entrance is on via Tommaso Marino), **www.fpettinaroli.it**. Four generations of a family of stationers and fine-art printers have served the gentry of Milan since 1881.

L'Oro dei Farlocchi 13 via Madonnina, in the Brera district, **www.lorodeifarlocchi. com**. Antiques from many periods, including the mid twentieth century. This is one of the wittiest sites on the web, especially if you are fond of dogs.

ERIC MATTHEWS

Bally 8 via Montenapoleone, **www.bally.com**. The superb quality and faultless service bring Eric back every time he sets foot in Milan.

Malo 7 via della Spiga, **www.malo.it**. Malo is for those of us who revere cashmere. Although the prices are breathtaking, the quality here is 'magnificent' according to Eric. 'Turtlenecks and cardigans in the most exquisite colours, natural tones, greens, greys and navy blues.'

Illulian 41 via Manzoni. Inspirational interior design store with 'the most sublime rugs including Odegard. Some of the best rug designs in the world.'

Boffi 11 via Solferino and 19 Corso Monforte. 'The ultimate in kitchen and bathroom design.'

B&B Italia 14 via Durini. 'The place to see why Italian furniture design is legendary.'

Spazio Armani 31 via Manzoni. Every category to which maestro Giorgio has attached his name is represented on 6000 square metres over three floors. No wonder Eric is enthralled. Furniture, fashion, accessories, fragrance, flowers, books, hi-fi, are all accommodated, along with the Emporio Armani cafe.

CRAIG MARKHAM

10 Corso Como 10 Corso Como, **www.10corsocomo.com**. This concept emporium named after its address is the brainchild of Carla Sozzani, whose sister Franca is the editor of Italian *Vogue*. For Craig, the packaging is almost as good as its contents, which might turn out to be 'fashion, home accessories, books, music, magazines, fragrance, jewellery, or almost anything that's currently hot or cool. It has a great restaurant and art gallery.' You can even sleep there, in one of three double rooms decked out in mid twentieth-century iconic furniture (Eames, Saarinen and such). This mini-inn made up of three rooms is called 3 Rooms, what else? (See chapter 5, 'Sleeping around'.)

Hogan 23 via Montenapoleone. Craig loves the 'preppy style of the trainers and I have them in a few colours. The store was created by the son of the owner of footwear designer Tod's, but it's younger and more casual.' There are great bags there, too.

Four Seasons Hotel 6/8 via Gesù, in a former fifteenth-century convent, **www.fourseasons.com/milan**. There's nothing ascetic now about its 118 exquisite and costly rooms, although some are so big, they must have been the Mother Superior's.

Bulgari Hotel Milan 7B via Privata Fratelli Gabba, between Montenapoleone and via della Spiga, **www.bulgarihotels.com**. For Craig, 'it's the most fabulous place to stay in Milan now.' Designed by Antonio Citterio, it's a serious rival to the Four Seasons. (See also Ilana Katz's recommended hotels, page 49.)

MICHAL MCKAY

An absolute must for Michal McKay is **Prada**, 21 via Sant'Andrea, **www.prada.com**. 'What I love about Prada is that it's slightly offbeat. Fashion cannot be too serious.'

JANE ROARTY

10 Corso Como (See also Craig Markham's comments on page 139). Although Jane prefers Paris to Milan for shopping, this place is an exception. 'Being a journalist [in the fashion industry] you get a discount for buying things at Prada, but I would rather go here because Carla Sozzani has this unique ability to buy things that you haven't seen before. You'll go there and she'll have not only the most contemporary pieces from Comme des Garçons and Yohji Yamamoto, which are hand-picked and absolutely brilliant and unique; she'll also have the Bonds T-shirts that Akira did and that nobody's seen. She has the best perfumes, the best menswear, the best books, the best candles, so it's like stepping into an exotic world of extremely bohemian things, but with ultimate taste. She is the one who brought Azzedine Alaïa back. She was famous for bringing back Zandra Rhodes vintage. She sells Vivienne Westwood but she does it in her own way.'

LUCINDA MENDEL

Lucinda is another fan of 10 Corso Como, particularly the bookstore upstairs. 'It's one of the most impressive bookstores I've ever seen.' She recently bought a hefty tome on Francis Bacon for her husband there and blessed the fact that she'd packed lightly so there was room for it in her suitcase.

BELINDA SEPER

Mercatone dell'Antiquariato on the banks of Il Naviglio Grande, the oldest canal in Milan, between viale Gorizia and via Valenza. An outdoor flea market is held on the last Sunday of each month, except for July. Belinda tries to time her trips to coincide with it. She and her colleague 'push all our other appointments out of the way because it is just a brilliant thing to do. You can find the most staggeringly beautiful things, from vases and glassware to old plates and vintage clothing, handbags, umbrellas, jewellery, buttons, clips, posters, chandeliers. It's just endless. If you were furnishing an apartment you could do it quite brilliantly from here. And there are streets of it. Put on your good walking shoes, don't look like you've got too much money, bargain hard. They know you're a foreigner, so they put their prices up. But they're fun and generally everyone speaks a bit of English. You get by.'

Belinda is also a great fan of Pettinaroli (see also page 138). For the past six or
so years, she has been collecting their notebooks, each one covered in a different
decorative paper. In these, she records anything she sees that is interesting or relevant
to her business. 'I sketch very quickly what I'm buying. Some of the people are kind
enough to give me little swatches and I stick all the swatches in. Every note about
every season, every shape that we've bought is recorded in all these little books.' More
than a dozen of them lined up on a shelf at home attest to her diligence.

Hotel de la Ville 6 via Ulrico Hoepli, between the Duomo and via Montenapoleone,
www.delavillemilano.com. Belinda is such a regular, she gets the same room every
time. 'It's not the Four Seasons but, you know, I don't want to see all the people I'm
going to see during the day. I don't need to sit in the lobby and see all the fashionistas
parading. I would prefer not to see anybody from the world of fashion.' Her loyalty
to the hotel pays off in the exceptional service she receives there. 'I leave my scarf
in a restaurant and, two days after I get back to Australia, I ring them and tell them.
They say, "It's okay, we pick it up for you and we give it to you next time." And then
the minute I arrive, out comes the scarf.' If she goes for a stand-up coffee in the bar
opposite the hotel in the morning, the doorman knows that's where she is and when
her taxi arrives, 'He'll sing out, "Signora! Signora!" gesturing for me to chuck my
coffee down and run for the taxi.' No wonder she feels at home there.

It's not all work and no play on Belinda's four trips a year to Milan, though. 'At the
end of the day we always have a fabulous meal and really beautiful wines', often at a
little restaurant around the corner from the hotel. If Belinda is on her own, they'll
re-cork her unfinished bottle of wine and put it on her table the following night. She
realises that some people might think frequenting the same restaurant is boring, but
she finds it 'a confirmation that everything is as you need it to be, in order to do what
you've got to do', especially when you are there on business.

Local knowledge – Antonio Berardi's hot spots in Milan

If you want to know the best places in any city in the world, ask a trustworthy
inhabitant of that city. So it was that **Tempe Brickhill**'s colleague Piera in London
asked her brother, the fashion designer Antonio Berardi in Milan, for tips on his city
of residence. See more about Antonio at **www.antonioberardi.com**.

SHOPPING

Anaconda 7 via Bergamini. 'The most amazing jewellery to be had. Modern with a nod to the past. Must see.'

A&B 7 Piazza XXV Aprile. 'The best sneakers under one roof.'

Casolari 2 via Verri. 'Fantastic perfumery. Tiny but full of wicked little surprises.'

Lab 19 via Arena. 'Unknown designers, amazing knits, bags, trinkets and antique *objets d'art*. Eye-opening.'

10 Corso Como 'Multi-brand designer store. Music, books, gallery, cafe and restaurant – possibly the most exciting store in the world.'

La Vetrina di Beryl 4 via Statuto. 'Shoes, shoes, shoes!'

Viktor & Rolf, via Sant'Andrea, **www.viktor-rolf.com**. 'New flagship store that turns the concept of shopping upside down, quite literally.'

RESTAURANTS

Dar El Yacout 23/25 via Cadore, **www.darelyacout.com**. 'Like being in a Moroccan riad in the centre of Milan. Stunning.'

Antico Ristorante Boeucc Piazza Belgioioso 2, **www.boeucc.com**. 'Old-world chic. Very Milanese. Food amazing. Expect to see diplomats and old money.' (It's been going since 1696.)

Paper Moon 1 via Bagutta. 'Open late, great for pizza and light food. Expensive and IN.'

Le Langhe 6 Corso Como. 'Great food. A favourite with the fashion set.'

Rangoli 36 via Solferino. 'Indian – the best there is in Milan.'

Compagnia Generale dei Viaggiatori Naviganti e Sognatori 4 via Cuccagna. 'Japanese. My favourite place in Milan. Food is wonderful, the staff are great and the sake cocktails with prickly pears are 2die4.'

Giulio Pane e O'jó 10 via Muratori. 'Roman osteria. Spaghetti caccio e pepe is a must.'

BARS

Absolut Icebar 12 Pizza Gerusalemme, **www.townhouse.it/icebar**. 'Inside is totally made of ice; the best place to be during the summer in Milan.'

The bar at the hotel **Principe di Savoia**, 17 Piazza della Repubblica, for 'the best vodka sour in town'.

Hotel Diana 42 viale Piave. 'Very in and very relaxing; an oasis in the centre of town.'

G-Lounge 8 via Larga. 'Happening bar on two floors with great DJs.'

CLUBS

La Nuova Idea 30 via de Castillia, at the corner of via Melchiorre Gioia. 'Perhaps the most surreal club I have ever been to. Milan's oldest gay club, with a floor dedicated to cheap house music and one to ballroom dancing. Very Quentin Crisp. Has to be seen to be believed.'

Magazzini Generale 14 via Pietrasanta. 'Milan's supper club, the best night being Friday. House (and fashion) upstairs.'

Plastic viale Umbria. 'Cool and trendy, Sunday night jams being the best.'

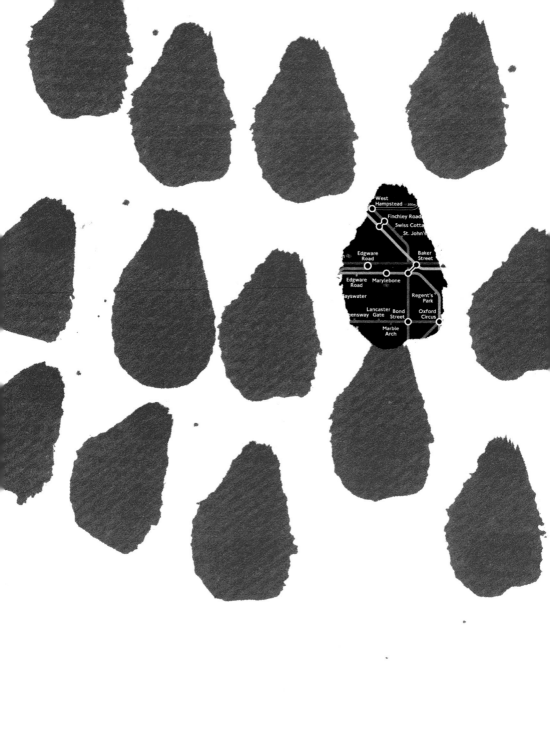

14
LONDON
HIGHLIGHTS

ANY CITY WHERE you have lived for more than a couple of years remains a kind of surrogate home for the rest of your days. London has that effect on me. I lived there for seven years at an impressionable time in my life, when I was between the ages of twenty-four and thirty-two. While I adjusted quickly to my work as an advertising copywriter, it took about two years for me to feel completely at ease with the people and the climate. After that period of adjustment, I adored it and thought I'd never leave.

Then, as now, it was expensive. I couldn't save a penny. There was too much to spend it on: reasonable digs at a decent address; seats at the Old Vic and Royal Festival Hall; sales at Liberty and Dickins & Jones in Regent Street; Danish kitchenware at Heal's in Tottenham Court Road; midweek lunches at Olmi's (my co-workers dubbed it Filthy's) in St Martin's Lane and at Terence Conran's Soup Kitchen, where the speciality of the day was served in Cornish blue-and-white pudding bowls; dinners at Schmidt's or Bertorellis in Charlotte Street or, if we were flush, at Sheekey's in St Martin's Court or Rule's in Maiden Lane where notables, Charles Dickens among them, had been welcomed since 1798; stolen weekends and necessary summer holidays on the Continent. When I decided to come back to Australia, I had to borrow the airfare from my parents.

It's even less affordable now, especially if you're not paid in pounds sterling but in Australian dollars, because they don't go very far once you land at Heathrow. That's why you have to be selective in London, more than in any other city I know. So, rather than buy or experience things that are universal, I prefer to stick to what is rarely or never found in cities other than this one. London has depth, richness and cultural complexity based on 2000 years of history. There is a lot to see and do there, and some of it is free.

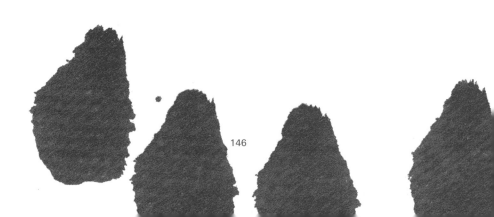

The best purchase I ever made in London is a paperback, as thick as a brick and just as heavy, called *The London Encyclopaedia*, edited by Ben Weinreb and Christopher Hibbert (published by Papermac, an offshoot of Macmillan). If I were you, the first place I would visit after I'd unpacked and settled into my lodgings is Hatchards at 187 Piccadilly, **www.hatchards.co.uk**, for a copy of this treasure of a tome. (Having sold books in Piccadilly since 1797, Hatchards is such an institution it has merited a listing in the *Encyclopaedia*.)

You'll be compensated for the inconvenience of lugging the book around by the knowledge it imparts, whether about something regal (Buckingham Palace, Clarence House, Kensington Palace), venerable (Westminster Abbey, St Paul's Cathedral, the Brompton Oratory), theatrical (the Apollo, Aldwych, Gaiety, Haymarket, Wyndham's), arboreal (Hyde Park, Green Park, Epping Forest), botanical (Holland Park, Richmond Park, Regent's Park) or cultural (the British Museum, Victoria & Albert Museum, Courtauld Institute), and that's not the end of it. It also covers the snooty (White's, the oldest gentlemen's club in St James's), eccentric (Dogs' Cemetery in Kensington Gardens), humble (Cock Lane, Coal Hole, Billingsgate Market), macabre (Whitechapel, where Jack the Ripper wielded his knife) and creepy (Holloway Prison, Wormwood Scrubs). You'll never be able to see more than a small percentage of what it contains but at least you'll know what you missed. And what great reading when you're too footsore from sightseeing to get out of bed.

As for where to shop, you'll have to look elsewhere, except for the places you already know, such as Fortnum and Mason, **www.fortnumandmason.com**, Liberty of London, **www.liberty.co.uk**, Harrods, **www.harrods.com**, and Marks & Spencer, **www.marksandspencer.com**.

Even on a fleeting visit to London, I'd be sorry to miss Harvey Nichols, **www.harveynichols.com**, the only department store there that I would put on a par with the best of New York, although Selfridges, **www.selfridges.com**, has an enthusiastic following since Christian Liaigre (see Craig Markham's favourites on pages 150–51) gave it a makeover. When decision fatigue has overtaken me on the lower floors of Harvey Nichols, I revive myself at the bar, cafe or restaurant beside the splendid food market on the fifth floor; if brussels sprouts are in season, this is where you'll see how tiny they can be – about the size of your thumbnail – when they're picked at the peak of perfection.

The series of quaint shopfronts under the name of **Browns** in South Molton Street hides a very rewarding place to train your eye on what's newest from the edgiest English fashion designers and their counterparts wherever they happen to be, **www. brownsfashion.com**. Browse at Browns for Alexander McQueen, John Galliano, Paul Smith, Matthew Williamson, and goodness knows who else. This is also the place to buy Liz Earle Naturally Active Skincare, a very successful botanically based range developed by an enterprising young woman on the Isle of Wight.

Speaking of enterprise, the **Jo Malone** skin preparations that grew from their namesake's expertise at giving facials at her flat in Walton Street are now big-time in beauty and fragrance, so don't miss her flagship store in Sloane Street, or browse **www.jomalone.co.uk**. But if you do, no need to despair. In 2006 a Jo Malone store opened in Sydney at 110 Queen Street, Woollahra, telephone (02) 9362 5555. For the handiwork of another English achiever, drop in on **Stella McCartney** at 30 Bruton Street, or log on to **www.stellamccartney.com**.

London has always been offbeat, fertile ground for new ideas; eccentricity is at home here. That is why, like her or not, we students of fashion owe ourselves a visit to one of **Vivienne Westwood**'s three London boutiques, preferably the one at 430 Kings Road, World's End, where she started in 1970. Back then she was a rock 'n' roll chick, selling 1950s records and related items in partnership with the performance artist Malcolm McLaren at their shop called Let It Rock. In 1972, the shop was renamed Too Fast to Live, Too Young to Die and it sold leather and T-shirts with pornographic images which, by 1974, had morphed into all-out sadomasochistic wear; the shop was then called SEX, to make sure people got the message. When The Sex Pistols went on stage in 1976 wearing the paraphernalia of bondage from the shop, which was then called Seditionaries, Punk was born, with Vivienne Westwood as its deity. A T-shirt with an image of the Queen with a safety pin through her nose appeared in 1977, but Her Majesty is clearly not one to harbour a grudge, for she awarded the wayward Westwood an OBE in 1992. Westwood's evolution has been uninhibited, wide-ranging and extraordinarily influential. It's all there on her excellent website, **www.viviennewestwood.com**. Such a phenomenon could only have happened in London. Can you imagine Punk in Paris?

I couldn't leave London without a visit to one of the **Conran** establishments, and not just for old times' sake. Whether marketing furniture or food, Sir Terence has always been a trailblazer in style, and he still is, **www.conran.com**. On the subject of interiors, the **General Trading Company** at Sloane Square is a store I wish would open a branch around the corner from where I live. Have a wander through **www. general-trading.co.uk**.

The venerable **Burberry**, **www.burberry.com**, maker of outfits for a South Pole expedition in 1911 and famous for its military trenchcoats with checked linings, now has Christopher Bailey as its hot designer, which accounts for renewed excitement in a brand that's been going since 1856. The quality has always been there; now there's currency as well, and a lot more to try on than a trench (although who'd be sniffy about that?).

Upholding lofty traditions is something London does extremely well, and I don't just mean the pomp and pageantry of royal displays, such as Trooping the Colour and the Changing of the Guard at Buckingham Palace. I love to window-shop in the Burlington Arcade, off Piccadilly, which is just as exclusive now as when it opened in 1819. It was designed by the architect Samuel Ware for his boss, Lord George Cavendish of Burlington House, specifically to house traders in exquisite objects for the elite. His lordship employed liveried beadles to keep out roughnecks and maintain a civilised tone, a practice that still prevails. So don't run, sing, put up your umbrella or lug ungainly packages in this elegant covered passageway, or you'll be chastised by a beadle. See **www.burlington-arcade.co.uk/home.htm**. My favourite shops here are Irish Linen, at 35 and 36; and Penhaligon's (I have a weakness for their Bluebell bath oil) at 16; closely followed by the specialists in cashmere (see page 79). You might prefer the St Petersburg Collection of objects designed by Theo Fabergé (grandson of Carl, of the famous eggs) and his daughter Sarah at 42. If you're a chap who yearns to mingle with the blue bloods, Ascot & Henley at 51 has the correct dress for you, whatever the occasion.

Local knowledge

CRAIG MARKHAM

There's not much going on in London that misses the eye of Craig Markham. He recommends two areas worth exploring. The first is Brompton Cross. 'I lived in Walton Street for seven years, so this was my neighbourhood. The area, at the junction of Brompton Road, Sloane Avenue and Fulham Road, is defined by the flagship Conran shop [in the Michelin Building] and Joseph [the legendary fashion retailer].' Although Craig concedes that the Conran shop is 'an obvious choice, I love browsing there after lunch on a Sunday, especially in the book department.' Other worthwhile ports of call at Brompton Cross are: 'The Library, for alternative men's fashion and books; Interiors Bis for modern French furniture; Isis for the best eyewear including their own designs; B&B Italia for the best of modern Italian furniture design by Antonio Citterio; and Santa Maria Novella, the London outpost for the famous Florentine perfumery. A wander will reveal all. Have lunch at Tartine, Joe's Cafe or Le Brasserie.'

His advice about Notting Hill is also worth heeding. 'Avoid Portobello Road unless you are a diehard antique fiend. Instead, head for Westbourne Grove and Ledbury Road. Have lunch in the Nicole Farhi store [202 Westbourne Grove] or at Tom's Deli, then wander about. The highlights are: Matches, for the right pieces from best designers such as Prada, and men's shirts from Dries Van Noten; Heidi Klein swimwear for women; Aime, for clothes and home accessories; Paul & Joe and Ghost [for designer Tanya Sarne's 'real clothes for real women']. Cross to the corner of Kensington Park Road to Paul Smith's Westbourne House and an edited selection of his collections for men and women.'

While you're in Kensington Park Road, call in on Coco Ribbon, **www.cocoribbon.com**, the lifestyle boutique set up by Sophie Oliver and Alison Chow (a Sydneysider) in 2002. It has earned accolades, not only for its imaginative goods and chattels (from knickers decorated with Swarovski crystals to Italian chandeliers), but also for the way in which they're displayed. Fond of vintage? Rellik, at 8 Golborne Road (at right angles to Portobello), **www.relliklondon.co.uk,** is worth a rummage, because you never know what big-name wearables there might be in a collection spanning the 1920s to the mid 1980s.

Connolly at 41 Conduit Street is another of Craig's favourites. 'The shop was designed by Andrée Putman, and the leather goods are the best. I buy gifts there all the time, often leatherbound copies of *London A–Z*, and travel notebooks for friends.' Connolly leathers have awesome credentials; they've been used in upholstery at Windsor Castle and the House of Commons, and in swish carriages, such as Rolls Royce, Aston Martin, Ferrari and Jaguar.

The fragrances of the moment in London come from an exceptional Scottish 'nose' called Lyn Harris through her company, Miller Harris, now headquartered at 21 Bruton Street and at her original shop at 14 Needham Road, Notting Hill; see **www.millerharris.com**. Apart from her regular wardrobe of fragrances, Lyn will create one just for you (if you can spare 4000 quid, roughly $10 000). Craig describes her as 'an extraordinary perfumer who trained at Grasse in France. I love what she does because it is chic, low-key but has a strength of character. I buy her great range of body products in her signature scents.'

Thanks to John Smedley at 24 Brook Street, Craig owns 'about fifty wool and sea island cotton sweaters. I buy them in black, navy, grey, chocolate and blue and they last forever. My mother loves the twin-sets, so that's a great gift to send home.' See **www.john-smedley.com**.

For inspiring interiors, Craig goes to Christian Liaigre, 68–70 Fulham Road. 'I love his aesthetic, his furniture design and style of architecture, but it's all very expensive. So I've bought the exquisite coffee-table book [*Maison – Christian Liaigre*, Thames & Hudson] compiled and written by Herbert Ypma. It is simply beautiful.'

TEMPE BRICKHILL

'I can spend hours in garden centres,' says **Tempe Brickhill**, so she is a regular at Petersham Nurseries, off Petersham Road, at Richmond in Surrey, **www.petershamnursery.com**. Apart from the horticultural delights, there is the 'wonderful' and rather bucolic Petersham Cafe, run by Skye Gyngell, an Australian chef noted for her use of organic ingredients and her impressive client list as a private caterer.

Tempe also frequents **Sarah Raven's Cutting Garden** in Sussex, for its marvellous array of bulbs, seeds and seedlings, **www.thecuttinggarden.com**. As well as being an expert gardener and florist, Sarah Raven is a columnist, writer and lecturer. Another out-of-town excursion takes Tempe to the Cotswolds and the **Daylesford Farm Shop**, **www.daylesfordorganic.com**, which is 'packed full of marvellous organic food, books, garden pots, plants and it has a wonderful cafe'.

Then there is **RK Alliston** at 173 New Kings Road, Parsons Green (and at the beguiling address of 6 Quiet Street, Bath), **www.rkalliston.com**. This is not a nursery but a place which, with delicious understatement, describes the goods it carries as 'simple, practical and stylish products for people who enjoy being in the garden'. For 'plants, pots and gardening tips', Tempe logs on to **www.crocus.co.uk**.

Another passion of Tempe's is browsing in bookshops. While she often visits **John Sandoe Books** in Blacklands Terrace, Chelsea, **www.johnsandoe.com**, Tempe's 'favourite shop in the whole world' is **Daunt Books**, 83 Marylebone High Street, **www.dauntbooks.co.uk**. It specialises in literature for the traveller who wants to read more about a destination than run-of-the-mill guides provide. Therefore, everything – novels, biography, historical works, poetry, as well as travel guides – is organised by country. 'It's one of the most beautiful shops in London, a panelled gallery on three floors, redolent of an old college library – a bibliophile's delight.'

Because Marylebone High Street has been smartened up over the past decade, Tempe suggests you stay awhile. 'There are lots of good coffee shops and bakers, a **Conran** shop, plus a plethora of spa-type shops. One of my favourite shops is **Skandium** [at number 86, **www.skandium.com**] specialising in wonderful, classic Scandinavian design. **VV Rouleaux** [at number 6, **www.vvrouleaux.com**] sells every button and braid you could dream up. Yet the street still retains its essential "English High Steet" normality, with newsagents, the fishmonger and [a branch of the supermarket chain] Waitrose.'

Tempe is also fond of **Smythson** (see also chapter 25: 'A place for everything'); **The Rug Company** at 124 Holland Park Avenue, **www.therugcompany.co.uk** (log on to this site for a magic carpet ride to the most exotic places); and **Couverture**, 'An eclectic and lovely small shop owned by Emily Dyson' at 310 Kings Road, Chelsea, **www.couverture.co.uk**. (The website is worth viewing for its freshness and humour – who can resist those goosedown duvet socks?)

East Enders

There is another side to London, a gritty yet fascinating alternative to the
settled grace of places with area codes that begin with W followed by 1, 3, 5 or 7.
Gentrification is gradually moving east, modifying the character of streets and squares
that lie beyond Bloomsbury. Clerkenwell, Hoxton, Shoreditch and Spitalfields have
become deeply desirable addresses for the kind of movers who, in New York, would be
living in SoHo lofts, Chelsea brownstones or Hell's Kitchen warehouses.

So, if I were in London for more than a flying visit, I'd love to explore areas whose
names are familiar only because I've seen them on double-decker buses and maps of
the Tube. This is the East End, heartland of the Cockneys and Pearlies. I might stay
in one of ninety-seven rooms at the **Malmaison London** in Charterhouse Square,
near the Barbican Centre, **www.malmaison-london.com**. But I'm also attracted
to a nineteenth-century former warehouse in Clerkenwell bought by restaurateurs
Michael Benyan (an Australian chef) and Mark Sainsbury (son of super-grocer Lord
Sainsbury), who opened it as **The Zetter**, a 59-room hotel and restaurant in March
2004. It's very hip. I believe you can buy champagne there as easily as you can Coca-
Cola – from a slot machine. You will find The Zetter at St John's Square, 86–88
Clerkenwell Road, **www.thezetter.com**.

Not far away is one of London's best contemporary eating houses, particularly if you
are a carnivore: **St John Bar & Restaurant**, near Smithfield Market (which has
been trading in meat for 800 years). Co-owner and chef Fergus Henderson's bold
ways with humble cuts are not limited to his celebrated signature appetiser of roast
bone marrow and parsley salad. He also dishes up ambrosial offal that might sound
iffy (lambs' tongues, calf's heart, pig's spleen, tripe and onions) but, according to
those with seriously refined palates, the food here, whether vegetables, puddings,
fish, fowl, flesh or innards, is masterly. The restaurant is located at 26 St John Street.
Farther east, **St John Bread & Wine** – an eat-in and take-out bakery, bar and
kitchen – opened under the same ownership in May 2003 at 94–96 Commercial
Street, opposite Old Spitalfields Market. You can read about both establishments at
www.stjohnrestaurant.co.uk.

In Fergus Henderson's hands, eels have come a long way from the jellied variety sold by the costermongers in the East End in Victorian times. Yet old-fashioned dishes such as pies with mash and liquor (gravy), hot stewed eels and jellied eels are still around, if you know where to look for them. In 1995, The Pie 'n' Mash Club of Great Britain was established by a Stepney family named Smith. Its objective, according to its Constitution, is 'To keep alive the unique traditional recipes & rituals associated with thy regular visit to your favourite shoppe'. If you'd like to tackle the grub that is as important to the Cockneys as haggis is to the Scots, try F Cooke, which has been trading for more than a century at 9 Broadway Market, Hackney, or G Kelly at 414 Bethnal Green Road.

Among restaurants more attuned to contemporary tastes which have opened in these parts in the past few years are The Light Bar & Restaurant, in a converted 1893 power station at 233 Shoreditch High Street; and The Clerkenwell Dining Room and Bar at 69 St John Street.

In March 2006 Kate Evans, sometime fashion buyer for Harrods and Harvey Nichols, gave Spitalfields a fashion fillip with her swish salon Precious at 16 Artillery Passage.

Markets

Whenever **James Gordon** is in London on a Sunday, you're likely to find him at the Columbia Road Flower Market at Bethnal Green, **www.columbia-flower-market.freewebspace.com**, sometime between 8 a.m. and 4 p.m. He loves the flowers, but that's not the end of it. 'There's a cake shop at 160 Columbia Road called Treacle, with the best cheese-and-onion pasties and the daintiest of cupcakes, about the size of a 50-cent coin, iced and decorated beautifully.' You can log on to the 'Homepage of the Cupcake' at www.treacleworld.com. 'A few doors away is a really fab hat shop called Fred Bare. I purchased a black, sort of crocheted pull-on with a white Swiss cross on top and I was very keen on many more. Almost next door is a gallery kind of shop with amazing felted bits of this and that, and jewellery. I bought a marvellous little marcasite frog with sapphire eyes.' These stores open only on Sundays,when the plants and flowers attract big crowds, so go early.

15

SYDNEY —
MY STAMPING
GROUND

Casting a cold eye over what I've written so far, I see that you might have the impression that I am so besotted with the outside world, I have neglected my own territory. To some extent that is true, although there are local gems tucked away in most chapters. The place where you live never seems quite as glamorous as the glittering attractions on the other side of the world. That's why so many of us can't wait to get on a plane and skip the country. It is also true that, while we in Australia are well supplied with desirable goods, we don't have the choice that exists in New York, Paris, Milan and London – mainly because we don't have the population to sustain it. Apart from that, it's much easier to find out where to shop in your home country than to track down the best places abroad; our newspapers and magazines are full of on-the-spot information.

Nevertheless, I can't pass myself off as a passionate shopper without paying attention to my home base. To help me in this enterprise, I rang **Alison Hanson**. She has a superb eye for a really good thing. Not obvious, very particular. It's amazing what you find out when you spend some time with Alison.

Alison Hanson's pick of Sydney

No matter where she goes, whether it's into a stationery store in Paddington, a bookshop in Potts Point, a homewares boutique at Fairlight or a flower stall at a growers' market, everybody knows Alison. Such is the power of an inquisitive mind and an outgoing personality.

Paper Couture (see also chapter 25: 'A place for everything'), 284 South Dowling Street, Paddington (near Oxford Street), telephone (02) 9357 6855. 'I love it to bits,' Alison told me when she first took me there and, true to her word, she is there on the slightest pretext. This is the source of her clever custom-made visiting cards that double as gift tags. Alison especially loves being able to order small quantities instead of the big numbers you have to commission if you go to a regular printer.

Herman & Herman Interiors (no relation to Hermon & Hermon of Melbourne) 62 Kings Cross Road, Rushcutters Bay, telephone (02) 9357 6684. 'Well-bred' is how Alison describes the pieces showcased here. There is refinement and polish to every piece. Many are designed by Walter Herman himself, who (with his sister, Sharon) opened the shop in late 2005 after twenty years' involvement in interior design and decorating, notably with Ros Palmer Interiors in Queen Street, Woollahra. The retro dining table of European beechwood, the chocolate cotton-velvet armchair with silver studs, the ottomans in cowhide and woven leather, the sofas, side tables and lamps, the updated 'Louis' chairs painted white and covered with candy-striped Paul Smith fabric are, says Alison, 'the modern we want'. Conveniently for her, a cup of excellent coffee is waiting right next door at Café Hernandez, a Kings Cross institution and cab drivers' hangout that never closes.

Ganimtextiles **www.ganimtextiles.com**. As soon as Alison laid eyes on Rae Ganim's hand-dyed and hand-loomed textiles she wanted to get her hands on the yarns, bolts of cloth, cushions, throws and scrunchy bags from this gifted Melbourne artist and former fashion designer. Rae's infallible instinct for colour and texture makes her work irresistible and somehow timely; there's nothing mass-produced here. She literally cooks up colours and designs in her own backyard and sends them to a family of weavers in India. Sydneysiders can buy her bags from Carolyn Rowe Design, Harris Arcade, 12 Cross Street, Double Bay, telephone (02) 9363 2947; and at Museum Shop, 140 George Street, The Rocks, telephone (02) 9245 2430.

Palm Beach Cupcakes 1109 Barrenjoey Road, Palm Beach. **www.palmbeachcupcake. com.au**. The cupcake's moment has come, especially with a glass of champagne, advises Alison. Dieters beware. These are proper old-fashioned cakes – full of butter and eggs and cream – which used to be made at home before word got out, prompting the setting up of a professional kitchen and 'cupcakery' at 30 Whiting Street, Artarmon. These ambrosial little morsels are tiny, so one wouldn't hurt, would it?

L.A. Design 26 Queen Street, Woollahra, telephone (02) 9326 2888. Between them, sisters Louise and Belinda Murray source and produce lighting, furniture, window treatments, jewellery, vintage clothing and an assortment of decorative objects. They also specialise in gilding and painted finishes. When Alison introduced me to this fascinating little treasure house, I found the lamp base I'd been looking for without having realised what I wanted: a single simple black rod rising from a small and sturdy circular black iron base.

Farmers Markets on Wednesdays 10 a.m. until 4 p.m. at The Entertainment Quarter, Moore Park. Despite the dreary name for the former Fox Studios (which muscled out our endearing old Sydney Showground), the market is a rewarding place to shop for food, plants and flowers. Just ask Alison. She regularly calls on: Tessa Bradford, who brings back hand-woven seagrass shopping baskets from her regular trips to France; Chris, wrapping bunches of blooms non-stop at Mayfarm, a battalion of buckets filled with some of the freshest and cheapest flowers in Sydney; Lisa at Brilliant Food, for mouth-watering marinated salmon, wasabi crème fraîche to go with it, and pickled red onions; David Borg, for creamy Willowbrae chevre cheese made by his wife Karen back home on the farm at Wilberforce; and Frank, for strawberries and peaches in season. The market is also open on Saturdays, but we prefer midweek.

Eclettica (see also page 102), **www.eclettica.com.au**. Alison is so enamoured of the work this talented twosome produce, it took her months to make up her mind about which bag to buy. She wants them all. It is a common problem for Eclettica admirers. For stockists, email info@eclettica.com.au.

Bandigan Art 39 Queen Street, Woollahra, telephone (02) 9328 4194, **www.bandigan. com**. In an intimate two-storey gallery, John Colquhoun and Suzanne Lowe mount exhibitions of indigenous art and ceremonial pieces from remote communities in the north. Their passion for Aboriginal art and culture developed more than two decades ago, when they lived in the Northern Territory. Suzanne began to collect sculptures from Yirrkala in Arnhem Land, while John built the house Glen Murcutt designed for Banduk Marika, one of Australia's most important women artists. They actively support community art centres and their artists in whatever way they can, including mentoring young talent.

The Bay Tree 40 Holdsworth Street, Woollahra, telephone (02) 9328 1101, **www.thebaytree.com.au**. It's difficult to believe that 12 500 items can be crammed into this tiny corner shop that's been a local landmark for decades, but the organised clutter is one of its charms. Apart from basics, ranging from excellent kitchen knives to hard-to-find cooking muslin, there is whimsy and wonderment in much of the selection. Last Christmas, I could not resist tree decorations in the shape of frivolous Manolo-esque high-heeled shoes. Says Alison, 'This is far more wonderful for wedding presents than the mainstream stores.' Yes, it does offer a wedding registry.

Honey Bee Homewares 178 Sydney Road, Fairlight, telephone (02) 9948 9908.
Virginie Fontes, the charming young French woman who owns this rich little store
of covetables, travels to Paris each September to source supplies of whatever makes a
nest beautiful and comfortable: bedclothes, tableware, lamps, mirrors, old-fashioned
coathooks, baskets, candlesticks, towels and bath mitts. The pieces have originality
and wit, and many are surprisingly affordable. When we shopped there before last
Christmas, Alison's loot included a green-and-white berry wreath for the door.
I couldn't resist the journal sticks – those newspaper-holding batons found in cafes all
over France.

Vivalino 489 Darling Street, Balmain, telephone (02) 9555 8855, **www.vivalino.
com.au**. Another store that rises above the norm, Vivalino expresses the ideas and
personalities of its two owners, Linda Martin and Rhonda Townsend, who have
dedicated their brainchild to 'indulgence at home'. That means quilts in patterns
and colours, as well as pristine embroidered white, and all the trappings that go with
a beautifully made bed: soft furnishings, room accessories, nightwear, bath and body
products. Vivalino also caters divinely for babies up to the age of one.

My Island Home 5 Transvaal Avenue, Double Bay, telephone (02) 9362 8760. When
Alison feels like fleeing the city to a tropical retreat, she goes here instead, where the
mood is 'holiday-in-town, the occasional Pacific Island fantasy': wicker chairs and
sunbeds, seagrass mats, bamboo door curtains, caftans and shifts, beach umbrellas,
bags, baskets, bedcovers, and more. Log on to **www.myislandhome.com.au** and see
what she means.

City Recital Hall Angel Place, Sydney, box office telephone (02) 8256 2222,
www.cityrecitalhall.com. Although it opened with a gala concert on 30 October
1999, this superb, purpose-built recital hall plays second fiddle to the Opera House
when it comes to publicity. What it lacks in harbour views, it makes up for in
acoustics. Like many other music-lovers, Alison and Jack have spent 'perfect evenings'
here with the Australian Brandenburg Orchestra and the Australian Chamber
Orchestra. The Australian String Quartet and Sydney Philharmonia Choirs also
regularly perform here to audiences of 1238, maximum.

My own beat

Even when we live in big cities, most of us routinely move in little pockets close
to home. These cosy hamlets within the great urban sprawl have developed unique
characteristics through their history, their shifting demographic and the businesses
that establish themselves successfully there. We gravitate to places compatible with
our needs and personalities. For some, that means lawns, trees and swimming pools.
Others prefer vistas of beaches and water. City slickers, like me, are sticklers for the
Big Smoke.

When people learn that I've lived in Surry Hills for thirty years, they often say, 'You
must have seen some changes.' I suppose I have, although the process has been so
gradual that for a long time I barely noticed it. We were attracted to this former
slum in 1976 by its intact Victorian terrace houses, its proximity to the city and its
affordability. The disreputable nature of it never bothered me, and I am happy to
report that it has not been entirely obliterated by young professionals moving into
converted warehouses and couples beavering away on the renovation of houses
that hadn't been touched for decades. Multiple bathrooms having been acquired,
converted attics are now all the rage.

REIGNING CATS AND DOGS

Whenever I'm at Bondi Junction I look for an excuse to call into **Oxford Pet Supplies** at
350 Oxford Street, telephone (02) 9389 9294. It's wonderfully no-nonsense and crammed
to the rafters. I was once faced with the need to buy a present for Louie the Labrador,
who lives in Los Angeles. Whatever do you give a dog who lives in America, land of the
pampered pet? I found the doggy equivalent of a Driza-bone, lined in sheepskin. I am told
Louie is so pleased, he thinks he's the dog from Snowy River.

Shabby shopfronts have been given over to cool restaurants and designer boutiques. Since its ambitious makeover, one formerly notorious pub is so flash you can't buy cask wine in its bottle shop. Trees, shrubs and flowers have changed grungy streets and back alleys into botanical showpieces that attract all kinds of birds, including big ones such as kookaburras, currawongs and sulphur-crested cockatoos. A couple of years ago, an industrious pair of crows built a nest in a gum tree in the backyard of a house across the lane from me and successfuly raised four squawking young; at dawn, the cacophony made us feel we were living in a real jungle instead of an urban one. Over the past decade, the district has evolved from down-at-heel, to up-and-coming, to having arrived. Similar gentrification has transformed the other side of Cleveland Street at East Redfern, which we prefer to call the Paris end of Redfern. Now it's spreading to Waterloo and beyond.

The result of all this is that, whatever I need in an everyday way, I can now usually find in my own backyard. Following are my favourite local ports of call.

Ici et Là 588 Bourke Street (at Parkham Street), telephone (02) 9699 4266, www.icietla.com.au. In a seasoned atmosphere at what I remember as a corner grocer, you can now find treasures brought in from France by Geraldine Manivet and her husand Andrew Forst. Pre-loved outdoor furniture, pots, dishes, tablecloths and bric-a-brac, striped deck-chair canvas, espadrilles, bags and cushions are presided over by Marcel, a brindle-and-white French bulldog of the kind immortalised in the writings of Colette. Sometimes I pretend I'm there for the loot, but it's really to say *bonjour* to Marcel, who gazes at me with rolling eye, flattened nose and tongue sticking out from his impressive jaws. One day when a customer tethered a young Airedale to the front bench outside, there was a bit of a French farce when Marcel demonstrated just how much he fancied her.

Cafe Niki 544 Bourke Street (corner of Nobbs Street), telephone (02) 9319 7517. Whenever I go to this time-honoured local hang-out, I can't go past its superb eggs Florentine: two perfectly poached eggs on a bed of baby spinach, smothered in a true hollandaise sauce.

Bourke Street Bakery 633 Bourke Street (corner of Devonshire Street), telephone (02) 9699 1011. Closed Mondays. Until Paul Allam and David McGuinness took over this little space after it was vacated by Chrissie Juillet's La Passion du Fruit,

Surry Hills was missing a top-grade bakery. The day it opened, the neighbourhood streamed in and we've never left. At the start, you could sometimes commandeer one of the three tiny tables in the window for coffee and the best croissants, brioches and pain au chocolat outside France. Alas, they're rarely unoccupied now, whatever the time or the day. The queue for take-home – baguettes, rye and sourdough breads, raisin and pistachio loaves, flourless chocolate cake, seasonal fruit tarts, praline twists dusted with icing sugar, coffee, warm pies made with ox cheek, coffee, and so on – trails out into the street. You have not tasted the apotheosis of the sausage roll until you've eaten the pork-and-fennel variety they bake here. The soy-and-linseed loaf has my name on it. The bakery's success has spawned a sibling at 130 Broadway.

When David Campbell opened **The Book Kitchen** at 255 Devonshire Street, telephone (02) 9310 1003, **www.thebookkitchen.com.au**, just across the street from the Bourke Street Bakery, it was the finishing touch to this attractive tiny pocket of Surry Hills. His bright idea to attract food-lovers was to offer them not only a choice of light or substantial dishes from 8 a.m. until late afternoon, but to stack the place with new and vintage cookbooks. You can buy them or just borrow one to read while you eat your tucker at a table inside or under an umbrella on the footpath. No reservations during the day but you can book for dinner, Thursday to Saturday, and it's licensed. Everything on the menu is cooked to order; the salads are wonderful, so are the veal and ricotta meatballs.

Well within walking distance of where I live is **Billy Kwong**, for me the most exciting Chinese restaurant on the planet, not just because I know and love its co-founder and owner, Kylie Kwong, but because of the scallops. I never knew how succulent a scallop could taste until I tried one here. Since then, I never eat them anywhere else. You don't need to know that Kylie is an active advocate of organic ingredients at their freshest – you can tell when you taste the food her chef, Hamish Ingham, and the team toss together in the homey open kitchen, where orders are strung over the worktable, like washing pegged to a clothesline. No bookings. Join the queue for a six o'clock opening at 3/355 Crown Street, telephone (02) 9332 3300.

If you are in need of good sustenance in this vicinity at lunchtime, it's worth remembering that **Bills Surry Hills** is virtually next door at 359 Crown Street, telephone (02) 9360 4762, **www.bills.com.au**. Don't ask me about the full menu because I can't resist Bill Granger's sweetcorn fritters with avocado salsa, whether I eat them here or at the space he took over from Margie Agostini at Queens Court, 118 Queen Street, Woollahra, telephone (02) 9328 7997. Further south along Crown Street at 381–385 is **The White Horse**, telephone (02) 8333 9900, **www.thewhitehorse.com.au**, a sleek and civilised retreat at lunchtime with good food and wine, and what I truly believe to be the best chips in Sydney.

Orson & Blake at the corner of Devonshire and Riley Streets, telephone (02) 8399 2525, **www.orsonandblake.com.au**, and **Parterre Garden** at 493 Bourke Street, telephone (02) 9356 4747, **www.parterre.com.au**, both have floorspace generous enough to show off large pieces of furniture in imaginative settings. For the latest trends in interiors and exteriors, look no further.

When I'm out of ideas for interesting gifts, I rely on three boutiques in Crown Street, between Foveaux Street and Withers Lane, opposite the Clock Hotel. Among the tableware, cushions, candles, artefacts, clothes and accessories at **Atmosphere Concepts**, telephone (02) 8354 1571, **www.atmosphereconcepts.com**, is the tactile FLATOUTbear made of sheepskin in koala or teddy style. Sisters Prue Trollope and Sarah Novati, whose **FLATOUTaustralia** gift shop is at 107 Mansfield Street, Rozelle, telephone (02) 9555 6434, are the brains behind the bear that has been cuddled by the offspring of Sarah Jessica Parker, Gwyneth Paltrow and even Crown Princess Mary of Denmark. Instead of being stuffed to make them solid, they are languid, like Linus blankets with ears, eyes, arms, legs and neckties. Irresistible to the child in all of us. For stockists, log on to **www.flatout.com.au/bears.htm**.

Although **Chee Soon & Fitzgerald**, 387 Crown Street, Surry Hills, telephone (02) 9360 1031, **www.cheesoonfitzgerald.com**, is a place to find serious elements of interior design – wallpapers, fabrics, lights, carefully chosen pieces of furniture – it is peppered with affordable decorative objects that make exciting and imaginative presents.

The tiny shop called **Mrs Red & Sons**, behind an appropriately coloured door at 427 Crown Street (corner of Withers Lane), telephone (02) 9310 4860, is run by a pair so welcoming, it's a pleasure to linger there to browse among the Asian offerings, from chopsticks and pots to candles and T-shirts. It's even more fun to watch your purchase being beautifully wrapped, whether or not it's a gift. Better ring before you go, because they keep gentlemanly hours.

The conversion of a warehouse at 500 Crown Street, between Arthur and Rainford Streets, has given us two welcome new restaurants: **Pizza e Birra**, telephone (02) 9332 2510, endearingly Italian with more on the menu than the name indicates; and **Bird Cow Fish**, telephone (02) 9380 4090, **www.birdcowfish.com.au**, a superior bistro and espresso bar. They both have an easy informality that augurs well for them in a district that spoils us for choice. Aren't we lucky?

Southward to **Fratelli Fresh** at 7 Danks Street, Waterloo, telephone 1300 552 119. Barry McDonald's two-level white-painted warehouse, with the incongruity of elegant Gothic windows, is filled with fresh produce, imported foods from Italy and a cafe/restaurant called Sopra (Italian for 'above', which is where it's located). This place is based on a brilliant idea: until 10 a.m. it's wholesale, but after that it's open slather for the rest of us. When my friend Lana Dopper and I meet for a day out we often start here, stocking up on virgin olive oil (Ranieri for cooking, Paradiso di Lara for salads), carnaroli rice, organic chicken and red meat, cheeses (pecorino pepato, gorgonzola and parmigiano), bread, flowers, and the best of seasonal fruit and vegetables. The produce marks the seasons as precisely as a calendar on the kitchen wall: the pencil leeks, artichokes, broad beans and barely formed garlic in spring; the stone fruit and tomatoes called 'Johnny's Love Bites' in summer; the quinces in autumn; the blood oranges in winter. Parking is a nightmare but the gains are worth the agony of finding a spot. Next door is Vicino (Italian for 'nearby') where you can stock up on basic Italian kitchen utensils and tableware. Both places are closed on Mondays.

Having filled the boot with food, do Lana and I then take it home and prepare lunch? Goodness, no. Sometimes we go upstairs to Sopra, where the food is always good because the best ingredients are downstairs for the chef's picking. When we're in the money, we treat ourselves to a glass of Bollinger and a succulent fillet steak with bearnaise sauce at Damien Pignolet's matchless **Bistro Moncur**, behind the Woollahra Hotel, corner of Queen and Moncur Streets, Woollahra, telephone (02) 9363 2519, **www.woollahrahotel.com.au**. We do have a good time on these stolen weekdays.

Since we are in Woollahra, let's stay here for a while. Queen Street is another beguiling pocket of Sydney, one that owes its charm to the human scale of old-established houses in settled gardens and shopfronts that are well kept and shaded by awnings and trees. This is **Carolyn Lockhart**'s neighbourhood. **Lucinda Mendel** is also a local who is often tempted by 'follies that I don't need' at Orson & Blake, 83 Queen Street, telephone (02) 9326 1155.

Carolyn is a regular at Lesley McKay's bookshop, telephone (02) 9328 2733, in Queens Court, in the same complex as Sotheby's at the corner of Moncur Street. (There is also one at 14 Macleay Street, Potts Point, telephone (02) 9331 6642.) Bookish types love to congregate at Lesley McKay's because its owner has the instinct and the intellect to know exactly what you'd like to read. Carolyn buys casual clothes at Reads of Woollahra, 130 Queen Street (telephone (02) 9328 1036, **www.reads.com.au**), gifts for children at one of several adorable shops in Queen Street, and bio-dynamic food ('The soy bread is to die for, all nutty with big chunks of soy beans') at Whole Foods House, 109 Queen Street, telephone (02) 9363 9879. When friends are looking for superior accommodation, she recommends Kathryn's on Queen, a small, comfortable and charmingly decorated B&B at 20 Queen Street, telephone (02) 9327 4535, **www.kathryns.com.au**. Kathryn Bruderlin, who owns and runs this desirable place to stay, also offers Apartment 8, a self-contained two-bedroom flat with air-conditioning and double-glazed windows in the neighbourhood. While you're in Queen Street, don't miss Robert Burton at 42–44, telephone (02) 9363 9848, for what he does best: meticulous shirts and jeans.

There are other big attractions for me in Queen Street. One is Churchill's Butchery, telephone (02) 9363 1052, an old-established purveyor of fine meats at number 132, where I'm often tempted to buy a shoulder or rack of succulent lamb. Once a year, I place my order here for the Christmas ham. Nearby, at number 124, Pan D'Arte, telephone (02) 9362 0414, does brisk business in exquisite cakes and sweet pastries, pizza by the metre and a barrage of breads including the crustiest ciabatta that has ever crackled under a serrated knife. (Damien Pignolet told me that, to bring a ciabatta to the table in perfect condition, re-heat it first in a 200°C oven for eight minutes.)

BOUQUETS

In every city, there are one or two florists you can
trust to send flowers that will not only be fresh
and perfect, but superbly put together without
trickery, much less skewered with wires and other
instruments of torture. For me, **Grandiflora** heads
the list in Sydney. Visit them in person at 12 Macleay
Street, Potts Point, telephone (02) 9328 2733, or
online at **www.grandiflora.net**.

If you're in Macleay Street and you're feeling hungry,
turn into Challis Avenue and hope to find a table
at number 12–16, **Fratelli Paradiso** (telephone
(02) 9357 1744) for *autentico* food and service that
makes you think you've been spirited to Italy. It's
tiny and popular, so be patient, or go at off-peak
times. Around the corner is another Potts Point
foodie favourite, **Yellow Bistro & Food Store**,
57 Macleay Street, telephone (02) 9357 3400,
famous for its date tart.

NOTES

16

MELBOURNE
À LA MODE

HANS AND I arrived to live in Melbourne in 1968 with $1000 between us. We did have good jobs to go to, though, and the temporary tenancy of a self-contained penthouse at the Palm Lake Motel on Queens Road in Albert Park; our rent there was paid by the advertising agency that had brought us south. Because we were partners in life as well as work, but had yet to tie the knot, we were considered quite risqué. Behind our backs, they called us Hansel and Gretel.

When we were able to marry, the agency was so relieved, the board of directors offered to pay for the wedding. (We didn't know until later that 'What happens if they split up?' had been a regular question at board meetings since we'd arrived.) At the marriage ceremony conducted by the Reverend Raymond Sprigg at South Yarra Baptist Church in Chapel Street, the general manager gave the bride away and the creative director was best man. We spent our honeymoon with a client and the account director in Sydney making television commercials. We all stayed at The Sebel Town House and drank Dom Perignon dispensed by Ted Curtis in the bar. They were the days.

One day, a colleague persuaded us to have a look at an empty boarding house in South Melbourne that had been on the market for some time. Most of South Melbourne then was either industrial or fairly run-down, but our agency was in Kavanagh Street and it made sense for a couple as work-centred as we were to live nearby. Besides, we couldn't afford an impressive address.

Though it was shabby, the house was beautiful. Freestanding, graceful and generously proportioned, it was like a drop-in from East Melbourne, where many of the glorious survivors from the Victorian era had been built with gold-rush money. It had camellias in the front garden and old nectarine trees in the back. With the nod from our management, The Bank of Adelaide agreed to fund us. It was not the first house Hans had ever owned, but it was a first for me.

South Melbourne

How appealing to the vanity, to think you've been in the forefront of a trend. I have a sentimental attachment to South Melbourne, a feeling of possessiveness, although

I haven't lived there since 1976. How it's come up in the world! Along with Albert Park and Port Melbourne it's now among the city's most vibrant young districts. The signs were always there, if you were plugged in. One of them was Tony Rogalsky's Hot Pot Shop in Clarendon Street, where hearty casseroles, such as burgundy beef and bacon, were dished up in glazed and rimmed terrracotta plates designed – and signed – by Gus McLaren. We were good customers, so they often let us take our dinner away in Gus's handiwork; I think I still have one of those rustic relics in the back of a cupboard downstairs. A decade or so later, this humble bistro had morphed into Rogalsky's, which merited three chef's hats in *The Age Good Food Guide* of 1987/88.

MEGAN MORTON'S FAVOURITE PORTS OF CALL

While the Town Hall and the Markets are still South Melbourne's abiding landmarks, the streets around them have changed beyond recognition, at least by me. This is a hunting ground for stylists such as **Megan Morton**, whose job it is to track the trends. She's a regular in Coventry, Park and Clarendon Streets, and you can't keep her away from the vintage finds at Empire 111 at 63 Cardigan Place, Albert Park, telephone (03) 9682 6677, **www.empirevintage.com.au** (see also page 235). Here are her other favourites.

Manon 294 Park Street, telephone (03) 9686 1530. The best of imported ceramics, glassware, candles, linen, bath accessories and body products. If something is precious and indulges the senses of smell, sight and touch, you're likely to find it here.

Nest Homewares 289–291 Coventry Street, telephone (03) 9699 8277. Minimalist decor, maximum temptation, especially if you are susceptible to tactile linens, luxurious blankets and the innumerable other comforts that help feather the nest and beautify the body.

Truc Pour La Maison 249 Coventry Street, telephone (03) 9696 9161. Francophile heaven. The furniture, jewellery, decorative objects and gifts here can save you an airline ticket to Paris.

Fragile 285–287 Coventry Street, telephone (03) 9686 4111, **www.fragile.com.au**. Once this clever store captures a pregnant woman by dressing her stylishly, it keeps her coming back, well after delivery, with all things bright and beautiful for babies and children. Check the website for other addresses.

Husk 123 Dundas Place, Albert Park, telephone (03) 9690 6994 (and 557 Malvern Road, Toorak, telephone (03) 9827 2700, and 176 Collins Street, Melbourne, telephone (03) 9663 0655), **www.husk.com.au**. These stores might easily be re-named 'Haven'. They are sanctuaries, offering not just selected desirables to wear and handmade objects to live with, but respite over a glass of juice, a plate of vegetables or a cup of house-brand tea, in settings that are both urban and earthy.

Before leaving the district, Megan treats herself to a scrumptious cupcake or two at **Let Them Eat Cake**, 147 Cecil Street, telephone (03) 9686 0077; and, if she's not rushing back to Sydney, a perfect posy from **In Full Bloom**, 280 Clarendon Street, telephone (03) 9696 1688.

But, wait, there's more. Since you're in the district, take a look at these tempting traders.

RG Madden 269 Coventry Street, telephone (03) 9696 4933, **www.rgmadden.com.au**. Where once was a bakery is now a bastion of contemporary design from big-time names such as Alessi, Jacob Jensen and MoMA NYC.

Paperpoint 259 Coventry Street, telephone (03) 9682 9414, **www.paperpoint.com.au**. More than a stationer, this is such a serious supplier of papers, it stocks more than 600 kinds, ranging from hemp to archival paper they reckon is guaranteed to last half a millennium. (Since we won't be around to check, I guess we have to take their word for it.)

Saulwick Bros. Susukka 258 Park Street, telephone (03) 9690 9333. Little Guatemala comes to South Melbourne with the handiwork of artisans and craftspeople from the Central American republic that was once the seat of the Mayan civilisation.

Fitzroy

The fact that I have a soft spot for South Melbourne doesn't stop me from appreciating certain other pockets of the city on Port Phillip Bay. By now you might have noticed that I'm trying to avoid taking us on shopping expeditions in districts we know all too well (though I'm desperate to get to **Ipanema Boutique**, telephone (03) 9827 4665, and **Issey Miyake**, telephone (03) 9826 4900, both at 177 Toorak Road, South Yarra; and to **Cose Ipanema** at 113 Collins Street in the city, telephone (03) 9650 3457, and **Cose Plus** at Shop 3, 286 Toorak Road, South Yarra, telephone (03) 9826 5788).

So here we are in Fitzroy.

If you were a stylist like **Megan Morton**, or an art director looking for props, or you'd just bought into Tribeca (Philippe Starck's conversion of eight old East Melbourne brewery buildings into warehouse apartments), you'd go straight to **Industria**, 202 Gertrude Street, Fitzroy, telephone (03) 9417 1117, in the hope of picking up the odd metal hospital trolley, surgical lamp, instrument case or ophthalmologist's reading chart, or some other highly desirable addition to an offbeat interior.

Ever on the scent of exotic essences and unguents, Andrea Burnie has given **Kleins Perfumery** at 313 Brunswick Street, telephone (03) 9416 1221, a unique aura for anyone in thrall to fragrance. Megan can't tell which she likes best: the forget-me-not scents from Florence, soaps from Syria or body cream scented with marigold and rose from Milan. While you're in this stretch, pop in to **Venus and Mars**, 319 Brunswick Street, telephone (03) 9415 9416, and riffle through the racks for something suitable to wear with your chosen scent.

You happen to have run out of stationery, storage boxes or wrapping paper, for all the odoriferous presents you've bought at Kleins? You are in the right place. Find your way to **Zetta Florence**, 197 Brunswick Street, telephone (03) 9417 6211, and hope you have enough arms to carry to your car or taxi all that you desire from this serious supplier; or log on to **www.zetta.florence.com**.

We cannot leave Fitzroy without a bit of Jewish mothering at Babka, a famous old bakery at 358 Brunswick Street, telephone (03) 9416 0091. As a change from buying bread and shoo-fly buns over the counter, you can sit down to breakfast or lunch (if you can grab a table) on the irresistible yield from the ovens out the back, plus trimmings such as scrambled eggs, Russian borscht and good coffee.

Hawksburn

Was it called Hawksburn when I lived in Melbourne? I never knew Hawksburn existed, but I was a blow-in from the north, so what would I know – I was lucky to find my way home. I certainly knew South Yarra (Dorothée Bis smocks at Masons, Edouardo's for a good steak, Maxim's for dinner) and Toorak, which we were quickly advised to pronounce 'Trak', as assured a sign of being a Melburnian as barracking for an AFL team.

Melbourne has many very, very long streets and one of them is Malvern Road. It begins at Chapel Street, South Yarra, and stretches south-east, touching Prahran, Toorak, Armadale, Malvern, Glen Iris and Malvern East, where it exhausts itself and gives up at Waverley Road. I only recently discovered that the bit that lies between South Yarra and Prahran is in the district known as Hawksburn.

This is rich turf for shoppers looking for children's wear and gifts. Although **Oilily**, 590 Malvern Road, telephone (03) 9510 8885, **www.oilily.net.au**, sounds like a good place to go for a salad dressing, do not be deceived. It's an old-established Dutch company that makes delightful, boldly coloured wearables for children and their mothers. **Jacadi**, 546 Malvern Road, telephone (03) 9521 1569, **www.jacadi.com.au**, imports from France the outfits you've seen on tiny tots with red balloons in the Bois de Boulogne in Paris. If you like the thought of that, don't miss **Mon Bébé**, 540b Malvern Road, telephone (03) 9530 2300. Inside a storybook kind of house at 582 Malvern Road is the fabulous small, small world of **Mill & Mia**, telephone (03) 9510 5275, **www.millandmia.com**, full of Australian-made basics and little luxuries. Pretty and practical children's rooms start at **House for Kids**, 584 Malvern Road, telephone (03) 9533 2995, **www.houseforkids.com.au**.

Co-habiting with these stores are lots of others with more grown-up tastes in mind. Trelise Cooper, 580 Malvern Road, telephone (03) 9521 2411, **www.trelisecooper.com**, is both a designer and the label on foxy fashion for women. At Empire Rose, 586 Malvern Road, telephone (03) 9521 2357, the clothes are more romantic, with influences from Japan. For good-quality knits, call on Faye Officer, 510 Malvern Road, telephone (03) 9510 8220. AK Traditions, 524 Malvern Road, 9533 7576, **www.aktraditions.com**, has a wonderful and varied hoard of treasures in textiles made by craftspeople of the Kyrgyz Republic in Central Asia using the traditional techniques of their nomadic heritage. As its name implies, Tango Boutique, 513 Malvern Road, telephone (03) 9827 0411, showcases clothing and accessories from Argentina. Not on Malvern Road, but not far from it, is In The Bag, 521–523 High Street, Prahran East, telephone (03) 9525 0120, **www.inthebag.com.au**. This mini emporium of affordable and imaginative gifts, homewares and accessories is run by Edwina Chartres and Karen Owen, who enjoy their work so much they call it 'The Ministry of Fun'.

Before you leave Hawksburn, pick up some fresh pasta from Donnini's, 525 Malvern Road, telephone (03) 9826 9199, and bio-dynamic health food from Organica, at the back of 546 Malvern Road, telephone (03) 9510 6787, **www.organica.com.au**.

Fashion in seclusion

Melbourne loves being furtive about its fashion. Some of its most avant-garde boutiques tuck themselves away in such obscure places, you'd think they were trying to hide from you. I'm not just talking about Christine (see page 103) down that dingy alley. There is a hushed and polished little salon called Marais, **www.marais.com.au**, with panelled walls, chevron parquetry flooring and a hand-picked selection of special pieces from here and overseas. But how would you ever know it was there? To get to it, you have to find an obscure stairway that leads to the first floor of the Royal Arcade, 314 Little Collins Street. Better ring them up on (03) 9639 0314 for detailed instructions.

Less difficult to find, but still underground (in more ways than one), is Assin with its slogan, 'by The Girls from Ipanema'. They are, of course, Francelina Pinto and her two daughters, Fernanda and Lucy, who led us to associate the name Ipanema more readily with avant-garde fashion boutiques in Melbourne than with a beach in Rio de Janeiro. I have always felt that the Ipanema stores alone, with their daringly original threads, were worth a trip to Melbourne. Having cut their ties with Ipanema (except for the one in South Yarra), the girls opened Assin in 2004, with Fernanda as its buyer, designer and driving force. Against a clean, industrial space with few distractions, the aesthetic of the clothes is self-expression rather than sexual attraction; art over prettiness, exemplified by a mixed bag of audacious designers. They include the Dutch duo Viktor & Rolf, whose ideas are keenly watched by fashion forecasters; the intellectual Turkish Cypriot Hussein Chalayan who, on graduating from the Saint Martin's School of Art in London, showed a collection of clothes that had been buried and dug up and, while he has since moved on to a more polished output, he never fails to innovate; and Project Alabama, the yield from a cottage industry in the American South where hand-sewn embroidery and quilting, along with other homespun techniques, are applied to contemporary fashion. There is also Assin's own line designed by Fernanda. Venture beneath 138 Little Collins Street, between Russell and Exhibition Streets, telephone (03) 9654 0158, for a journey into the future.

If that's not quite your scene, Hollie Sweet might be, but you'll have to go over to 535 Church Street, Richmond, telephone (03) 9421 4408, **www.holliesweet.com**. It's a girlier groove. Things that are comely and cute in clothes, accessories, bags and other items, including chocolates, find their way here to sugarplum fairyland.

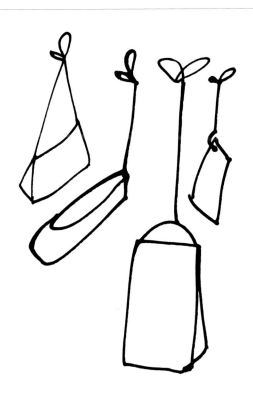

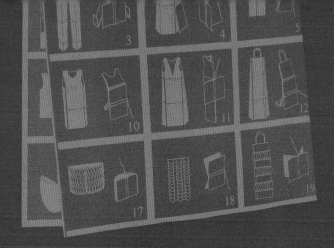

17

DO WE LOVE
A BARGAIN?

Keeping an eye out for marked-down items at favoured local pricey boutiques is the only way many of us can afford to hold our own in the social swim. There is another way, too: travel overseas when end-of-season sales are on. For those to whom shopping is a blood sport, only one thing matches the thrill of being in London, Milan, Rome, Paris or New York at such a time. What is that? Knowing how and where to find factory outlets that have real bargains at any time. Sure, the merchandise is hit-and-miss and you often have to search through a lot of mediocre things before you find a standout, but scrounging is part of the fun.

Somewhere in the vicinity of Scottsdale, Arizona, I acquired ten padded pink satin coathangers for US$20, and a Karl Lagerfeld choker of giant fake (faux is the fashion euphemism) pearls for only a few dollars more. Far from feeling somewhat ridiculous at having ten coathangers in my suitcase, I only wish I'd bought more. Have you seen the prices on those things here? That is, if you can find them. I wish I could give you the name and address of this clutch of outlets, but I don't think I ever knew it – I left that to the cab driver who took us there. Wherever you happen to be in America, ask the concierge at your hotel where to find the local fashion outlets.

On a more ambitious scale, **Lucinda Mendel** snapped up a black Prada trench and a pair of black Sergio Rossi boots last time she shopped at her favourite factory outlet in Palm Springs, California. Her husband, Charles, a lawyer, whose dress is quite conservative, in keeping with his profession, treated himself to what Lucinda describes as 'lairy red lizard-skin Prada boots'. I don't imagine he wears them to court, though.

To avoid being caught up in the kind of unseemly feeding frenzy that characterises some sales and often leads to expensive mistakes, Lucinda is a seasoned shopper with a strategy. 'I say to my husband, "I'll meet you back here in an hour and a half." I don't go into every store. I know exactly which ones. It's just experience. I buy things that I would have bought anyway. I don't buy them because they're cheap. I don't buy things that are too big or too small and need a lot of alterations because then you lose the discount, really.' Her other piece of advice is to be open-minded because you never know what you'll find. 'Never go with a wish-list – three pairs of jeans and some black cashmere sweaters – because you won't find them.' You'll find **Desert Hills Premium Outlets** at 48400 Seminole Road, Cabazon, Palm Springs, California, or log onto **www.premiumoutlets.com**.

When you log on to Premium Outlets, you'll find they crop up all over the United States, including Hawaii, which is temptingly close to our shores. **Waikele Premium Outlets** near Pearl Harbor, 30 minutes from downtown Honolulu, has more than fifty stores, including Barneys New York, Max Mara, Tommy Hilfiger, Calvin Klein and Polo Ralph Lauren.

There is much more to spend your money on in Las Vegas than one-arm bandits. Half an hour south of the city is **Fashion Outlets Las Vegas**, 32100 Las Vegas Boulevard South, Primm, Nevada, **www.fashionoutletlasvegas.com**. Among its hundred-plus stores are Burberry, Gianni Versace, Gap, Banana Republic and a Neiman Marcus Clearance Center. Saks Fifth Avenue is among the seventy-plus stores in **Belz Factory Outlet** at 7400 Las Vegas Boulevard South, Las Vegas.

For a comprehensive guide to 285 outlets across the United States, log on to **www.outletbound.com**. It lets you search by location, brand name, store name or product category.

Once you're a regular reader of Daily Candy's emails from New York (see page 211), you'll be alerted to snap sales of samples at various places in the city that's never stingy when it comes to discounts. If we'd been there, we could have joined the scrum a few months back at the **Metropolitan Pavilion**, 123 West 18th Street, where Malo cashmere knitwear walked out the door for as little as a quarter of its regular price; there were similar discounts on superb Italian bedclothes from Frette. At 260 Fifth Avenue, Versace couture samples were marked down by 60–70 per cent, as were wrap dresses by Diane von Furstenberg. There were price-cuts of up to 80 per cent on some top Australian labels in the Elizabeth Charles 2006 Australia Day Sale at 639 1/2 Hudson Street, in the Meatpacking District. And these were just a few of the offerings. Be prepared, next time round; what you save could pay for your airfare there and back if you bought really big.

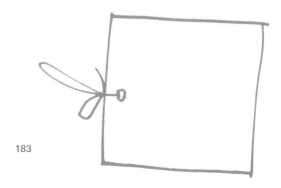

Of all the places in the world – with the exception of Japan – the country where I'd most like to find a bargain is Italy. Log on to **www.milanostyle.com** for fashion outlets in Milan and its vicinity. The magic names on sale at one called The Mall include La Perla, Ferragamo, Valentino, Armani, Bottega Veneta, Tod's, Prada, Gucci and Zegna. And there's a Max Mara outlet disguised as a proper shop called **Diffusione Tessile** at 2 Galleria del Corso, right in the centre of Milan.

Within an hour's drive of Florence is The Mall, 8 via Europa, Leccio Reggello, **www.outlet-firenze.com**, where you can flip through racks of discounted lines bearing such desirable labels as Gucci, Giorgio Armani, Bottega Veneta, Yves Saint Laurent, La Perla and Valentino. A few kilometres away at 69 Strada Statale, Levanella Spacceo, Montevarchi, you will find Fendi, Celine, Loewe and Dolce & Gabbana, as well as I Pellettieri d'Italia, for Prada and Miu Miu. Ask your concierge to check out the shuttle service that operates three times a day from Florence to The Mall. Or splurge on a car and driver.

A word of warning: disregarding alcohol and tobacco, the current duty-free allowance is $900 for each adult and $450 for people under eighteen. That doesn't go far if you have a taste for luxury. Shoes and bags made from the skins of certain protected species are forbidden. For details log on to **www.deh.gov.au** or **www.customs.gov.au**.

NOTES

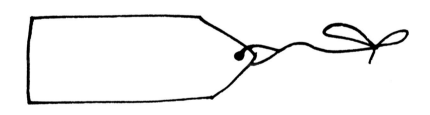

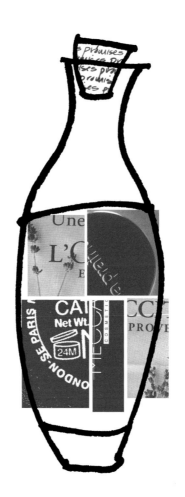

18

MIRROR, MIRROR

Surely, no overall product category in the world is as confusing as the one that covers skin care, hair care, fragrance and cosmetics. Glossy magazines owe their survival to multiple spreads of advertising that fill the opening pages with flawless faces flogging little pots, bottles and tubes, infinite in their promises of dewy perfection, instant radiance, complete renewal, diaphanous finish, visible results, luminous effects and best possible protection. Pseudo-scientific words, such as treatment, therapy and formula, are employed to reinforce the seriousness of product claims. Watch for the word 'helps'; it nullifies many a promise, especially that great perennial: 'younger-looking skin'.

Making an effort to look attractive is a sign of respect for yourself and of courtesy to others, but I've always thought that trying to look younger is a pointless exercise, doomed to failure; a waste of time, energy and usually money. You're either young or you're not. It's all relative, anyhow. The sensible thing to do is to look the best of what and where you are in life. Then you can relax and give your time, energy and probably money to something that at least has a chance of success.

Over untold decades I have dipped into lots and lots of skin-care brands in an effort to achieve dewy perfection in my visage, but whether the magic potion was labelled Oil of Ulan or La Prairie, Clinique or Jurlique, Neutrogena or Shu Uemura, I couldn't see much of a difference. Perhaps I didn't persevere for long enough? At present my skin-care routine could not be simpler – or cheaper, probably. I cleanse with Cetaphil from the plunge bottle with a blue label, and after it's washed off with a face cloth I moisturise with Cetaphil from the plunge bottle with the green label. They were recommended to me by a chemist and most pharmacies stock them. The magic formula that makes me look my best is a good night's sleep and a feeling of elation. But they don't come in a bottle.

What does come in a bottle is Clarins Liquid Bronze Self Tanning lotion. It helps (note the word) mask the flaws and cracks I prefer to think of as character lines on my face. Better still, a tanned countenance provides a contrast to my hair, which the passage of time has turned platinum blonde from dark brown. Over my fake suntan, I smoothe Chanel Teint Fluide Universel in the colour Doré. With the application of Nars Eyeliner in greige to my brows, Chanel Ombré Unique Shadowlight 21 to my lids, Shu Uemura Luminizer above them, Maybelline Lash Discovery Mini-Brush Mascara to my lashes, Elizabeth Arden Crayon Poudre pour les Yeux around the rims of my eyelids and

The Body Shop Lip Liner in Salmon Pink upon my lips, I scrub up quite well, if I've had a good night's sleep and I'm in good spirits. But what a performance.

Once about every five days – not daily as in the past – I wash my hair with L'Occitane Shampoo with Essential Oil. The naturally curly locks that were an advantage when I was a child have to be tamed but, instead of using a gel, I apply Pantene Pro-V Conditioner and leave it on rather than rinse it off. As well as exercising control, it gives the hair volume and body. Occasionally, I give my locks a boost of softness with L'Occitane Olive Paste, a kind of mask that's especially beneficial to dry hair like mine. My hairdresser comes to the house once a month to give me a clip. Ah, the luxury of not having to hang around in a salon flipping through magazines and listening to twaddle.

Anyone with eyes can see that I do my own nails. The only products I use on them are Nailtiques Oil Therapy and Nailtiques Formula 2 Treatment, which gives a similar finish to clear nail polish. When my hands become dry, as they often do in winter, I cup about a tablespoon of sugar in one hand, squeeze the juice of a lemon into it (bit by bit) and rub my hands together until the mixture becomes liquid, like glucose. After rinsing and drying, I apply hand cream to my newly baby-soft paws. That reminds me. I believe that certain Hyatt hotels in the United States offer the BlackBerry Balm hand massage for those who carry their offices in their palms and can't stop tinkering with them.

I'm uncomfortable being fussed over, which is why I'd do almost anything to avoid a massage. Too intimate. I'll never forget that Turkish bathhouse, somewhere in Russell Square, that a colleague in London persuaded me to go to, aeons ago. After I tiptoed about in dingy steam rooms clutching a covering the size of a tea towel, an alarming old woman with the longest arms and biggest hands I've ever seen on a tiny person pummelled me on a marble slab, then put me in a cage and hosed me down. Was I refreshed and invigorated afterwards? I've never felt so limp.

Following are some everyday products I would not like to live without.

- Luminous soaps in the colours of pink grapefruit and green apple, scented to match, from The Body Shop.

- Redwin Sorbolene Moisturizing Bar (from the supermarket).

- Revlon Hi & Dri roll-on anti-perspirant and deodorant.

- Issey Miyake L'Eau D'Issey.

- L'Occitane Soothing Body Ice Gel and Ice Hand Cream Gel with Organic Verbena Extract. Deliciously scented and incredibly cooling in summer. The Verbena Ice Eye Pads and a twenty-minute nap in the afternoon are a big help before a big night.

- Caldrea White Tea Hand Soap Liquid and Hand Lotion in plunge bottles. My friend Mindy Balgrosky, who lives in Los Angeles, sent me these luxuries from a shop in Santa Monica that stocks only the most exquisite and difficult-to-find items related to the culinary arts. I guess that includes pampering the hands. The store also carries chefs' jackets in *pure linen*. Mindy buys her French butter there. Le Sanctuaire, 2710 Main Street (between Hill Street and Ashland Avenue), Santa Monica, California, telephone 310 581 8999, **www.cookingbuddies.com**.

As you must have fathomed by now, I am no authority on beauty, but I have friends whose knowledge of this esoteric subject is either encyclopaedic or at least a whole lot better than mine. Listen to them; they know what they're talking about.

Karin Upton Baker

For all of the sixteen years Karin spent at *Vogue* Australia she was involved with the beauty industry and its products, whether as fashion and beauty assistant, beauty editor, beauty and health director or, finally, deputy editor. She has tried just about every product that exists at the upper (and not so upper) reaches of the market.

While she held those jobs, it would not have been ethical for Karin to go public with her personal preferences, but now that she runs Hermès Australia, she can open the door to her beauty cupboard. It holds a very interesting mixture of items, each chosen for performance rather than brand or price. Karin buys most of her beauty products at Mecca Cosmetica at David Jones, Elizabeth Street, Sydney. She also stocks up at Colette (see page 117) whenever she's in Paris.

Karin's everyday skin care routine:

1) Sorbolene in a pump bottle for cleansing with water.

2) Fresh face cloth to remove it.

3) Crème de la Mer lotion (a fermented distillation of sea kelp, vitamins and minerals developed by aerospace physicist Dr Max Huber, to treat the facial burns he suffered in a laboratory chemical explosion).

The best body products, says Karin, come in 'no-nonsense plastic bottles' from Kiehl's, an apothecary in New York since 1852. The flagship store is at 109 Third Avenue at East 13th Street in the East Village. You can also buy Kiehl's products at Mecca Cosmetica in Australia.

Every four to six weeks, Karin has a facial by Sylvia Deitch, because Sylvia 'doesn't give "formula" facials and she doesn't push products. Her facial massage technique is unique. If I had the time and her appointment book wasn't so jammed I'd go every week.' Sylvia Deitch Beauty Therapy, 3 Comber Street, Paddington, telephone (02) 9331 2626.

MAKE-UP

As Karin points out, 'There are hundreds of formulations on the market today.' The following, however, are her constants.

- T. LeClerc Bronzing Powder. You find it at 'most good pharmacies in central Paris' but not in Australia.

- Stila cream blushers and lip glosses. The Stila brand was launched in the United States in 1994 by Jeanine Lobell, a make-up artist who developed her technique by working on video productions. These days she embellishes famous faces for magazine covers and appearances at the Academy Awards.

- St Tropez Self Tanning Lotion which 'makes bare legs presentable. After all, "nude" hosiery is today's ultimate fashion faux pas.'

- Maybelline mascara. 'Cheap as chips and in the kit of nearly every professional make-up artist I've ever worked with.'

- Revlon Brow Beautiful. Karin still has a stash, although the line has been discontinued.

- Foundations: Chanel, Dermablend and La Prairie Skin Caviar.

HANDS AND FEET

Once a week, Melisa Silvestro from **Miss Frou Frou at Valonz**, 20–22 Elizabeth Street, Paddington, telephone (02) 9360 2444, arrives at Karin's office in the city to give her a manicure. At other times TeeJaye looks after her at Joh Bailey Spa, **www.johbailey.com.au**. If she had the time, Karin would return to Ana Aljinovic, 555 Old South Head Road, Rose Bay, telephone (02) 9371 9845. According to Karin, Ana is 'probably Sydney's best-kept manicure secret. She really is incredible and never written about.'

HAIR

Best chignon in Sydney: 'By Joh Bailey at Joh Bailey. Brilliant for formal events and done in five minutes.'

Best personal service: Geoffrey Smith at The Lounge, corner of Liverpool and Bourke Streets, Darlinghurst, telephone (02) 9331 0194.

Fastest blow-dry in Sydney: Diane at Joh Bailey Spa.

Best hair products: Hair Anti Age, 'especially the ampoule treatment recommended by Bruce Packer' at 494 Bourke Steet, Surry Hills, telephone (02) 9331 8282. 'You can also buy these products at Toot Hairdressing,' 426 New South Head Road, Double Bay, telephone (02) 9327 7163.

Hairdressers Karin uses on her travels: Cathou Duboc salon, rue Boissy d'Anglas, Paris; Il Colpo in the Grand Hyatt, Hong Kong; Bumble and Bumble in New York.

Lucinda Mendel

Because it's her job to try out new products, Lucinda doesn't have to commit herself to one label, although, 'I've had superb success with something recently, a salon brand called Environ, developed by a South African plastic surgeon. He works a lot with vitamins A and C. They make very small batches of the product because of the short use-by date. It's about working your skin up to a level, rather than throwing hard-core vitamin A on it, which would get a reaction. It's quite hard for me to get a noticeable reaction in my skin because it's so over-nourished but, since I've been using this, people at my Pilates class have been asking my teacher, after I've left, "Oh, has Lucinda had Botox?" I've noticed the difference in my skin, which is incredible.' Available through skin clinics, dermatologists and medical practitioners. Telephone 1300 888 708, **www.environ.co.za**.

Lucinda prefers to 'put myself in the hands of professionals. I have a very good hairdresser and, separately, a very good colourist. I have a manicure every week. I think those basics of grooming can elevate someone.'

BARGAIN BEAUTY
Whenever **Lucinda Mendel** finds herself in Hong Kong she goes to one of dozens of **Sa Sa** stores to buy fragrance and cosmetics at 'crazy prices'. The business, established there in 1978 by Simon and Eleanor Kwok, now has outlets throughout Asia. None of the 400 brands and 15 000 products is imitation, Lucinda assures us, and it hasn't 'fallen off the back of a truck' either. Shop online at **www.sasa.com**.

Eric Matthews

'It's a morning ritual I treasure,' says Eric, who uses the Erno Laszlo system, which involves applying pHelityl Oil to his face, then washing it with the special soap before he shaves. 'When you've been out the night before and you feel slightly under the weather, the kindliness of the water and the natural aroma is bliss. And you do the same ritual in the evening and apply a cream, which is emollient and nutritious.' See **www.ernolaszlo.com**. A great indulgence for Eric, when he has the time, is to take a shower, then run a bath with Jo Malone bath oil, open a 'glorious bottle of Billecart champagne and loll around in the bath listening to something exquisite, like Chopin on CD.' See **www.jomalone.co.uk**.

What is this thing called a spa?

Twinkle, twinkle little spa, how I wonder what you are. The spa has wandered a long way from its namesake, the town in Liége, Belgium, that's been famous for the remedial properties of its mineral springs since 1565. Today the name seems to be attached to any place that has running water and offers a range of therapies (some would say indulgences) for the body. It doesn't have to be anywhere near natural fountains of the kind that have turned Hepburn Springs in Victoria, Bath in England,

Baden-Baden in Germany and Evian in France into places of pilgrimage for people seeking cures for whatever ails them.

Spas are everywhere, in plague proportions. Day spas, weekend spas, retreat spas, city spas, country spas, beachside spas, mountain spas. They're in private homes and posh resorts. Fred Segal, the famous Melrose Avenue clutch of boutiques where Hollywood royalty shops, has opened a plush spa in its Santa Monica branch, **www.fredsegalbeauty.com**. Can a Belinda spa be next?

No hotels worth their stars are without their spas. I'm told that whether or not people use a hotel spa is beside the point; they just like to know it's there. Spa has become such a magic word, there's even one for clothes in New York. It's called, guess what? The Laundry Spa. Its slogan is 'Pamper your clothes' and you can have them scented with lime or lavender, if you like. Its website poses the question, 'Isn't it time you gave your treasured threads the spa treatment?' Log on, just for fun: **www.laundryspa.com**.

Because it seems that a spa is born every day, how can I give you an informed guide? I'll just point you in a few directions, with the help of our own spa addict, **Edwina McCann**.

One memorable spa treatment for Ed took place at Begawan Giri Estate at Ubud, Bali, **www.begawan-giri.com**, where she and her husband, Toby, stayed in one of the five self-contained residences with staff in attendance. 'They also do spas in your bathroom. I had a frangipani bath. In terms of indulgence, it was pretty amazing.'

At home in Sydney, Edwina goes to Leonard Drake at Shop 4, 551–555 Military Road, Mosman, telephone (02) 9960 5255. 'It doesn't sound very fabulous but it is seriously good. They use Dermalogica products [**www.dermalogica.com**], which I love.' Spa Chakra, on the Finger Wharf at Woolloomooloo, **www.spachakra.com**, also gets the thumbs up from Edwina.

New York, as Edwina rightly points out, 'is constantly changing. Bliss used to be amazing, but I'm not sure if that's the best one at the moment.' See **www.blissworld. com**. There are plenty of others. I doubt you could go wrong at Babor Spa at Takashimaya, 693 Fifth Avenue, because nothing in that store drops below first-rate. Otherwise, log on to **www.spafinder.com** for a world of choices.

19
WHEE-EBAY!

An online auction house for anything and everything anyone ever wanted to sell or buy in the world is called eBay, **www.ebay.com**. Once you register as a buyer – it's free – you just type in whatever you're interested in and the selection appears. The first time I typed 'Issey Miyake' I got nine pages of choices. True, most of them came in bottles and tubes, but among the multitude of L'Eau D'Issey bottles, collectible perfume posters and sewing patterns, I found a brand-new grey pleated cardigan I felt would instantly make itself at home in my wardrobe. The bidding in US dollars had reached $25. So I bid $30. It was like a slap in the face when an email came later to say I had been outbid. Who is this vulture, muscling in on my prey? I upped the ante to $40. I have just been foiled again. Now my bid is up to $55. We've got four days to go. I'll keep you posted.

Remind me not to get so caught up in the chase that I lose my sense of proportion, because once you bid, you're committed to buy if nobody outstrips your offer. I have just exercised admirable restraint over a few CDs of Martha Argerich playing piano pieces by Liszt and Schumann. Save those until after I know if that Issey cardi is mine. Oh, eBay. You are even more addictive than Freecell* (see page 203).

Fast forward three days . . .

Well, I lost the grey pleated cardigan because when the final bid came in I was out to lunch with people who know how to celebrate a birthday properly. It was just one lousy dollar higher than mine, which by that time had grown to $70. But my disappointment was short-lived. When I logged on to the Issey Miyake listing again – this time via the generic 'women's clothing and accessories', which eliminated all the bottles of scent – I came upon something that made that grey garment look very conservative, if a Miyake can ever be said to be so.

This glowing treasure is a pleated top, aptly described as 2DIE4, in shades of lilac over another layer in pale turquoise. When you turn the sleeves back, the turquoise shows. Heaven. The bidding had reached $199, so, having been bitten by the elusive grey, I raised the stakes to $250, which is where it has remained for the past two days. The bidding must end by 1 p.m. today. That puts me in a dilemma because that is when I plan to be having a glass of Bolly with my friend Lana at Bistro Moncur, and that is no Internet cafe. So, I have just been reckless enough to outbid myself by making $350 my limit, as a precaution against some snide Issey-stalker trying to pounce upon what is clearly meant for me.

Four hours later . . .

Well, 2DIE4 is mine, and I got it for $207 (plus air express postage at $29.50 and $2 insurance). You see, although you reveal to eBay your absolute top offer, clever eBay doesn't let on to anyone. You can trust them to take care of your interests even when you're asleep in bed, or toiling at work, or out shopping with a friend. The highest other bid must have been $206.

My prize resides in New York. I have paid for it on the web by a system called PayPal, which means you have to use a credit card. If you're worried about credit card fraud, the best thing to do is to get an additional credit card from your bank and ask for a low spending limit on it. How low is up to you, what you plan to buy with it and how high you're prepared to go. In any case, it's a sensible precaution because if somebody does try to diddle you, they can't get away with much. And your own excesses will be kept in control.

Six days later . . .

A box arrives by air express from Flushing, New York. Wrapped in tissue paper inside is my trophy, brand new and with labels attached to legitimise it. The size is perfect, the outside colour not so much lilac as uncompromisingly mauve. It suits me, though. It feels wonderful. But is it real? Why do I doubt it? Because it seems too good to be true, and I didn't walk into an authentic Issey Miyake shop to buy it. I do my best to imitate CSI forensics in poring over the texture and stitching of the labels to see if there's a hint of wear or tampering. My faith in my judgment starts to get wobbly. Is it really sensational or does it look like something from Paddington Markets?

Next day . . .

What would we do without our friends? Mine have pronounced my treasure authentic and sensational. I am at peace.

Six months later . . .

It's a fake. I think. It doesn't have the quality. It doesn't wear as well. A few little threads are coming off it. That would never happen with a genuine piece of Issey Miyake. Still, whenever I wear it – inside out, so the blue shows – somebody pays me a compliment, so I guess it wasn't such a bad buy, after all.

SNIPESWIPE

After **Megan Morton** was narrowly defeated in her bid for something deeply desirable on eBay one weekend, a friend told her about a wickedly wonderful service called SnipeSwipe. According to Megan, 'Seconds before the end of the auction, it swipes everyone else out by adding just 10 cents more to your bid, just in the nick of time. It costs a dollar [US] a swipe. What a fab idea!' No more waiting up to add dollars to John Smedley men's cashmere tops!' I wonder what would happen if more than one person paid SnipeSwipe to snatch the same item. Who would have the last swipe? See **www.snipeswipe.com**.

Selling on eBay

Online selling through eBay is a bit more complicated than buying. First of all, you have to register by providing details of your credit card and bank account. Then you need to establish how you want to be paid when someone buys your stuff. If you decide to accept PayPal, it means that the buyer's payment is electronically transferred straight into your bank account. Because you're paid immediately, you can pack up your goods and send them off a.s.a.p., which makes for efficiency and a satisfied buyer and seller.

All the instructions and fees are clearly laid out at **www.ebay.com** and there's even an audio that takes you through the whole process, step by step. You have to make decisions about which category to list your goods in, and how long you'd like them to appear. The best bit is finding out how persuasive you can be in creating your own advertisement to attract competition among bidders.

I haven't gone in for selling anything, though, because what would I sell? Certainly not an Issey. A fake Issey Miyake? Do not tempt me. Besides, I'd have to buy a digital camera so I could take photos and add them to my listing. Hmm, there's a thought. Think I'll log on again and see what's doing in digitals.

Spiderwoman: Life on the web

Only one person I know is as nuts as I am about spinning her way around the world wide web: **Megan Morton**. She does research there, she shops there and she logs on to certain sites just for the fun or the beauty of them. She is more patient than I am with the dreamy sites – usually European in origin – that tell you nothing but do it with enchantment through inspiring imagery, music and sound effects.

Megan's technique for sorting through what's offering on eBay becomes more refined the more often she window-shops there. For instance: 'I have a new tip. Instead of typing in "Romeo Gigli" or "Diane von Furstenberg", I now put in a favourite material; i.e., "bakelite" when I was searching for some fabulous bakelite buttons to update all my cardigans. Or "milk glass" because I love it and collect it. Sometimes I put in "blue" and see all those beautiful turquoise pieces, or "white" or "green". Another one I've been searching is "cameo", because I love cameos and there are some fab things out there, namely a black cameo ring that is totally modern, not a bit Victorian.'

Here are some of Megan's other favourite websites.

www.bonton.fr 'A very beautiful infants brand. Look at the most beautiful turquoise high chairs and heavenly wooden coathangers painted in milkshake shades for children.'

www.abercrombieandfitch.com 'Over the weekend I bought lots of beautiful vintage washed jeans and American-pie-style polos as gifts for friends. It was very easy. They ship to Australia, no problems.' This iconic outfitter, established in South Street, Manhattan, in the late nineteenth century, equipped President Theodore Roosevelt with everything he needed – snake-proof sleeping bag and all – for a safari into Africa in 1908.

www.garnethill.com 'They have some lovely fair-isle hats and scarves in the kids' section. There's a great flannel sheet set called Jacks Flannel in the sale section that I'm going to buy for my nephew's new bed. The last thing I tried to buy were these gumboots striped in olive green and red, but it didn't work out because they were too expensive to ship. They were gorgeous. If I were a gumboot I would be them.'

www.katespade.com Her shops are in major cities in America and her goods, whether sunglasses, bags, shoes, stationery and anything to do with living, are the last word in style.

www.fornasetti.com 'It's the official website, although you can't buy anything from it, but it shows you combinations of colours that you never thought of. Because they're so proud of their artistic heritage, they have a little advice section where you can say, "I'm about to buy a tray on eBay, or through a dealer," and they help you suss it out' to determine its authenticity. Megan also looks at this site for inspiration in her work.

www.tajan.com 'When I'm depressed or when I'm blue, I don't go to Tiffany's, I just go to Tajan and look.' L'Espace Tajan is a swish fine arts house in a 1925 former banking hall at 37 rue des Mathurins in Paris. You never know which important collections might turn up for auction by Jacques or François Tajan.

www.davidsequeira.com 'I saw David Sequeira's exhibition at the Object Galleries. It's a lovely website. I guess if you're an artist you need that to be a big calling card. He loves orange, talks about his obsession with orange.' Like Megan herself, 'he's just a mad colour-lover'.

www.tse-tse.com A brilliantly inventive French site that opens with a light bulb, buzzing flies and chirruping crickets before presenting an amazing assemblage of goods in a fresh and whimsical way by 'two girls who have a studio in the Marais'. The playful pair are Catherine Lévy and Sigolène Prébois.

www.jcrew.com 'An American outfitter that's good for really basic things but with nice details.'

www.llbean.com This American company started out by selling huntin', shootin', fishin' gear to backwoods men through mail-order catalogues. Then its plaid shirts and windcheaters started appearing on the backs of city trendies at weekends. Now L.L. Bean is online with some deeply desirable clothing and accessories for men, women and children. Megan's favourites are the canvas totes trimmed (and monogrammed, if you like) in delicious colours, such as wild berry, lime, flame or turquoise.

What is Freecell*?

If you want to squander time – fortunately, not money – log on to **www.freecell.com**, which proudly claims to have been 'draining workplace productivity since 1996' with addictive games, such as the online version of Solitaire, also known as Patience. Certain obsessive–compulsive types like me can't keep their fingers off it. I have to ration myself, like some people have to limit their chocolate intake or curb their dependency on Sudoku. It is a deeply satisfying way of putting things in order, a tendency I exhibited at the age of two-and-a-half when I participated in a bubs' chorusline on stage at the Jewel Theatre in Bankstown. I wore a pale yellow fairy dress with a tulle skirt, a satin bodice and a glittering corsage. Halfway through our number, when my fellow hoofers fell into disarray, I took it upon myself to push them all back into line. If, like me, you love watching the television series *Monk*, you will understand what I mean. If you don't know that series, do watch it for the hilarious antics of Tony Shalhoub as the fastidious Adrian Monk, an ex-cop whose preoccupation with detail is so neurotic, he can solve crimes that no sane person would be able to fathom. Nutty? He makes perfect sense to me.

Cast

...no Robertson, *a Puritan officer* .. .. .. John Kentish *(English)*

..., *daughter of Lord Walton* .. .. .. Joan Sutherland *(Australian)*

...Arthur Talbot *(Arturo), a Cavalier* ..Nicola Filacuridi *(Italian)*

...orge Walton *(Giorgio),*
Puritan, brother of L... ... Giuseppe Modesti *(Italian)*

...hard Forth *(Riccard...* Erne...

...Walton, *a Puritan* ... D...

...Henrietta of France... Mo...

The scene is laid in a...
during...

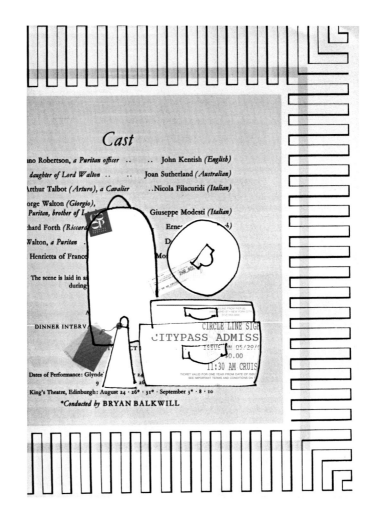

DINNER INTERVA...

... CT ...

Dates of Performance: Glynde... ... 2...
9 ... 2...

King's Theatre, Edinburgh: August 24 · 26* · 31* · September 3* · 8 · 10

Conducted by BRYAN BALKWILL

CIRCLE LINE SIG...
CITYPASS ADMISS...
ISSUE...N 05/29/0...
...0.00
11:30 AM CRUIS...
TICKET VALID FOR ONE YEAR FROM DATE OF ISU...
SEE IMPORTANT TERMS AND CONDITIONS ON U...

20

VIRTUAL TRAVEL — WEB'S WONDER

Le nozze di Figar

The part of Dr Bartolo will be sung
performances on June 28, 30, July 7, 9 ar
by CARLO CAVA, and in the performanc
July 13, 16, 18, 24, and 27 by MICH
LANGDON (English), and not as prev
announced.

EXHILARATION IS MINE. I have just bought a birthday present for a friend at the poshest stationer in London and I didn't have to move from the Ethiopian tribal chair upon which I rest my bottom when I tip-tap at the iMac in my workroom at home in Sydney. I went on a shopping spree and I didn't have to speak to anyone or go anywhere. I didn't have to dress up in an effort to impress the kind of snooty-nosed sales assistants that shops dealing in expensive goods so often attract.

I didn't have to spend twenty-four hours strapped into an airline seat, as helpless as an infant in a cot or a patient on a trolley in Emergency, having spent two hours before that being frisked for weapons and pacing the antiseptic nowhere called an international airport terminal, having a last-minute pee in a cubicle where I hope the bowl is clean, the seat is dry and the paper hasn't run out. My nail file is here beside me instead of being buried in the hold. Tonight I'll eat my dinner with a proper knife and fork instead of wobbly, unworkable plastic implements. I do not have to put my hand up like a schoolchild for permission to get into the loo, which I guess must be the custom on flights across the Pacific now that you're not allowed to loiter there for a chitchat anymore. I didn't have to risk the ordeal of being handcuffed and interrogated for five hours at Los Angeles Airport, which is what happened to those perfectly respectable young Australians not so long ago. People pay money for this?

It's not that I don't want to be there. I'd adore to see the polished new Berlin, the fashionification of Hell's Kitchen in Manhattan, the East End now that trendsetting Londoners are drifting there, and to revisit my favourite beautiful places in Venice. I just don't want to have to go through the ordeal of travelling there and back. I can remember when getting there was half the fun. Isn't that idea so yesterday?

So, until I can be sure of doing it not only in style but in comfort, I think I'll just switch out of reality. Fantasy is often better than reality anyway. If anything nasty creeps into your dreams you can just zap it as swiftly as you trash the spam; in real life you have to put up with it. No packing or unpacking. No noisy hotel rooms, lost luggage, tired feet, linguistic misunderstandings or relentlessly cheerful tour guides. No suspicion that there's a terrorist at the terminal, a suicide bomber in the square, a hijacker in the next seat – today's versions of yesterday's red under the bed. No long journey home with overweight bags full of dirty clothes, bargains bought on a whim that turn out to be follies, and presents for everybody and their dog. The American comedienne Lily

Tomlin was only half-joking when she said, 'Reality is the leading cause of stress among those in touch with it.' How true.

You don't have to be there to experience it. Virtual travel is the go. You can sit in front of your computer with a Darphin masque on your face and nothing on your feet, getting tomorrow's grocery shopping out of the way before you read *The New York Times* – it's free on the web at **www.nytimes.com** – without humping the real thing home, as you'd have to if you bought it at a newsstand in Manhattan.

Then you can go for a virtual-reality trip somewhere, say, to Normandy or Marrakesh or Charleston or Buenos Aires. Learn all about Sicily at the click of your mouse at **www.en.wikipedia.org/wiki/sicily**. Then log on to **www.ateliersulmare.it** for the fantastic Albergo L'Atelier sul Mare, a hotel in which a dozen or so rooms have been designed by notable artists. **Carolyn Lockhart** has stayed there. Some are sublime and some are so scary you wouldn't want to sleep in them. On the web you can dream without the nightmares. 'Reality is something you rise above,' said Liza Minnelli, who's been trying to prove the theory all her life.

Ah, but what about the poetry of being there to see the sun rise over Mont Blanc, or the moon hover above Mount Fuji? You can miss out on those in reality, too, because clouds and pollution do not necessarily disappear from the sky just because you travelled thousands of kilometres to be there. You've also got to get to the right vantage point and hope that six charabancs of others have not done the same.

Gawping hordes now clutter up anything remotely famous, not just the Taj Mahal in Agra, the Parthenon in Athens and St Peter's Basilica in Rome, which all lost their souls to the entertainment industry long ago. At St Peter's, Michelangelo's sublime *Pietà* is behind bulletproof glass and a loudspeaker summons the faithful to the next Mass in a way that's about as spiritual as the airport you've just come from.

In the golden years of travel, there was a slogan that urged us to do it 'Now, when your heart says go'. The words that comfort me these days are, 'Not now, thanks, my heart's saying no.'

21

A WHIRL
AROUND
THE WEB

ve the suit

cult to better the suit as the basis of your Monday-

fact, you could do worse than take a man's wardrob

t. You might decide to add a dress or two, and to e

ies of your suit by buying both a skirt and trousers

t. Fortunately, the decision on cut, colour and numb

tirely up to you and how much you are prepared to

current fashion. However, avoid skirts that are too sh

oo skimpy and colours and patterns more suited to

pics or an underground bar at midnight than to an

e might still be some companies with regulations preventing

mployees from wearing trousers but I cannot believe that such

d thinking can go on much longer. Well-tailored trousers are

good-looking, they are more comfortable and more practical

ts for many women.

e you are going to have to look your best, week after week, your

colours is best limited to those that team happily together.

IN THE FOURTH quarter of 2005, Australians spent $2 billion shopping via the Internet with their Visa cards. It doesn't take us long to recognise a good thing when we see it – more than four million of us have experienced the heady delights of buying from a sitting position in front of a computer. There's no doubt that shopping is one of the Internet's big attractions, but it's not the only one. The Net also provides a matchless voyage of discovery, whether for research or just for fun.

These are some of my favourite sites for sore eyes.

Fashion

www.net-a-porter.com It's right up to the minute in head-to-toe looks you can buy online, if you've got the cash flow to spray on a bag by Marc Jacobs or mules by Jimmy Choo. It's for big moneybags. Haven't got the wherewithal? Get in line for Mr Trump, next time round.

www.nytimes.com You have to register with *The New York Times* but no fees are involved, unless you want to delve into the archive. Click on 'Fashion & style' and search for those brilliant writers, Cathy Horyn and Ruth La Ferla, who cover fashion in all its forms, from haute couture to what's stalking the back alleys of Manhattan. Their viewpoints always come from the reader's angle, rather than spin from the designers, so I'm not sure how they rate with the fashion industry. In their book *Trading Up: The New American Luxury* (Portfolio), Michael J Silverstein and Neil Fiske mention a memorable piece Cathy Horyn wrote for *The New York Times* in 2002 when she covered the collections in Paris. Her sandals were admired by the man who runs Barneys. 'Are those Gucci?' he asked. 'No, Wal-Mart,' she was thrilled to say. And it was true. She wasn't the first of the fashion flock to notice what good stuff mass-market chainstores sell at a pittance compared to the luxury brands. For evidence, try: Wal-Mart, **www.walmart.com**; Zara, **www.zara.com**; H&M, **www.hm.com**; and Topshop, **www.topshop.co.uk**.

www.style.com Describing itself as 'the online home of *Vogue* and *W*' – meaning the two US publications that, along with *Harper's Bazaar*, are wooed by the international industry for coverage that can make or break a brand – this site has fashion shows, celebrities, profiles and trends but mainly in short bites to entice you to subscribe to the magazines. It's a skim across the surface, more style than substance.

www.dailycandy.com **Megan Morton** introduced me to this site, a classily illustrated, wittily worded daily update of what's cool or hot in your choice of cities, mainly in America. My Daily Candy comes from New York. Where else? London, too, since it came online recently. In reflecting current attitudes, Daily Candy brings fodder from a broader field of fashion than what to put on your back. It's irreverent and fun.

www.ebay.com When you know what you want to buy, make this your first window-shop. Study the offerings carefully, though. Some sellers have been known to tell whoppers about their goods, but most are fair dinkum and there are some terrific bargains. I always look at the customer satisfaction rating for the particular seller (top right-hand corner) before I bid on anything.

www.target.com Don't think I've gone off my fashion rocker. The volatile American fashion designer Isaac Mizrahi, whose own-label fashion runs to four figures apiece, designs a new and very affordable line for Target each season. There was that pink corduroy jacket marked down to something like US$30 that I was a moment too late to order online. Not only the price, but the timing is right – when end-of-season sales happen in America, that season is about to begin here.

www.gap.com I realise now how Gap got its name: it bridges the yawning chasm between cheap but awful and chic but unaffordable. Gap has basic stuff of great quality and in the range of sizes only America offers. I love the pants with pockets on both sides and two at the back. Crisp shirts in superb cotton and a decent length of sleeve. Bliss. Gap online doesn't deliver to Australia, so that's when an address in the US (a challenge, if ever there was one, see pages 218–9) could span that particular gap. Otherwise track down the stores next time you're overseas.

www.amazon.com This is a fashion site? It's an everything site, books on fashion included. I love Amazon like Jane Roarty loves Paris; it's an obsession. In its early days, every time the business pages reported that its founder Jeff Bezos was heading for

211

financial trouble, I rushed to order another book or CD, hoping to keep the company with us. Eric Matthews did the same. It seems to have worked. It's now a US$6 billion business, selling more than 20 million products. Sometimes I dare not log on to this site because it's too full of temptation. At this very moment, I await my copy of the *The Encyclopedia of New York City* (Yale University Press), to sit alongside *The London Encyclopaedia*, a truly marvellous work I bought at Hatchard's on Piccadilly twelve years ago. (That's available from Amazon, too; see also page 147.) Too indigestible for a fashionista? Then feast on *Allure* by Diana Vreeland (edited by Jacqueline Kennedy Onassis) or *A.L.T.: A Memoir* by André Leon Talley, the suave African-American editor-at-large for American *Vogue*. Or just type in the name of your favourite fashion identity and see what turns up.

www.trendychic.com Along with **Carolyn Lockhart** and **Lucinda Mendel**, those with an international fashion eye know that Petit Bateau is a label attached to a T-shirt that's tops for quality and style. Trendychic claims to be the largest online retailer of this most coveted of French imports. Petit Bateau started life at Troyes in 1893, made cotton knickers for French soldiers during World War I and, later, for children. It now specialises in cheeky knockabout clothes for children, and beautiful basics for women. Its website, **www.petit-bateau.com**, defines the brand but doesn't sell online.

www.landsend.com Terrific basic clothes well cut from superior fabrics.

More than fashion

www.greatbuildings.com A vast collection of inspiring structures spanning the millennia, from the ancient Egyptian Temple at Luxor, to Alvar Aalto's office in Helsinki; from Masai houses in Kenya to Château de Chenonceaux in France; from Antonio Gaudí's Sagrada Familia in Barcelona, to IM Pei's Bank of China Tower in Hong Kong. Search by architect, building or place.

www.timeandplace.com Find out how you can rent a nice little spread for a week or two. For instance, Twin Palms Sinatra Estate in Palm Springs, where Ol' Blue Eyes, after a tiff with Ava Gardner, his wife at the time, chucked all her belongings on to the driveway. Personally, I'd rather curl up in the one-bedroom penthouse overlooking Place St Michel in Paris.

www.fairtrade.org.uk Food for thought. The Fairtrade Foundation is a charity that works to end the exploitation of primary producers in the world's poorer countries. Having made progress with coffee, chocolate and fruit, it is now targeting cotton. Raising public awareness is one of its aims. Another is to put pressure on affluent countries that subsidise their own primary producers. According to a March 2005 report by Sarah Womack in the *Telegraph*, London, 'In 2002, the United States government provided $3.4 billion in subsidies to its domestic cotton sector, almost twice the total US foreign aid given to sub-Saharan Africa and more than the gross domestic product of Benin, Burkina Faso or Chad – the main cotton-producing countries in the region.'

www.vitra.com Go here for ideas for your workspace and to find out about key modern and contemporary furniture designers and their work. It's a very informative site, put together with style and polish.

www.flocabulary.com Hip-hop that elevates the mind? It's the easy way to memorise the meaning and pronunciation of forgettable words – peregrinate, ubiquitously, physiognomy – and it's so much fun you'd never have wagged school if English lessons had been like this. The music is catchy and tautology is the teacher. Examples: 'The vicissitudes of life, those ups and downs'; 'Time flows like waves, undulating'; 'I'm agoraphobic: scared of open spaces, claustrophobic: scared of confined spaces, so I'm doubly screwed, know what I mean dude?' I love the wit and the ingenuity of it but I'd like more. How about solecism and solipsism, eminent and imminent?

www.sparknotes.com Seems almost too good to be true to be able to download free online study guides covering a range of subjects, from literature and history to biology and maths. Print your own copies of the classics, such as George Orwell's *Animal Farm*, or Charlotte Bronte's *Jane Eyre*, or something current, such as selected editions of *Harry Potter*.

www.wwf.org.au/act/animaladoption Fifty dollars doesn't buy a lot these days, but it can help take certain species off the endangered list if you use it to 'adopt' Harriot the squirrel glider, Hubert the knob-tailed gecko, Sebastian the wedge-tailed eagle, Patricia the platypus, or Kiah the southern humpback whale. It's not about supporting a particular animal – your donation goes to save threatened native animals – although you do receive official adoption papers and a photograph from World Wildlife Fund, Australia. It's a lovely gift for children, and such a good cause.

www.wikipedia.org Simply type in whatever in the world you need to know.

www.gawker.com An irreverent and gossipy stickybeak at the news, the media, politics, celebrities and anyone and anything it sets its sights on.

www.crikey.com.au An enlightening look at the media and what goes on inside the newsroom. It's fearless, irreverent, as impartial as anyone is likely to be, and often entertaining.

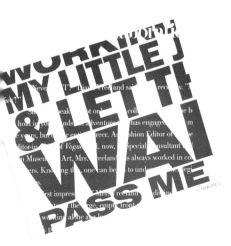

NOTES

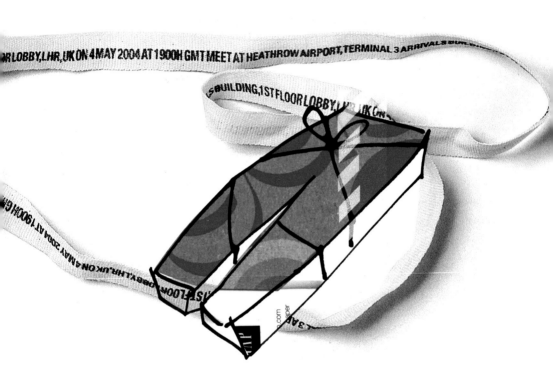

22

SNAGS IN
CYBERSPACE

AFTER AMAZON.COM opened up for me the wonders of shopping on the world wide web, it became clear that there was no way back. But in this celestial emporium there is one frustration. Many online stores that sell what you deeply desire don't ship to Australia.

It is a characteristic of commerce in America that for every need there is an entrepreneur. One Friday in 2004, an item in *The Australian* caught my eye. A crowd called **www.shopthestates.com** offered an address in the US and a forwarding service so the goods could be sent from there to here.

In a flash I logged on to **www.gap.com** because I needed summer clothes and it was end-of-summer sale time in the northern hemisphere. Soon after, four pairs of cotton strides and two cotton shirts at a total cost of $143.98, including freight, arrived at my Pittsburgh address. Six days later and at a shipping cost of $77.52, my Gap garb was out of its wrappings and on my body. That was one of my all-time great shopping experiences.

Then, in June 2006, a disaster of global proportions struck: Shop the States closed.

Nobody – except Lana Dopper, a friend in deed – knows what I've been through to find you another workable address in the US. Between us, we tackled the task like terriers. While I gained an address in Florida through Access USA, **www.myus.com** ($35 set-up fee, plus $132 annual membership), Lana drew up a shopping list at Macy's so I could test my new address. Topping her list was a man's Polo Ralph Lauren Pinpoint Yarmouth shirt.

I had a great time filling my basket at Macy's, until I typed my credit card numbers and everything stalled. I was told to telephone 1800-289-6229 (880-289-6229 from here). But I had to order during US working hours. That meant around 6 a.m. Sydney time.

Picture me in icy winter, in towelling robe and Uggs, spelling out the list to an order-taker in Missouri. The sale goes smoothly until I give her my card numbers. Macy's does not accept payment by credit card unless it is issued by a financial institution in America. What a start to the day.

Then Lana found she could establish a friend's address in the US as her own second billing address with American Express. That meant she could shop online at Macy's, pay with her AmEx card, and her friend would send them on. All you need is that kind of friend.

Meanwhile, I had not been idle. Access USA has a Personal Shopper service: they buy your goods and charge it to your credit card. Saved! I placed an order for the elusive Ralph Lauren shirt from Macy's. My order was confirmed. I called Lana. We crowed in triumph. Fools that we are.

Next day, an email delivered the startling news that Access USA cannot place orders with Macy's because it has been identified a 'reseller'. Same goes for Saks and Bloomingdale's.

By then, I'd come too far to give up. There was another possibility in Mailbox Exchange, **www.mailforwarding.biz**. What did I have to lose? Only the $25 set-up fee, plus $42, for three months' membership. My address was set up swiftly but, to have goods shipped, I needed to fill in Form 1583 to satisfy US Customs. It required me to proffer two forms of identification. Credit cards and birth certificates did not qualify. I am not a driver, so all I could offer, apart from my passport, was a copy of the title deeds to my house.

That is when my publisher called a halt to the whole sorry saga. 'You are not sending a copy of the deeds to your house anywhere,' she said.

Macy's might be the biggest department store in the world, but it's not the only one. Lots of specialty stores ship to Australia – or to a US address – and accept payment by cards issued here. Of course, there are other methods of sending money overseas, including bank transfers and online services such as PayPal and PayMate. But sometimes there are simpler ways to find what you seek. Lana found the Polo Ralph Lauren Pinpoint Yarmouth shirt at the signature store in the Queen Victoria Building in Sydney and it cost about the same as having one shipped in from Macy's.

Prices quoted here are in US dollars.

23
NESTING

B&B Itali
of endles

With the Bulgari
partner, Tyler Brû
their marketing ar
ten new showroo
within a year, the
on design and inr
1966 is ready to t

SPACE

IT CAME AS no surprise to me to read in *The New York Times* a while ago about the growing trend in the United States for people to turn the interiors of their houses into clones of chic hotels, such as The Hotel Montalembert in Paris and the Delano at Miami Beach. I know the feeling. After trips abroad on assignments that required me to report on every exquisite detail of sumptuous hotels, I would unlock my front door, survey my habitat and think: How Can I Live In This Squalor?

The main difference between the environment in a hotel and in a private house is not so much in decor, but in upkeep. At the 400-room Emirates Palace in Abu Dhabi, ten full-time staff are employed just to clean the 1002 Swarovski crystal chandeliers. Try as we may to ape the soothing perfection of a suite at a much smaller establishment, say the 124-room Raffles L'Ermitage in Los Angeles, it won't work unless we hire half the staff as well. Otherwise, who's going to take the fluff out of the corners with a pin and change the sheets and towels every day? Who's going to buff the brass the moment it gets a smudge and repaint every little scratch on the woodwork? Who's going to keep the floors and windows immaculate? I think I know the answer. I won't even mention outdoors, where leaves collect in gutters, slugs eat the roses and lawns turn into a savanna the minute you turn your back.

Living is messy. Perfection lies in the grave. So, I tell myself, we might as well accept imperfection as a way of life and stop pretending otherwise. We can always dream, though, especially when we know it can't come true.

My ideal nest is a corner of the nobly proportioned second floor of some palazzo in Venice. Its gothic windows overlook a small canal, where I can see the plumbago spilling over balconies, washing strung on clothes lines, water traffic that is strictly domestic and I can buy my artichokes from the vegetable barge moored beside the arched bridge in view of my balcony. The walls are rough and white, the furniture painted in fanciful patterns, or stripped and waxed, and there are no built-in cupboards, not even in the kitchen and bathroom.

Like all princesses, I have always felt I could live in a castle. Not an opulent palace of the Versailles type, all gilding and ornamentation; goodness no! Nor could I feel at home in anything as twee as Ludwig II's fairytale Neuschwanstein in Bavaria, the one that had such an effect on Walt Disney. I have in mind something more austere.

The ruins of Dunluce Castle, towering majestically from a black basalt cliff on the North Antrim coast of Northern Ireland, is the most dramatic ruined castle I have ever seen. (Have a look at **www.northantrim.com/dunlucecastle.htm**.) Swathed in mist, what a marvellous, moody setting it would make for the last act of Wagner's *Tristan and Isolde*. What's left of this mighty citadel dates from the sixteenth and seventeenth centuries but it is roofless and uninhabitable. A bit scary, too. One evening in 1639, during a dinner presided over by the resident Duchess, the kitchen fell into the sea and the staff along with it. Perhaps it's just as well it's not for sale. In any case, I don't have the cash flow, at the moment.

The sale of the odd castle in Europe is not all that rare, as you will see if you type **www.sothebysrealty.com** into the space provided by your trusty Google search engine, then click on 'Find a Property'. Don't expect to find Dunluce, but I bet there'll be one or two others in Ireland. In much the same league is another seductive site I discovered recently – **www.forbes.com**, the online version of the magazine for real and wannabe billionaires. Avoid the serious financial coverage, click on 'Lifestyle' and have the time of your life.

Under the ironic slug 'Home Improvement', journalist Sara Clemence recently listed the most expensive penthouses for sale in the United States in 2005. Guess what topped the list? The triplex crowning The Pierre in New York that Lady (Mary) Fairfax sold to the Wall Street financier Martin Zweig for a bit less than US$22 million in 1999. It was back on the market at US$70 million – might still be, in case you're interested.

Greedy for more, I looked up Forbes' listing of the priciest islands for sale in 2005 and warmed to one that came with a bucolic house, the remnants of an eighteenth-century cotton plantation and a couple of shipwrecks in the US Virgin Islands – all for US$25 million. For a million or so more than that, you could buy a whole community along with Isola Santo Stefano in the Gulf of Gaeta, off Naples. I use the pronoun 'you' not 'I' deliberately here, because I am not in the market for this sort of thing at present. I am but an enthusiastic voyeur (a kinder word than stickybeak).

Rubbish-dump architecture

What my cash flow might be able to stretch to is an Earthship, an ecologically sustainable house built to a concept developed over the past three decades by American architect Michael Reynolds in New Mexico, **www.earthship.org**. Through his company Earthship Biotecture he builds houses out of the rubbish that clutters up our environment: walls are made of used tyres, staggered and filled with rammed earth, the gaps stuffed with bottles and cans, the whole thing masked by adobe. There are variations on this theme, depending on where the house is sited and the needs of its owners, but, in general, each is solar-powered, perhaps with a fireplace with hot water stored above. Its temperature is controlled naturally, its waste and water are recycled and it costs almost nothing to run because it's not connected to municipal utilities.

Models of sustainable living such as these take us into a responsible future by spiriting us back to mediaeval hamlets that materialised from available stone and the wood of local forests. In that sense, they are just like mini castles. For a very persuasive testimonial from a couple who built their own, log on to **www.gradyallengooch.com**. If you'd like to try living in an Earthship you can rent one for a night, a few days or longer – just as you'd book a hotel room – in Taos, New Mexico. For further information and bookings, email amyklay@earthship.com.

Within our own shores, architect Ken Latona's Smart Shax, **www.smartshax.com.au**, make self-sufficiency in the bush a possibility in simple, good-looking and well-designed huts that can generate their own power, store water and compost waste.

Some of the planet's most thoughtful and ingenious architects have been working on ways to turn old shipping containers into housing. One of them is the much-awarded Melbourne architect Sean Godsell, **www.seangodsell.com**. Although he designed his Future Shack as housing for people displaced by disasters of all kinds, plenty of well-heeled people have shown interest in it as a weekender. His prototype of the re-invented rusted steel box went on show in 2004 at the Cooper-Hewitt National Design Museum, Smithsonian Institution, 2 East 91st Street, New York, **www.ndm.si.edu**. I find Sean's Park Bench House his most endearing invention: it opens to provide cover for someone with no other place to sleep, but so far, no council has shown interest in picking up the idea. He has also designed a bus shelter that converts to housing after hours. I guess it will be a long time before we see that around, too.

Current trends? Ask David Harrison

For now, though, most of us live in pretty conventional structures. Whether they are houses or apartments, a lot of them lack architectural individuality, so we have to be clever and courageous enough to give them character by what we put into them in the way of furniture, decoration and colour. In principle, decorating a room is the same as dressing a person: you emphasise the good points and mask the bad ones. You're careful to assess passing fashions for their suitability to your own looks and style before you take them on, so the same goes for your home.

According to **David Harrison**, our enthusiasm for twentieth-century furniture is being tempered by 'a more eclectic approach to interiors in general. At one point it became a bit silly in that every piece of furniture had to be a design icon from the twentieth century. Now there's a blend of a few twentieth-century pieces that are interesting or fit well within an interior, with some of the better contemporary pieces mixed with other items from a different era altogether.' He acknowledges that making disparate items coherent is not as easy as adopting a period and sticking to it, but 'it's a lot more complex, it's got a lot more depth. And really, whether a house is completely furnished in twentieth-century design icons or in Ikea, the end result is much the same: it's very one-dimensional; it feels forced and looks like a film set, definitely not a house that people live in. The whole idea of bringing in different eras and ages in furniture shows that the owner has collected things over time and that the house has evolved, as opposed to being pristine and new. That's a real plus, in my book.'

One way of doing this is to hang on to some pieces you love and make them work with new acquisitions. David believes that 'a lot of people are encouraged to dump their past when they move into a new, modern apartment because they don't feel that anything of theirs works there. A lot of the time, most of it doesn't. But a good interior designer will be able to see what elements of your old interior can be brought into the new one. Even if it's just photographs or some kind of artwork, small elements which give the interior the personality of the people who are living in it rather than being completely created.'

There's a lot of encouragement out there to jettison the past and start again. Showcase apartments in new developments are kitted out with whatever the look of the moment happens to be; a developer may even offer to sell you the furniture as well as the flat – all you have to do is get rid of your old stuff and move in to a ready-made environment that may not be unlike the hotel rooms we discussed earlier in this chapter.

Similarly, some big furniture retailers offer pre-selected furniture ranges at different price levels. David explains: 'You, as a punter, could go in and say, "I'm thinking of replacing all my lounge room furniture" or "I'm moving into a new apartment, what can you show me for $20 000?"' He acknowledges that this makes good sense, particularly if you've mortgaged yourself to the limit on the property and there's not much left over to furnish it, but the downside is, 'You end up with a lot of apartments looking very much the same.' Not much personality comes through and 'a few years down the track, it can look much more dated than a house which has evolved and has different eras within it, even if they're quite close eras. The biggest thing that magazines like *InsideOut* are trying to push as a concept is not to just throw huge amounts of money at the problem but to carefully and selectively choose your pieces so that within an interior that might include Ikea pieces and junk-store finds, you can indulge in a few expensive key pieces. One great chair can lift the quality of everything else. If you choose the mix correctly it's a very personal and cost-effective way to go.'

How to Choose an Investment Piece

1. Untold tomes have been written about twentieth-century furniture, so study the reliable ones to teach yourself the difference between the real thing and the fake. Charlotte and Peter Fiell have put together a series of books for the publisher Taschen, covering design from the 1920s through to the 1970s. 'If you had a set of those,' says David, 'you'd probably be able to recognise 80 or 90 per cent of the best items of the century.' His trained eye almost got him thrown out of a junk shop in Redfern where he spotted a copy of the famous Eames 670 lounge chair. He asked the price and when the owner said $2500, David replied, 'That's quite a lot for a copy.' It had been sold to someone who hadn't done their homework.

2. Auction houses sometimes attribute something to a famous name because nobody can prove otherwise. If you have any doubts, David's advice is to ask the auction house to put it in writing, particularly if it has a high estimate.

3. Buy from a trustworthy source.

DAVID HARRISON'S LIST OF RELIABLE STORES

For vintage furniture

Copeland & De Soos Antiques Dealers, 66 Queen Street, Woollahra, telephone (02) 9363 5288. They've been established for more than thirty years and, while their pieces are usually costly, 'You have the certain knowledge that you have a product which is well restored and only restored if it needed to be. A lot of people do a bad restoration job, which actually reduces the value of the item, rather than leaving it with the original patina. You have to pay for the knowledge of the people running the business to know what to buy in the first place. The quality of their product is always very high.'

Kenneth Neale Mid Century Modern Furniture 138 Darlinghurst Road, Darlinghurst, telephone (02) 9331 2033. 'He's quite an eccentric fellow. He charges good money for his things, but rumour has it he's had two or three warehouses full of the stuff for years. He's just been collecting and storing it, watching the general value of it all go up, waiting for the right time to release it back on to the market. He was buying things when nobody else was interested in vintage modern, not just from Sydney or Melbourne, but going out to the countryside in a truck and finding stuff. That takes a lot of dedication and hard work, so that you are able to rock up to a showroom in the centre of Sydney and purchase it. You've got to pay for that.'

Fifty Sixty Seventy 308 Trafalgar Street, Annandale, telephone (02) 9566 1430 or 0413 764 101. The man who owns this store 'learned his stock-in-trade from Ken Neale and does the same thing, goes out into the countryside in his van to deceased estates and elsewhere. He works really hard, too, but his scheme is quite different [from Ken Neale's], in that he turns it over as fast as possible. You can get some good bargains there but often you have to figure in the restoration. He's at the cheaper end [of the market] and it's much more cluttered, a jumble of stuff that spills out of his tiny shop on to the street outside.'

Geoffrey Hatty Applied Arts 296 Malvern Road, Prahran, telephone (03) 9510 1277. 'Something of a Melbourne institution, Geoffrey has been displaying his eclectic mix of twentieth-century objects and art for more than twenty years. African, Asian or French touches are combined with modern classics and turn-of-the-century curios. His ability to mix pieces from different eras and styles is a lesson in how it should be done.' This kind of presentation makes browsing there an adventure.

Khai Liew Design 166 Magill Road, Norwood, telephone (08) 8362 1076. 'This shop combines Asian antiques, vintage mid-century Danish and Khai Liew's own refined furniture designs. The emphasis is on beautiful timber and joinery in a fine and delicate style. The look is extremely pared down and quite exquisite.'

Plasma 2A Cecil Place, Prahran, telephone (03) 9525 1271. 'This small shop off Chapel Street always manages to dig up good-quality and interesting furniture and lighting pieces from the 1950s through to the 1980s. The owner, Dean Angelucci, knows his stuff, and whether the pieces are Danish, American or Italian they are always reasonably priced.'

For new furniture

Anibou 726 Bourke Street, Redfern, telephone (02) 9319 0655, **www.anibou. com.au**, is a specialist in Finnish furniture, particularly the designs of Alvar Aalto manufactured by Artek. It also imports the avant-garde Italian label Gervasoni, and supports young Australian designers.

Corporate Culture 21–23 Levey Street, Chippendale, telephone (02) 9690 0077, **www.corporateculture.com.au**, imports, distributes and retails Fritz Hansen, Erik Jøergensen, Carl Hansen & Son and other predominantly Danish manufacturers.

De De Ce Design Centre 263 Liverpool Street, Darlinghurst, telephone (02) 9360 2722, **www.dedece.com**, owned and run by the Engelen family, imports, distributes and retails Cappellini and Knoll and other top names, such as Moooi and Minotti.

Design Farm 1000 Hay Street, Perth, telephone (08) 9322 2200, **www.designfarm. com.au**, is the main outlet for quality contemporary furniture in Western Australia.

FY2K Furniture 4 Foster Street, Surry Hills, telephone (02) 9281 1771, represents Italian furniture brands Emmemobili and Ferlea an Tissetanta, as well as Noguchi lights and small New Zealand designer names, such as Purple South and David Trubridge.

Hub 63 Exhibition Street, Melbourne, telephone (03) 9650 1366, **www.hubfurniture.com.au**, represents Italian companies Accademia, Emme B, Moroso and Molteni & C, and imports modern accessories from around the world.

Space 84 O'Riordan Street, Alexandria, telephone (02) 8339 7588, **www.spacefurniture.com.au**, represents most of the major Italian contemporary furniture labels from B&B Italia, Cassina, Edra, Kartell and Zanotta.

24

DECORATING

HAVE YOU EVER stopped to count how many places you have inhabited in your entire life? As time goes by, the list becomes awesome. Not counting the houses where I lived with my parents, the number for me has by now reached eighteen.

How many walls have I painted myself or caused others to paint and paper on my behalf? How many floors sanded, tiled or carpeted? How many shutters screwed into place and curtains hung? How many colour schemes have I seen lose their bloom and be replaced? It has taken me more than half my life to discover what I truly love to live with: white walls, tiled floors, white shutters and old, worn, seasoned wooden furniture (lovingly buffed-up every so often). And I do like a shiny pot. What I truly do not want to live through, ever again, is a house full of tradesmen knocking down walls and never quite finishing what they promised they would. I like shabbiness. I'd better. Des the painter, Craig the electrician and Eddy and Matt the plumbers are the only tradesmen permitted to cross the threshhold of my house ever again.

I am no longer tempted to go in for the great Australian passion I call RRS: Repetitive Refurbishment Syndrome. I've done it too often. Well I remember that divine Thames Green (we nicknamed it murk-and-sludge) feature wall I painted in the sitting room of my maisonette at Swiss Cottage in London in the early 1960s. The other walls were white, the floorboards were stained almost black. One spindly chair, picked up at the market in Edgware Road, was placed against a white wall. I painted the attic white – with one wall in French navy – hung striped polished-cotton curtains in the window and rented it to a Swiss nurse who, conveniently, worked the night shift.

The delights of doing it myself went into eclipse soon after. By the time Hans and I bought a freestanding Victorian boarding house in South Melbourne in 1968, an army of artisans arrived to gentrify it. The main task was to clear out all the add-ons

that blocked the fireplaces and obscured the top half of the French windows upstairs. When I realised that the painter liked classical music, I kept him wielding the brush by playing Beethoven, Brahms and Vivaldi long after his workmates had packed up their toolboxes and gone home.

Megan Morton's styling tips

Because **Megan Morton**'s job entails propping and decorating rooms for the camera, she knows a lot about creating effects without spending a lot of money. 'I've got a theory,' she told me when I asked her for some tips for putting instant style into a room. 'Houses have a colour. There's a colour palette that they're meant to have. You've got to sit out a winter and a summer to see where the sun comes, where the light goes, or where it's nice to have a cup of tea. When you find the colour, if you're doing a room from scratch, then totally chase the colour to the end. Not that you'd have, say, powder blue everywhere, but powder blue looks great with cherry red, with brown, hessian and oatmeal. It also looks beautiful with white.'

Once you settle on the colour, other decisions come easily. Megan collects paint swatches of each chosen colour scheme from a hardware store and keeps them in her bag. 'If I'm in a shop and I'm about to be overwhelmed, or I'm going to waste my money and have to return something, I go, "Do you live in this scheme? Yes you do," and then I buy it. Shopping is quicker. All your decisions are done.' It's also a sensible idea to record the dimensions of the whole room and the spaces you need to fill, and keep the measurements with you, because you never know where or when the perfect thing will turn up.

What would Megan do if she were given $100 to spend on decorating a room? 'I would buy paint. I've just painted a room in the country with blackboard paint, not because I wanted to do a blackboard but because it's got that lovely chalky finish. Paint colour is so important.' Her work takes her into many private houses that find their way into the editorial pages of glossy magazines. In one of them that she recalls vividly, 'There was a beautiful chocolate-y, licorice-y coloured feature wall, and dusty pink and brown on the bed. I said, "How did you get that colour?" And [the owner] said, "I couldn't afford to buy the $40 tins just for one wall, so I asked for all the mis-tints in brown." I thought, "You clever girl."' (Mis-tint is an industry term for paint with incorrect colour, so it's sold off very cheaply.)

Megan remembers another house where the woman wanted to paint the bedroom pink but her husband insisted on minimalist white. So she painted the insides of the cupboards hot pink. 'Her shoes and all her clothes looked beautiful against the pink. I said, "You got the better deal."' Ingenuity will find a way.

The simplest way to lift a room is with flowers. 'I think wonders can be done with a vase full of hydrangea, ranunculus, daphne or floppy tulips, even in the drabbest house. Or greenery in that silvery grey.'

Just like breeds of dog and periods of furniture, flowers are subject to fashion, although I would never take that seriously myself. Remember when that white orchid, phalaenopsis, was the must-have? Then we had a run on gerberas which, I am told, are out now because they've been overdone. Although saturated colour has been around for a while, I prefer white or blue flowers. Think of the simplicity of snowdrops, masses of white daisies with blue or yellow centres, bundles of blue forget-me-nots, stacks of scented white stock and – luxury of luxuries – cream peonies.

Where Megan shops for homewares

Space 84 O'Riordan Street, Alexandria, telephone (02) 8339 7588, **www.spacefurniture.com.au**. 'I never had a taste for modern furniture, but Space makes you want to throw everything old out and get plastic. I thought it was just for boys in penthouses in Potts Point, but it's not. It's just so exciting. There's such a range of palettes. [The Italian brand] Kartell is fantastic for bathrooms.'

Planet 419 Crown Street, Surry Hills, telephone (02) 9698 0680, **www.planetfurniture.com.au**. Ross Longmuir, the man behind it, has expanded the store's merchandise from furniture to include other crafts, such as ceramics. 'He is a real ambassador for the arts community.'

Spence & Lyda 16 Foster Street, Surry Hills, telephone (02) 9212 6747, **www.spenceandlyda.com.au**. 'They've got the serious-name furniture, but the way they merchandise it is joyous. It's all punchy and beautiful. Eames chairs in gorgeous colours – bumblebee yellow or powder blue. And Missoni towels, bed linen, throws and feature cushions, because they add colour to what is good, expensive, modern furniture. I also like the Bridget Riley-ness of the black-and-white towels, the perfect fix of modernity in a functional disguise.'

Home Furniture on Consignment 23 Doody Street, Alexandria, telephone (02) 8338 8000, **www.hfoc.com.au**. 'The whole idea here is bartering designer furniture. I guess this is such a Sydney syndrome, isn't it? Get furniture in, sell your house, make the money, move on, oh-I-don't-like-that-anymore-because-I'm-totally-over-it. So if you go in here you always find something you could love. Eames. Noguchi. Really distinctive pieces. You can get a buzz on someone else's misfortune or real estate success.'

Positively Curlewis Street 11 Curlewis Street, Bondi Beach, telephone (02) 9365 6000. 'Two guys, woodmakers who love old things, go on the road all around Australia to places where you think you could get an old oilcloth school map for $20, but they get it for you. They might get an old toolbox but paint it a beautiful lime green. They're very clever.'

Husk 123 Dundas Place, Albert Park, telephone (03) 9690 6994, **www.husk.com.au**. 'Adobe walls, tea with mint and cardamom – and that's just the little bonus cafe bit down the end. They've got a beautiful homewares section where they've gone beyond the Moroccan teacup. Lovely ceramics. It's all organic. It's all about wellbeing.'

Empire 111 63 Cardigan Place, Albert Park, telephone (03) 9682 6677, **www.empirevintage.com.au**, describes its offerings as 'painstakingly selected vintage clothes, furniture and objects'. The shop is the brainchild of Megan's friend Lyn Gardener. 'Her shop is Australian industrial, so there are big old sleeper benches, old hat blocks, shoe lasts and lots of things in white.'

Ikea Homebush Bay Drive, 1 Oulton Avenue, Rhodes, telephone (02) 9313 6400, **www.ikea.com.au** (log on to the website for details of stores throughout Australia). 'It is brilliant; the biggest one in Australia of international standard.'

When **Bodum** closed its store at Westfield Bondi Junction, Megan was devastated, until she discovered that by calling 1800 209 999 she could track down other stockists. She loves Bodum because 'every single thing has been re-thought and turned upside-down. Their tumblers are double-glass so you can have a hot or a cold drink in them. Bodum makes everything seem completely simplified. And it's all about the good things, like coffee, tea, big plates to share with people in this lovely Danish design.'

Auction houses

Stanley & Co 9–15 Alberta Street, Sydney, telephone (02) 9283 3838, **www.stanleyandco.com**, boutique valuer and auctioneer of fine and decorative arts. 'Dalia Stanley is the auctioneer who goes to people's deceased estates and gentlemen's residences. I always go to her auctions because they're fantastic properties.'

Mitchell Road Auctions 76 Mitchell Road, Alexandria, telephone (02) 9310 7200. You might remember it as Gavan Hardy, the clever auctioneer who paved the way for flash furniture showrooms and galleries to move into what was primarily an industrial area. Now it's abuzz with designer-driven shoppers.

Raffan, Kelaher & Thomas Pty Ltd 42 John Street, Leichhardt, telephone (02) 9552 1899, **www.rafkelauctions.com.au**. You never know what you'll find here, from antique furniture and paintings, to precious jewellery and bric-a-brac.

LAMPS AGLOW

The waxed lampshades decorated with botanical motifs that you might have seen at Copeland & De Soos are the handiwork of artist Rosine Grosmougin, who comes from a family of candlemakers in France and now lives at Berry. The wax finish softens electric light to give the effect of candlelight, moody and romantic. 66 Queen Street, Woollahra, telephone (02) 9363 5288.

Out of town

'Really good crap' is the way **Megan Morton** describes vintage treasure, and she finds
plenty of it in the Southern Highlands of New South Wales, where both she and
Belinda Seper have houses. Apart from being a desirable place to own real estate,
the district is a fabulous hunting ground for anyone addicted to fossicking among old
wares. That is why these two bowerbirds often find themselves bidding on the
same item.

Following is a list of places where you're likely to find the two of them scrounging.

The Shed 120 Old Hume Highway, Mittagong, telephone (02) 4872 2295.
So dark and cavernous, when Megan buys, it's 'almost like going to the
Easter show and hoping you've got the right show bag'. One trophy was a
weathered-grey three-legged French ladder that was used for picking apples.

The Crystal Palace The Igloo at The Milk Factory, Station Street, Bowral, telephone
(02) 4861 6444. 'This place is very cute and 1950s, with lots of stuff from different
design genres: Austrian chandeliers, rococo bedheads, old Louis chairs but in teal.'
It is owned and run by Jasper and Michelle Foggo. 'He's just finished an upholstery
course and she is an interior designer.'

Nostalgia Traders Corner of Main and Victoria Streets, Mittagong, telephone
(02) 4872 3770. 'Gorgeous' is how Megan describes it. 'I've bought old Chanel soap
boxes, just the packaging that still had the tissue paper. I found a gorgeous little
knitted black Jemima doll with earrings and a big brooch.'

Peppergreen Trading Company The Market Place, Berrima, telephone (02) 4877
1488. Belinda describes it as 'A giant barn of a place. There are stacks of plates,
glassware, a whole wall of cutlery, all old kitchenalia. Doilies, throws, mixmaster
covers, tea-cosies, milk-jug covers. But I love the curtain room upstairs: brilliant old
curtains, all carefully organised by size. It's like stepping back in time.' Owner Carina
Cox hand-picks whatever she fancies – vintage quilts, Spode china, bread boards,
copper pans, buttons – on her regular shopping expeditions overseas.

The Cottage Hume Highway, Berrima, telephone (02) 4877 1298. It has 'knitwear piled high to the roof,' says Belinda, 'and the most extraordinary environment, with the biggest range of Liberty fabrics, some made into beautiful shirts. Everything the country squire and squiress could desire.'

Berkelouw Book Barn Bendooley, Old Hume Highway, Berrima, telephone (02) 4877 1370, www.berkelouw.com.au. Bookworm heaven. Browse among more than 300 000 secondhand titles, some of them rare. There is also a cafe to tempt you to idle there.

Other personal preferences

Because **James Gordon**'s work involves the use of lots of colour, his personal world is 'pretty much a monotone'. His apartment is a white backdrop for his art and the pieces he loves to collect. 'I never stop shopping. I'm never happier than when I'm in a shop.' Look around his living space and you'll see what he means. It is filled with tables of various heights to display selections from his hoard, most of it housed in cupboards, with the spillover in the garage. 'I like surfaces, so the stuff can come out,' to be arranged, re-arranged and enjoyed: a small white Buddha and cushions from Sri Lanka, chairs and a cupboard from Bali, a plaster crab from the British Museum, a cupid from San Francisco, a vintage painted tin vase from 'a country town near Bathurst, I think', fine bed linen from many sources, white porcelain in the shape of crushed paper cups from New York. He has such a good eye, he spots treasure in an instant.

A white table in front of the window in his living room doubles for dining and working. 'I sit here to read a magazine, read the paper, have coffee. I've actually thought of making a longer version of it to run right across the room because no-one sits on that sofa, no-one sits in that chair.' Everyone gravitates to the table and the view.

The merits of an oversized table were recognised some years ago by Melbourne architect Sean Godsell, who designed one 7 metres long, to run from the galley kitchen to the living area of his family home in Kew. Art advisor Amanda Love in Sydney also has a new 7-metre kitchen table designed by David Katon. Can this be The Next Big Thing?

One of **James Gordon**'s favourite shops for homewares is **Sanders and King**, 13 Morey Street, Armadale, (03) 9500 1150. Taimi Sanders and Elissa King – each a designer and mother of three sub-teen children – have an instinct for sourcing wonderful bedclothes and bath products for their tiny shop. Pure linen sheets and pillowslips from Libeco of Belgium; cotton sheets and pillowcases, hemstitched in a contrasting colour such as cherry, from Vietnam; Australian Bemboka alpaca and angora blankets and cushions; linen/cotton quilts from Shades of India; Côte Bastide soaps – so inviting, you'll feel like curling up in that beautifully made bed in the window.

This little pocket of shops in Morey Street beside Armadale Railway Station is one of the most charming in Melbourne, with the **Tiggywinkle Baby Boutique**, telephone (03) 9500 0098, and **Carolyn Lockhart**'s favourite shop in Australia, **Market Import**, at number 19, telephone (03) 9500 0764, **www.marketimport.com**. Carolyn lived for a time in Mexico and still has a passion for the vitality of its craft, which is what this lively store specialises in, along with Italian pieces and some from the Finnish label Marimekko. The whole place sings with colour and informality. Carolyn loves the way 'they wrap things so beautifully, always in these mad colourful tissue papers with masses of raffia'. Across the road is another temptation for her in the enchanting children's wear boutique Seed, number 8, telephone (03) 9509 3878, **www.seedchild.com.au**. Its adorable outfits are designed and made in Australia. A little cafe with outdoor tables and chairs, often occupied by mums with baby carriages, completes the village-like scene in this cosy corner of Melbourne. Ride there on a train from Spencer Street, but be prepared to take a taxi back with all your packages.

Lemon Tea No Sugar 98f Bellevue Road, Bellevue Hill, telephone (02) 9363 1811. Pamela Albaytar imports only the best antique French linens that she finds through the network she describes as 'my ladies' in France. **James Gordon** is her greatest fan.

You can also find him inspecting the latest European imports at Kalinka Antique Gallery, 281c Old South Head Road, Bondi, telephone (02) 9300 0406, **www.kalinkagallery.com**.

Parterre Garden – either the original tiny shop at 33 Ocean Street, Woollahra, telephone (02) 9363 5874, or the capacious warehouse at 493 Bourke Street, Surry Hills, telephone (02) 9356 4747, **www.parterre.com.au** – crops up among the favourites of not only **James Gordon** but also **Belinda Seper** and **Megan Morton**. Inspiring things to live with, brilliantly presented.

Susan Kurosawa homes in on India

If boho is your bent, India is your nirvana. Surround yourself with handmade textiles and decorative objects from the Indian subcontinent and your habitat can never be said to lack warmth and character.

For what **Susan Kurosawa** describes as 'the ultimate in market experiences', venture into the labyrinthine streets of Chandni Chowk in Old Delhi, where there are 'bargains galore, from jewellery to artefacts'. Because it's easy to get lost in the snaking streets, she suggests you 'hire a rickshaw or auto-rickshaw and have the driver stay with you. Some markets close either Sundays or Mondays. Check with your hotel concierge.'

Susan loves 'trawling through fabric shops (which usually include a tailor or two in the premises running up "suitings, shirtings and underwearings") for sari offcuts that can be transformed into scarves and shawls or covers for cushions and bolsters. Western women rarely cut an elegant swathe in a sari, but the long-top and loose-pants punjab suit (*salweer kameez*) is a flattering alternative. It is known as "The Jemima" in Sloane circles, in deference to the ex-Mrs Imran Khan. There are such shops aplenty in Delhi, Mumbai (Bombay) and Chennai (Madras). Some even have counters proclaiming "Secret Fashion" (silk underwear) and "Bollywood Presentation" (extra sparkle).

'Don't overlook Indian grocery stores for brightly packaged goods that make terrific presents. Cakes of Rani sandalwood soap, with a pouting princess on the cardboard wrapper, cost 20 cents. Wooden stamps and cooking moulds have designs of birds and lotuses and are beautiful objects, as well as useful ones. I stamp my Christmas card envelopes with a handsome Rajasthani peacock. You'd be hard-pressed to spend more than 50 cents for a stamp or mould.'

Central Cottage Industries Emporiums are government-run and easily found in India's major cities. Their prices are fixed, so there's no bargaining. 'The one in Delhi, opposite the city's Janpath strand of shops, is particularly cavernous, with six floors of low lighting and yawning clerks (don't dare interrupt their lunch pails). Don't be put off by the aircraft-hangar proportions and the lack of service. Browse for hours among counters and arched rooms that are roughly segmented, state by Indian state, or according to specialities, such as brassware, sari silks, ceramics and wooden goods. The papier-mâché boxes, made in troubled Kashmir, are particularly fine (all shapes and sizes; designs ranging from flowering vines to elephant polo), as are the lengths of hand-loomed cotton in fashionably sludgy colours of oatmeal, caramel and milk coffee. You will also find good-value silk-mix pashmina wraps and inexpensive souvenirs (best portable bulk buys: papier-mâché letter-openers, journals with hand-printed covers, Darjeeling tea in silk pouches). Last visit, my friends and family all scored an exquisite pen from CCIE, clad in brass, with insets of coloured glass gleaming like a maharani's jewel box. Less than $2 a pop.'

Janpath Lane Just off Delhi's central Janpath thoroughfare. 'Thick with stands of traders selling intricately worked Rajasthani bedspreads, throws, tablecloths and cushion covers made from sari offcuts.' No fixed prices here, so be ready to haggle.

Fabindia Stores in Dehli, in Nelson Mandela Road and Greater Kailash, **www.fabindia.com**. 'Brimming with village-made dhurries, wall hangings, cushion covers, bolts of hand-looms and jacquard, and "ethnic" pyjama-style kurta sets.'

Seasons Furnishings Feroze Gandhi Road, Lajpat Nagar, is Susan's favourite textiles shop. 'The quality is wonderful, the designs contemporary and sufficient fabric to upholster a two-seater lounge and a pair of armchairs costs less than $200. The store also sells picture frames, brass wall plaques, delicious-smelling candles, silk cushion covers with Swarovski crystal detailing and fabulous quilts in two dozen colours.'

Brigitte Singh is the widow of a Sikh 'from a princely family. She bases her designs on stylised motifs, mostly floral compositions, from the eighteenth- and nineteenth-century Mughal empire. Each print run is different, usually with a creamy background and featuring garnet-red flowers such as poppies and tulips. The wooden blocks are re-carved after use. Her designs have been described as "William Morris goes to Goa" and appear on cushion covers, cool and roomy clothing, tablecloths and light bedcovers.' Most of the gorgeous fabrics designed by this Jaipur-based Frenchwoman are exported, but she does see selected shoppers by appointment. Susan advises you to 'stay somewhere classy, such as Rajvilas or Rambagh Palace, and you may be lucky. The former has Brigitte Singh bedspreads in its rooms and you can order them at an inflated price through the hotel gift shop.' **Soshu's Gallery** at Palm Beach, telephone (02) 9974 1573, is the sole Australian distributor.

Anokhi Showroom 2 Tilak Marg, Jaipur, **www.anokhi.com**. Set up in Jaipur in 1984 by Faith Singh, the British-born wife of a cousin of the Maharajah of Jaipur, Anokhi 'more-or-less pioneered block-printed Indian-style clothing in Western sizes, including crushed cotton skirts in vegetable-dye hues. The shop is now run by the Singhs' son, Pritam, and his British-born wife, Rachel. Fabrics, dyes and blocks are sent out to artisans in villages close to Jaipur who return the finished materials to the Anokhi factory. It's a decentralised system that involves whole communities, including women who can only work from home. There are eight Anokhi shops in India and a swag in the United Kingdom and continental Europe, but the real bargains are in India. Aside from clothing, look for commodious cloth bags, table runners and cushion and bolster covers.'

NOTES

25

A PLACE
FOR EVERYTHING

NOT LONG AGO, when I was idling over the web searching for ideas on storage, I came upon a piece of information that thrilled me. The moulded unit screwed to the wall beside my desk, its fifteen pockets and five hooks holding office clutter, is a notable piece of twentieth-century design. When I bought it in a shop called Cabana at North Sydney in the 1970s to organise my pens, pencils, tape measures, stanley knife, letter-openers, scissors, staplers and all that, I did not realise that its name is Utensilo and it was designed in 1969 by Dorothée Becker, who worked with Ingo Maurer, the famous German lighting designer.

I have always loved a tidy space to work in. A pernickety person's paradise lies at the American site **www.containerstore.com**. For proof, click your mouse on 'Closet', then on 'Drawer Organizers' – have you ever seen tidier drawers than these? I do love stacks of boxes for different items, such as writing paper, envelopes, cards, ink cartridges, fax paper, paperclips and rubber bands. The moment I laid eyes on kikki.K's shiny boxes, binders and magazine holders in pastel blue and pastel pink at Orson & Blake a few years ago, I knew that it marked the end of the dull work station. According to the grapevine, once when Rupert Murdoch returned to Australia to find the offices at *The Australian* had been painted grey, he ordered a re-paint because, he said succinctly, 'Grey walls, grey newspaper.' No excuse for grey areas anymore if you log on to **www.kikki-k.com.au** or visit the kikki.K concept store at Shop 5009 Westfield Bondi Junction, telephone (02) 9386 0804.

The office colour revolution must have started with iMacs in jellybean colours (minus the black). My iMac is old now, but I couldn't bear to trade its Schiaparelli pink for something sane and conservative. Certainly not grey. Even the revered London stationer Smythson of Bond Street, which has served successive generations of the aristocracy since 1887, has broken the colour barrier with its portable writing bureau in powder blue, colour coordinated with notebooks and wallets. Smythson diaries, notebooks and other personal and business paraphernalia now come in candy pink, tangerine, amethyst and lipstick red, as well as black, bronze croc and the company's traditional mid blue.

I could never have imagined Smythson taking such a giant leap into contemporary marketing when I visited the venerable old store in London in the 1980s. I had volunteered to buy writing paper on behalf of my friend, the stylish Betty Keep, and I thought it would be a flying visit, in and out in a tick. But no. The atmosphere was quite hallowed. I was eyed with some suspicion, then invited to sit down at one side of an antique desk while the gentleman seated on the other side opened a great ledger to check that the writing paper I requested was, indeed, the kind Mrs Keep preferred. Now you can even shop online at **www.smythson.com**. (I have always pronounced the company name as Smithson and, though I am mortified to find that I've been wrong, I'm also disappointed. I still can't bring myself to utter such a pretentious word as Sm-eye-thson.)

Precious paperwork

When, in the same week, the Daily Candy websites in London and New York featured the makers of exquisite invitations, Robert Burton launched **www. robertburtonstationery.com** and my sister-in-law requested writing paper for her birthday, I realised something quite profound was happening. Stationery has replaced real estate as the new sex. Pen and paper have risen up against computer and mouse. Just as slow food has challenged instant gratification, snail mail is fast gaining ground over email as the choice of civilised people in their private lives.

In logging on to Daily Candy's London recommendation, Oh So Inviting, **www.invitin.com**, I discovered that it promises a delicate compromise between tradition and innovation, especially when it comes to the tricky matter of wedding invitations. As for Tiger & Jones New York, **www.tigerandjones.com**, it soars into the stratosphere of style with extravagances such as hand-dyed silk ribbon and 18-carat-gold engraving.

Some of the most creatively refined ways with paper that I've ever seen in Australia are the work of Jo Neville of **Paper Couture** in Sydney. Whenever I go there, I'm stultified by overchoice, a sensation I've always associated with shopping in New

York or Paris or Rome. Her signature-stitched greeting cards, deckle-edged papers, personalised blind embossing, cloth-covered journals, albums, boxes and the kind of ribbons you thought disappeared a century ago are displayed on narrow shelving, or in big glass jars, or tucked into pigeonholes, or stacked in angular baskets, as though in a lolly shop. High on a wall, garments made from crumpled brown paper are a kind of witty logo. The whole presentation, in a light airy atmosphere, is as superb as her handiwork, much of which takes the form of custom-made invitations to weddings and other personal milestones. In mid 2005, before I'd had a chance to take **Megan Morton**'s advice and visit the shop at Northbridge, Jo moved Paper Couture and her workshop to 284 South Dowling Street, Paddington, near Oxford Street (telephone (02) 9357 6855), just up the road from where I live. Lucky me.

Another superbly innovative graphic designer in Sydney with particular expertise in wedding and event planning is Phoebe Gazal, the clever person behind Papier d'Amour, Shop 2, 4 Cross Street, Double Bay, telephone (02) 9362 5200, **www.papierdamour.com.au**. Her work is subtle and refined, with hand-made paper and envelopes, monogrammed rubber stamps and masses of marvellous ribbons among the temptations. She supplements her personal couture service with what she terms her 'pret-a-porter' collection of French designs. In Melbourne, Paper Impressions is another source of exquisite personalised writing paper and invitations; you will find them at 1221 Malvern Road, Malvern, telephone (03) 9824 7955, and online at **www.paperimpressions.com.au**.

Bookbinders Design is a Swedish company that makes a huge range of beautiful paper-based products, from address books and diaries, to photo albums and wrapping paper. See these covetables in reality at the concept store in The Galleria, 385 Bourke Street, Melbourne, or log on to **www.bookbindersdesign.com**. Pepe's Paperie on Level 5, Westfield Bondi Junction in Sydney, is a cheerful place to browse through brightly coloured imports, **www.pepespaperie.com.au**.

Remember when we used to have to go abroad to find Italian marbled papers? Il Papiro now brings them to Melbourne and Sydney wrapped around photograph albums, frames, diaries, boxes, address books and by the sheet, along with inks and sealing wax. You will find them at Shop 5, Degraves Street, Melbourne, telephone (03) 9654 0955; and 87a Macleay Street, Potts Point, telephone (02) 9361 6252; **www.ilpapirofirenze.it**.

Thinking of sealing wax reminds me that the only thing I like as much as a stationer is an art supply store, because I indulge in the time-whittling habit of making my own Christmas cards. I find shopping for the raw materials as much fun as turning them into one-off creations designed around sealing wax into which I have pressed my ring. The ritual of lighting a candle, melting the wax, licking the stone, then stamping it firmly but briefly into the wax is indescribably satisfying, like making paper chains and collages was in childhood.

I collect sealing wax in as many colours as possible, apart from traditional legal-document ox blood. At present, I have sticks and stumps of it in blue, gold, green, silver, cream and black. As a good customer of Eckersley's Arts, Crafts and Imagination, I am spending my way up to $500 on sealing wax, paper, cardboard, pens and ribbons, so that I earn a $50 gift voucher. Visit 93 York Street, Sydney, telephone (02) 9299 4151, or **www.eckersleys.com.au**.

When inspiration fails, or loving hands at home are not appropriate, I hope to find greeting cards with Laura Stoddart's imaginative and amusing illustrations of elongated people doing eccentric things. I also adore the work of Erika Oller, who captures winsome fat ladies and their cats in water colours.

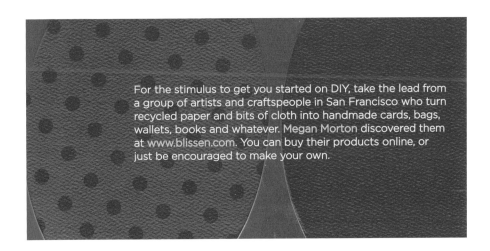

For the stimulus to get you started on DIY, take the lead from a group of artists and craftspeople in San Francisco who turn recycled paper and bits of cloth into handmade cards, bags, wallets, books and whatever. Megan Morton discovered them at www.blissen.com. You can buy their products online, or just be encouraged to make your own.

0002-000060

EGGS		$8.95
FRUIT		$3.94
FREEZER	*	$10.75
50%		
DISCOUNT	*	-5.38
DELI FOODS		$2.85
VEGETABLES		$1.96
VEGETABLES		$2.88
BREAD		$0.85
FRIDGE		$6.95
VEGETABLES		$4.40
VEGETABLES		$3.99
VEGETABLES		$1.27

26
EATS

THE CONTEMPORARY SCOURGE known as road rage is not the only hazard on the high street. There is also footpath fury. Because we walking classes are without the weaponry of wheels, do not assume that all our encounters are benign. We can be belligerent, too, when we have to share a narrow pavement with skateboarders, cyclists, oversized baby carriages, unleashed dogs, abandoned supermarket trolleys, and packs of people spread out and advancing towards us like an army. Footpath fury is alive and well, just around the corner from where we live. I fell into its trap myself the other day.

When I went out to shop, there were two ladders sticking out across the pavement of an inner-city thoroughfare notorious for its heavy and chaotic traffic. Nobody was up either ladder, but the two were minded by a young man who stood there indolently as pedestrians, like me, had to weave our way between them.

On my way back half an hour later with my green bag of comestibles, a sexy pink enamel bucket from McKenzies Hardware and two bunches of pink lilies from the greengrocer in Crown Street, the ladders and their keeper were still there. At my instigation, words were exchanged. Were mine a bit vehement? Maybe so, because his voice trailed me for two blocks shouting, 'You live in a high-class area and you're just a piece of shit . . .' (It was news to me that I live in a classy area, but that's beside the point.) This is reality, a very good reason to stay out of it.

One of the many virtues of virtual shopping over the real thing is that you do not have to risk ugly incidents arising from footpath fury, road rage, check-out churlishness or potholes in the pavement.

About once a month, I travel to the supermarket via my computer. It started a few years ago when **www.greengrocer.com** was first set up. The quality of its fruit and vegetables was outstanding and its system of grading individual items ingenious and amusing: instead of stars, they used green apples for regular produce, mushrooms for organic. In other words, five granny smiths or five shiitakes meant superlative quality, but if an item had only one or two, you knew to give it a miss.

Pencil leeks were always on my shopping list. They are so named because they are young and slender, unlike the overgrown and overpriced whoppers widely available. I don't know where my passion for this elongated onion comes from, although it might have stemmed from my role as the personification of Wales in primary school one Empire Day: I wore Welsh national costume and carried a daffodil which, along with the leek, we were told, was Wales's national symbol.

I'd never tasted leeks until I lived in London as an adult. At The French House Restaurant, upstairs at 49 Dean Street in Soho, they used to serve leeks – Poireaux à la vinaigrette – as a first course. This delicious dish is called Poor Man's Asparagus in *Jane Grigson's Vegetable Book* (Penguin), where she points out that leeks don't taste remotely like asparagus, but they do look a bit similar. I've tried without success to make this dish with big old leeks, but it's a tender triumph with pencil leeks.

Anyway, just when I was getting confident in scanning my granny smiths, greengrocer.com was sold to Woolworths. Goodbye pencil leeks. Hello big old coarse ones.

It was then that I began to rely on **www.shopfast.com.au**. I didn't expect pencil leeks, but there were compensations. Shopfast has always been dependable for the stuff that greengrocer.com didn't sell, or didn't stock in a very wide range. Everything you expect of a big supermarket and liquor store: tins of tomatoes and packets of Weetbix, pots of yoghurt and bags of desirees. What pleased me most was that I could buy Max's Cat Litter in a 12.5-litre bulk pack, so I didn't have to buy it as often. Alas, before you could tap in your password, Shopfast was sold to Coles. Goodbye Max's Cat Litter in bulk. Hello 2.5-litre boxes of it.

There are trade-offs you have to make in shopping for food on the net. For instance, certain items on which your entire menu for that evening depends might be out of stock. Another disadvantage is that you can't be choosy about the size of your vegetables. When I shop for real, I pick out the tiny ones, whereas whoever packs up my order from the web invariably sends me giants. (When will we learn to harvest brussels sprouts before they start to look like cabbages?) Still, although the goods may be commonplace, sometimes it's just more convenient – it's certainly less time-consuming – to shop from a sitting position in front of your computer screen one day and have the delivery van at your door at a predetermined time next day. It sure beats running the risk of altercations out there in reality.

Old-fashioned farming

When I was in my teens, there was a big sign, visible to people seated on the left side of trains from the western suburbs as they neared Sydney's Central Station. While I have forgotten the brand of bread it advertised, I remember the slogan: What You Eat Today Walks and Talks Tomorrow. Unsubtle maybe, but nevertheless true. The food we eat, like the air we breathe, keeps us alive, so we'd better be sure that our intake is as pure, natural and beneficial as possible.

I grew up on organic food before it even had a name. My father, a country boy born in Gundagai, kept chickens and grew vegetables in our backyard. I can remember winter mornings when the steam rose from two buckets of pollard and bran, mixed with vegetable scraps and warm water, that he took to the chookyard. We knew when the cackle of hens meant they'd laid eggs and we collected them while they were still warm. My father gathered cow manure from local fields to be turned into compost to nourish the peas, beans, potatoes, carrots, tomatoes, cucumbers, radishes and lettuce that flourished in the garden. My brother and I liked nothing better than to pick the tiniest beans and eat them raw. (I still have to restrain myself from eating raw peas when I'm shelling them.) When tomatoes were in season, my mother kept a bowl of them on the sideboard and we ate them like apples.

That's one reason why I have never needed persuading that ancient farming methods produce food that is better for our bodies than anything that's been exposed to artificial growth stimulants, synthetic pesticides and other poisons. It's now also clear that these natural methods are crucial to the health of our planet.

Faced with the profusion of food on offer at supermarkets, farmers' markets, butchers, bakers, greengrocers, delicatessens and corner stores, how do we know the difference? It's getting easier, as the organics industry gathers momentum. The more we support organic farmers, the more they'll prosper and proliferate, which means their produce will be more abundant, more widely stocked and cheaper than it is now. And we'll be a lot healthier for it.

Until that day comes, the best way to find out more about organic food and where to buy it is through websites such as **www.cleanfood.com.au** and **www.theorganicsdirectory.com.au**.

SLOW CHICKEN SANDWICH

Do not make the mistake of thinking that a spoonful
of bottled mayonnaise over a few slices of takeaway
roast chook between slices of bread from the freezer
constitutes a decent chicken sandwich. Goodness no.
You must be prepared to make more effort than you
would over grilled steak and two veg.

It takes me two days to make a satisfactory chicken
sandwich. That's why I make them very rarely and for
only the dearest of my friends. I sometimes invite them
to come for an hour or two on their way home from
work, when they're hungry and in need of a reward.
If I'm flush, we have a bottle of Taittinger. Otherwise,
it's Kemenys Hidden Label Victorian Riesling 2004, an
excellent drop for the money.

Here's my performance, step by step.

Day 1
Cook a whole organic chicken according to Stephanie
Alexander's Cold Chinese White-cooked Chicken (page
294 of the second edition *The Cook's Companion*,
Penguin). This method of poaching results in
wonderfully moist flesh and a layer of jelly under the
skin. Cover the bird with cling-wrap and refrigerate.

Let 250 grams of butter soften in a basin. Chop one
whole bunch of garlic chives (bought in Chinatown) or
two bunches of regular chives as finely as you can, and
add them to the butter. Add a dessertspoonful of Dijon
mustard. Put the whole thing in the blender, if you like;
I just mix and and mash it with a fork. Taste and add
salt and pepper if necessary. Cover with cling-wrap and
refrigerate.

Day 2

Go shopping for a bunch of celery and a loaf of sliced bread, which must have been baked that morning. I buy a wholemeal loaf from **Baker's Bun**, where it's made on the premises at Shop 401a Cleveland Street, Redfern (the entrance is actually around the corner in Baptist Street).

Three hours before your guests are due, take the chive butter out of the refrigerator and let it soften. Break off two or three small stems from the heart of the celery, wash them and chop them finely.

One hour later, dismember the chicken and slice the breast and thighs finely and carefully so as not to lose the jelly. Now it is time to make the sandwiches. Be sure to spread the chive butter right to the crusts on both slices of each sandwich, then sprinkle one slice with a little celery. Spread the bits of chicken flesh, skin and jelly over the celery, right to the crusts; be generous. Sprinkle with salt and freshly ground black pepper, and lay the second slice of bread on top.

Flatten each sandwich gently with the palm of your hand, then take a very sharp knife and slice off all the crusts. Wrap the sandwiches, two at a time, in cling-wrap and refrigerate them.

Half an hour before your guests are due, remove the sandwiches from the refrigerator and slice each into three fingers. Marshal them on a serving plate, cut sides up, cover with cling-wrap and let them return to room temperature before you serve them.

Day 3

I always hope for leftovers, a nice little return on my
two-day investment. Sometimes I toast them for lunch.
As for the chicken carcass, it goes into the stockpot.

School sandwich

If all that is too much trouble, or if you simply don't have
time, mix together equal quantities of grated carrot,
grated tasty cheese and chopped parsley for a satisfying
and nourishing sandwich. This is my standby for lunch
midweek.

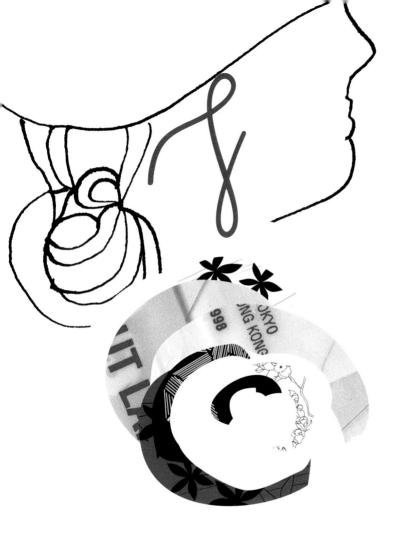

27

WHAT IS THIS THING CALLED LUXURY?

SOME TIME IN the 1980s, when June McCallum was Editor-in-Chief of all the *Vogue* titles published in Australia, she sent me to Europe to experience luxury so that I could write about it. Never have I applied myself more earnestly to an assignment. I began my research at the couture collections in Rome and Paris, interviewed the legendary, turbaned couturier Madame Grès in her salon at 1 rue de la Paix, hobnobbed with the gentry at the Ritz in London, boarded the Venice Simplon-Orient-Express (it was new at the time) and partied all the way to Venice, where I stayed in the suite at Hotel Cipriani that is usually reserved for James and Shirley Sherwood, the owners of this sumptuous resort hotel and the train that carried me there.

Wherever I went, I couldn't help noticing that not everyone shared my state of over-excitement. Bored expressions and petulant remarks were not rare, even on that glorious 24-hour train ride into nostalgia. I realised that the difference between them and me is this: they live permanently in this rarefied realm and I do not. It was the contrast to my everyday existence that made a taste of the high life so exhilarating for me. Would it be luxury if I had it every day? I don't think so. Besides, I'd die of exhaustion.

Luxury is an elusive thing. There was a stage in my life when my work as a writer was so all-consuming, the greatest luxury for me was to steal an afternoon at the ironing-board. After motoring through France for a week one balmy autumn, lunching and dining sumptuously at Relais & Châteaux properties every day, all I longed for was a lamb chop with peas and mashed potatoes. What I guess I'm saying about luxury is that, if we're not careful, we can spoil it for ourselves by being too greedy, whether we're gulping down experiences or having a feeding frenzy in the shops.

Binge shopping is an express lane to dissatisfaction, not to mention insolvency. So is the acquisition of status symbols in what Professor Barry Schwartz describes as 'a kind of arms race of exquisiteness' in his enlightening study of contemporary shopping, *The Paradox of Choice: Why More Is Less* (HarperCollins). Restraint and selectivity might not sound as thrilling as profligacy and recklessness, but they're better for body and soul in the long run. Your mother was right: you can have too much of a good thing. Don't ruin it for yourself.

Luxury can be a heart-to-heart with a good friend and a bottle of good wine, a new CD, a new book, the first crocus to flower in winter, an armload of pink peonies in November, the tuning-up of an orchestra, a night on the town, an evening at home, an outfit that makes you look and feel wonderful, cooking a favourite dish for people you love, or, to be absolutely honest, a beautiful designer shopping bag with something adorable that you truly want inside. Luxury doesn't always cost money, although quite often it does.

I once asked the glamorous Betty Keep – who at ninety still wore only carefully selected pieces by Yves Saint Laurent and Calvin Klein – for her idea of luxury. 'A surprise,' she said. I guess at four score years and ten, there are not likely to be too many of those left for you. So luxuriate in them, while you can.

LUXURY IS MANY different experiences for **Belinda Seper**. 'Doing a gym class on relaxation is luxurious to me,' especially when she should be at work, because it's a contrast to her normal life. 'I'd love to sit in a temple with Buddhist monks for a month, or challenge myself physically in some sense – climb some mountain or trek the Kokoda Trail. I know I'd have to physically prepare myself, so that would be luxurious in itself.' Not all her ideas of luxury entail making a big effort, though. 'I also like the experience of really beautiful restaurants. It's not about the money, it's about making the time to participate in those experiences.

'My idea of a holiday is palm trees and chairs beside swimming pools and men in white jackets who bring you an endless supply of little pink drinks with umbrellas in the top.

A handwritten note on someone's personal stationery I think is the epitome of luxury, with the right texture of paper and an ink pen. I fall about, because they've taken time to think about it, to put pen to paper rather than just bash off an email.'

James Gordon's assistant, Alex, is 'luxury in herself', and he likes nothing better than to give her presents, such as the 'diamondesque' earrings he brought home from his last trip. Apart from Alex, 'I guess true luxury for me is a great book or a terrific new magazine, a delicious big drink, a bowl of perfect roses, the view from my apartment and the Hills Hoist in the garden for drying sheets and towels.'

On the subject of laundry, as a break from doing the family wash herself, **Megan Morton** luxuriates in the sheets she takes home from Woollahra Laundry Service three or four times a year after 'a seasonal wash-starch-and-dry. It's such a small price to pay for such a beautiful, hotel-decadent bedtime situation. Sun-dried is best, but some professional TLC is magic!' On a less mundane level, 'Luxury can be a roomful of books – there is so much to learn.' Megan also indulges in the luxury of planning trips to Vietnam, knowing 'I'm never going to take them'.

When **Lucinda Mendel** turns her attention to the subject, 'Some things immediately fill my mind. Luxury is having a Kir Royale with my husband at Bistro Moncur, sitting at the bar chatting to the staff, whom we love. It's not just the fact of having Bollinger, it's about not having any cares, being with my husband, laughing with the staff. For us, it's access that you can't get just by going to dinner. It's the time we've spent there, the years of talking to them. I think it's a luxury that they share a bit of their working life with us.' Lucinda's other great luxury is to take the weekend newspapers to the little park near where she lives, to 'have my toes in the grass and think we're so lucky'.

Jane Roarty looks for luxury in 'objects of art rather than goods. Luxury is finding something that I instantly fall in love with: a unique pair of shoes, a fabulous jacket, even a raincoat; something I've had in the back of my head that I've wanted. It is also certain design things that I have always pursued, such as Christofle and Baccarat, for design rather than name. A beautiful Hermès handbag that I would live with forever. The Kelly is me and I also love the Birkin. I wouldn't even mind getting vintage. I'd go for the conservative colours, cognac in the Birkin, but I'd also adore the alligator.' Jane longs for 'an 18-carat huge gold charm bracelet, and I think the gold Rolex is to die for. I have great loves but they're usually very strong design concepts. I'm not a modernist. I'm much more traditional. When I lived in London, I used to go and look at Lobb's shoes for men, and I just adore to see a bespoke suit.'

Being at the right place at the right time on a trip to South Africa resulted in luxurious serendipity for **Eric Matthews**. He set out from his beachfront hotel in Durban one morning to walk through a seemingly endless sea of hawkers selling touristic kitsch when, 'as I was about to turn round, I saw, a few metres away, these long strips of exquisite Kuba fabric on the grass.' The Kuba people, who live in Zaire, produce intricately embroidered and appliquéd abstract patterns on raffia cloth that inspired the Cubists, notably Braque and Picasso. Each piece, woven by a man and decorated by a woman, takes months to complete, which is why Kuba cloth is rare and highly prized. Eric has always loved it: 'It's clothing, made in one long narrow piece. They just wrap it all around themselves and tie it with ropes. It is quite the most beautiful stuff.' He believes that fate was on his side that day. 'I was meant to keep walking; he was meant to be there. He had travelled from central Africa, carrying them in a fantastic woven grass rucksack. It must have taken him weeks to get there.' Did Eric bargain over the price? 'I didn't. I was so thrilled at discovering it, I thought he deserved whatever he wanted. He asked for 750 rand and I gave him 800 [roughly $155]. We bonded. He was rapturous at my response to this fabric. I'd have bought it all but I didn't have enough cash on me.'

To Eric, luxury is intangible. 'In my mind luxury can be defined by great things and also by simple things. It can be a sip of coffee, a view, an enduring friendship, a picture. I love the expression on people's faces, seeing their hands if they've toiled and created something.' One of his treasured experiences happened after he'd come out of the back door of the Forbidden City in Beijing, having spent a day there with a friend who is fluent in Mandarin. It was a beautiful spring afternoon, so they sat on a bench, listening to stories told by a very old woman who sold them beer and pork dumplings from her barrow. The privilege of just being there is what mattered to him: 'You couldn't buy that.'

Craig Markham's idea of luxury is simply 'space and time'.

Michal McKay is almost as succinct: 'The Four Seasons in Bali, that's my idea of absolute luxury, where you've got a spa and beautiful food. Not having to dress up. No pressure. You can read books when you want to, put on a sarong and go and have something to eat. My other idea of luxury is flying first class.'

'Time and comfort and warmth' are luxuries to **Carolyn Lockhart** and, 'If I really could afford it, I would only drink champagne. But the ultimate luxury – and it's never happened to me – is to have a driver at your beck and call, particularly for city things, when you're working and going to functions.'

Being coddled is **Edwina McCann**'s idea of bliss. 'I have a pampering addiction. I go to the hairdresser once a week but it's not really about being well groomed for me, it's the pampering thing. I like having my head massaged and being spoiled.' She reckons her predilection was 'made worse' by a year as beauty editor of *Harper's Bazaar*. Edwina's hairdresser is Valonz Haircutters, 20–22 Elizabeth Street, Paddington, telephone (02) 9360 2444. It's also the place to find Miss Frou Frou, boutique beautician, who does a pedicure that is, says Edwina, 'just divine. She puts your feet in this beautiful porcelain bowl with water, honey, rose petals and milk. So, to begin with, you bathe your feet. She does a foot scrub with salt, honey and olive oil. Then she rubs a bit of olive oil with lavender, or you can have citrus if you prefer, into your feet. It's not product-driven, it's total indulgence. There's no reason for rose petals to be floating in the water, but it's just divine.' Scented candles are another passion: 'Well, they're the new flowers, aren't they?'

Susan Kurosawa, who stays in more hotels in a year than most people will in their entire lives, looks for 'supreme comfort, absolute privacy, an eye for exquisite detail (beautiful soaps, lighting over the bathtub so I can read amid the bubbles, a menu of pillows, curtains or blinds that don't let in the dawn's first stab of light, lots of magazines) and, at a resort, a private plunge pool.' For travel in general, she wants 'time to myself, an unhurried timetable ("free afternoon" is my favourite entry on any itinerary), a hotel or resort that has some specific reference to the destination, in vernacular interior design and detailing.'

Luxury for **Ilana Katz** is 'to stay in a place that is better than home, a fantasy that I could never afford myself. I want to be able to admire it, to want it, but I couldn't have it because it might have antiques that are unique. To be able to do these sorts of things in comfort is something I know I can only do for a few days in my life. I can't have it every day. This is what I call luxury. It's like a treat. That's what I'm looking for, always.'

Tempe Brickhill's thoughts on luxury are likely to strike a chord with many of us because she has crystallised much of our own thinking: 'In London, there is a growing movement that considers it is time to re-evaluate the concept of "luxury". I believe that some women are growing increasingly fatigued with the idea of the "luxury brand", and that they are looking for something more authentic and individual, something that enhances their everyday lives, as much as the occasional treat.

'It has been fascinating to witness the re-invention of the "luxury brand" in the nineties . . . Their commercialisation is a huge success story, yet one that I would argue comes with a price. That price is the loss of individuality . . . Massive amounts of money are spent on advertising campaigns which develop a culture of must-have branding. But I do believe that, for many people, the thrill of the ownership has worn thin and empty. There is a hunger for authenticity, craftsmanship and to a certain extent principles.

'True luxury should be above "fashion", as all too often fashion is about the trend of the moment, with an undercurrent of disposability. True luxury for me is about beauty, craft, tradition and principle. Having said that I still think luxury is subjective, a state of mind, of being, of adapting. If you don't appreciate and feel grateful for the luxury, whatever it may be, then you fail to recognise its worth and it ceases to be one.

'I would say that what luxury means to me is gentility, comfort, harmony, beauty and nature, something that soothes or excites your own sensibilities, ideas or dreams. I don't think of it as a concept that is synonymous with wealth and consumerism, but rather with authenticity and personal values, of having the freedom to be able to choose how to live my life. Not everyone is that lucky.'

Let the last word come from **Akira Isogawa,** who wraps up all his luxuries in three little words: 'Peace of mind.'

ACKNOWLEDGMENTS

ONE SUNDAY, two years ago, my friend and publisher Julie Gibbs invited me to her flat for home-made fairy cakes and a flute of the Billecart-Salmon champagne with which she is often associated. 'I have something for you to look at,' she said, handing me a copy of a book titled *The Shops*, by India Knight, along with a newspaper cutting on the subject of packing for travel. 'Take them home and see if they inspire you' is all she said as she gave them to me.

So I did. The clipping was nothing to get excited about – packing being a subject that does not stimulate someone who has done so much of it and written about it so often – but the book was a different thing. The writing, by a vulnerable and endearing young woman, was free and funny. I just kept on reading. It made me want to loosen up my style, to shrug off formula writing and be myself. It set me off.

So my first thanks go as always to Julie Gibbs, muse, mentor and catalyst to all her writers. And my second thanks go to the talented India Knight, whom I feel I have met although I've never laid eyes on her. I have not copied her book, I have been ignited by it. My third thanks go to my friend and agent, the unflappable Fran Moore, who is always there when she is needed most.

Encouragement and leads came from many people, in particular (in alphabetical order) Mindy Balgrosky, Peter Bracken, Jean-Yves Bussières, James Carter, Judith Cook, Lana Dopper, Vivien Egge, Philip Engelberts, Mary Harper, Kylie Kwong, June McCallum, Frans Poppeliers, Kay Russell, Patrick Russell, Gene Silbert, David Tilley, Yen Tsai and Wanda Tucker.

Two brilliant fellow writers have been exceptional in their kindness and generosity. Shelley Gare not only alerted me to fruitful sources of information, but kept me buoyant when I felt bogged down or blue. And Marion Hume did me the enormous favour of agreeing to read my part-finished manuscript as she winged her way around New Zealand promoting her novel, *The Fashion Pack*. Their input has been invaluable.

In bringing the book together, where would I be without the team at Lantern/Penguin, particularly Claire de Medici, who edited the pages (with Alison Cowan standing in when necessary), John Canty coordinating the design and Nicole Brown guiding the whole production.

As we shoppers know, packaging can make or break a product, so my final thanks must go to eskimo, the graphic design company headed by Zoë Pollitt and Natasha Hasemer, responsible for the wit and refinement of the book's design. They were inspired in giving the task of illustrating it to Lyndal Harris, whose elegant and irreverent touch is all I could have wished. No points for guessing who commissioned them. Julie Gibbs, who else?

The author and publisher would like to thank the following people and companies for allowing us to reproduce their material in this book. In some cases we were not able to contact the copyright owners and we would appreciate hearing from any copyright holders not acknowledged here, so that we are able to properly acknowledge their contribution when the book is reprinted.

Alber Elbaz for Lanvin; Cacharel; Chanel; Cose Plus for assorted swingtags; Dolce & Gabbana; Editions Herscher, publisher for the Musee des Arts de la Mode YSL retrospective exhibition; Grandiflora; Hotel Ritz Paris; House of Cashmere; Ikea; Jo Neville of Paper Couture; Ladurée; L'Occitane; Marimekko; Smythson; Space; Transport for London; Vogue; Yves Saint Laurent.

INDEX